THE BOOK ON
INCENTIVE COMPENSATION MANAGEMENT

The Systematic Administration of Variable Compensation in the Enterprise

THE COMPENSATION ARCHITECT

WWW.COMPENSATIONARCHITECT.COM

THE BOOK ON
INCENTIVE COMPENSATION MANAGEMENT

The Systematic Administration of Variable Compensation in the Enterprise

DAVID KELLY

THE COMPENSATION ARCHITECT

2014

First Printing: 2014

ISBN 978-0-9960810-0-9

Compensation Architect
Santa Clara, CA 95050

www.CompensationArchitect.com

Ordering Information: Please email David@CompensationArchitect.com

Special discounts are available on quantity purchases by corporations, associations, educators, and others. For details, contact the publisher at the above listed address.

U.S. trade bookstores and wholesalers: Please email David@CompensationArchitect.com

CONTENTS

Contents 5

Dedication 7

Chapter One – About this Book 9

    Why This Book? 9

    Who is the Book For? 10

    What do I Hope You Will Learn from It? 10

    A Note about Style 11

Chapter Two – What are we Actually Talking About? 13

    Variable Compensation 13

    ICM vs SPM 13

    How is it supposed to Work? 14

    What is the Logic of ICM? 16

    Why is ICM hard? 20

    Time – the Hidden Challenge of ICM 26

    The Weirdness – It's a Technical Term 28

Chapter Three – Administering Variable Compensation 31

    How is it Done Today? 31

    Who Does ICM? 34

Chapter Four – What Do ICM Systems Do? 39

    Data 39

    Compensation Plans 56

    Reporting 57

    Workflows 59

Chapter Five – Planning for your ICM Project 61

    The Waterfall Methodology 61

    The Project Team 62

    The Sales Cycle 66

    Project Preparation & Kickoff 74

Chapter Six – The Project Commences 81

    Requirements Phase 81

    Business Consulting & Organizational Change Management 104

    Design Phase 107

    Build Phase 117

    Test Phase 119

    Deployment Phase 128

Go-Live Phase 130

Organizational Change Management Phase 130

A Note on Agility 132

Chapter Seven – ICM Functional Challenges & Issues 137

Transaction Processing 137

Sales Crediting 138

Aggregation 140

Incentive Calculations 141

Payment 151

Data Integration 151

Reporting & Analytics 152

Modeling & Forecasting 154

Exception Processing 156

Chapter Eight – Best Practices in Incentive Compensation 161

The Comp Plan Virtues 161

Gaming the Comp Plan 166

Chapter Nine – Conclusion & Rousing Call to Action 169

Appendix One – Glossary 171

Appendix Two – the Compensation Center of Competency 183

Appendix Three: Contract Hierarchies in Insurance & Financial Services 185

Appendix Four: Ol' Unka DK's Laws & Virtues 189

The Laws 189

The Virtues 190

Index 191

DEDICATION

Many thanks must be tendered to the people who made this book happen, wittingly or unwittingly:

- A lot of people over the years who have strongly suggested I write it. I can't say anyone in particular turned the tide in terms of making me do it, but a lot of people contributed;
- Rob Gillette, who hired me at my first consulting company, and then at my first ICM vendor company. A lot of what I know about business administration, consulting, and about ICM, has come about because of those two incomprehensible and probably indefensible hiring decisions;
- The engineers at Callidus Software (now CallidusCloud) and at Merced Systems (now NICE) who made me look at the problem in interesting ways and showed me some handy tips, including the DBAFI algorithm;
- The consulting managers who threw me into the deep end and made me pretend that I knew what I was doing even when I wasn't entirely sure I did. And of them, Jimmy Duan, who did the most to convince me that maybe I really did know after all;
- The "real" consultants who treated me like a respected peer and taught me how they thought about problems. Much of that knowledge appears in these pages as though it should be entirely self-evident;
- Sheryl Friesz who made partnership with customers a cornerstone of consulting engagements, rather than a nice-to-have;
- Tim Wald for reading and validating the first draft of the book, and for suggesting some clarifications that made it a much better tool for customers and consultants;
- Jeff Sanders who kept me honest, musically and syntactically;
- The customers who gave me interesting problems to solve, and sometimes some great anecdotes;
- And especially Tammy, in all of her incarnations and genders, all of whom keep the ICM wheels turning.

And oh yeah –

- Many, many thanks to Anne, who cheer-led constantly, and who only occasionally asked me whether I was planning to get a real job anytime soon. I wouldn't have done it without her support, so if you have any issues with anything inside, take 'em up with her.

CHAPTER ONE – ABOUT THIS BOOK

Why This Book?

Incentive Compensation Management is hard – let's just get that right out on the table. It is a strange business domain that requires odd combinations of skills from its practitioners if they are to be successful. Human language does not adequately express the concepts that make up ICM problems or solutions, and human math is sometimes only partially relevant in day-to-day ICM operations. ICM is a financial system that looks like it's based on hard numbers and data, but because it is all about getting inside the heads of the human beings it touches, it is full of squishy psychological practices and exceptions that make the data suspect and the numbers pliable.

There are tons of books on the art and science of selling and sales management, quite a few books on comp plan strategies and design, and a zillion more books on the various technical aspects involved in building complex systems – data integration, calculations, reporting, and project methodologies. But I haven't yet seen a book on the real world problems inherent in building and using ICM systems:

- That consistently get the right answer;
- That perform well;
- That are maintainable; and
- That are flexible.

I have worked in the ICM industry for 15-plus years, and in the decade prior to that I held various jobs that touched on and illuminated many of the concepts and issues that make up the ICM domain. What I have learned is that no one is born knowing ICM. No one was prepared for it when they arrived to start dealing with it. The learning curve to becoming useful in the domain is long and often painful, and everyone in the field has made many missteps and gone down lots of false trails. Everyone.

In its modest way, then, this book's reason for being is to try to prepare ICM practitioners for their journey. It won't change the underlying problems, but it might eliminate some of the surprises.

Please note, and I may regret saying this: there is very little agreement amongst the practitioners of ICM about anything. Colleagues get into shouting matches with each other in meetings over this stuff. We don't agree about what a best practice is, other than that we're pretty sure there must be an applicable one and that we will know it when we see it. We can't even agree on what the words mean. This book is proposing a view of the world based on what I have seen over the course of scores of projects in a dozen industries. But it is only as "right" as what I have seen and heard from my customers. Other customers, other consultants, will have heard or done some of the same things, but also some different things. I expect violent disagreement about a few fundamental things I'm laying down the as laws of the compensation universe.

So why should you read this book? Because it *is* based on a fairly broad representation of customer requirements and the system architectures that have arisen to meet them over the years. It may not map 100% to the world you know, but it will certainly give you a way to look at your world that can help illuminate what you are seeing. So let the fights begin, and take it all with a healthy dose of skepticism. Either way, I don't think you'll be any further behind from reading this, and you might be yards ahead afterward.

Who is the Book For?

If you are reading this book, the odds are that you have had Incentive Compensation Management inflicted on you in some professional capacity. You might be the Compensation Manager of a large company facing a system implementation of new incentive comp software. You might be in the IT department of that company, where you might find yourself required to support that system. Or you might be in the Program Management Office, where, come Monday morning, you could find yourself running an ICM implementation project.

On the other side of the coin, you could be a business or technical consultant, whether from an ICM vendor or from a Systems Integrator, who has to implement the system. One minute there you were, minding your own business and bothering no one, and the next you were assigned to an ICM project. And because large ICM projects can be multi-year affairs, after your first project you might become an ICM "specialist" – whether you want to be one or not. That has happened to a lot of good people who might have deserved better.

Whoever you are, I am guessing that you didn't spend your carefree youth dreaming of the day you would finally be allowed to implement and use a large and complex application to pay the commissions and bonuses for a professional sales force. In my years in the industry, I don't know if I ever met anyone who got into incentive comp on purpose. In MBA School they don't teach you that the fast track to the Executive Suite is by way of Sales Ops, though the education you receive managing compensation for a sales organization can be an eye opener to the way business is really conducted in large companies.

So if you're reading this book, it might be because you need answers to some foundational questions, like what is ICM, why is it so weird, and isn't there anything anyone can do to make it better? Maybe I can give you some of those answers.

What do I Hope You Will Learn from It?

I want to help you become a better planner, implementer, and user of whatever ICM system you either have or might acquire, even if it's not a very systematic system. This applies to both the customer side and the delivery side of the project relationship.

Because I come out of the system vendor and implementation side of the ICM world, I am using the word "customer" in this case to refer to the company that must manage the incentive compensation for its sales force or agents. It means the business operations staff – often (but not invariably) in Sales Operations or Sales Finance. It also refers to the technical professionals who must provide infrastructure and data to the system. And it could mean the consumers of data from the ICM system, including corporate Finance and Accounting folks who like to crunch numbers to get a handle on the state of the business.

By "delivery", I mean the project team that must make the system – a packaged application or home-grown – work to the specifications of the customer. This project team might actually be part of the customer organization, but it is equally or more likely that it refers to the vendor's technical staff, or the consulting staff of a large **Systems Integrator (SI)** or smaller "**boutique**" consulting firm. Even if the customer company is implementing its own system without help from SIs or vendors, the implementation staff on the delivery side will often not be the same folks who will have to operate or maintain the system moving forward. The agenda of the implementation project staff – to get signoff that the system they built works and was delivered on time and under budget – will generally be different from the agenda of the operations staff who will be defining the requirements for the system – to get a system that makes their lives easier than they are today, and that will also work next year and the year after.

So what does it mean to become "better" at ICM? I think it means a couple of things. From a customer perspective, it means understanding what an ICM system can – and cannot – do for you, and being able to clearly define your requirements and expectations to make full use of the capabilities on offer to build an operational system that will meet your business needs today and in the foreseeable future. What I hope to do in this book is to help customers learn how to ask for what they need and want from the system more crisply and in a way that will enable the delivery team to succeed.

From the delivery side, it means setting appropriate expectations about what you can – and cannot – do, and it means meeting those expectations by being knowledgeable, consultative, and creative about how you satisfy the customer's stated and unstated requirements with your system design and configuration. With this book I hope to help the implementers learn more about the incentive comp domain so that they can ask the right questions to drive out the real customer requirements, not just the ones written down in the comp plan documentation handed to them on the first day of the project.

Most importantly, I hope to show both sides how to bring a spirit of partnership to the ICM system implementation project. Without that partnership, the project might eventually be completed and there will be signatures on the handoff documents indicating that the letter of the contract has been met, but it probably won't be a success.

A Note about Style

You might have already noticed that I tend to write in a fairly casual style. While I am perfectly capable of writing in business language – really, I can! – I have chosen not to for this topic. It's a complicated enough subject to begin with, and honestly, it's no one's idea of a good time. Why make it worse with passive verbs and formal syntax? I hope it won't be off-putting to anyone looking for a more scholarly approach, but I just don't have it in me to inflict that on anyone where incentive compensation is concerned. So try to think of this as a 14-hour flight to Australia, the newly hired Director of Comp of a large company in the window seat, an implementation consultant starting out in ICM in the aisle seat, and I'm the handsome, charming, and knowledgeable fellow in the middle seat *who will not shut up!*

Figure 1 - Hour 11 of 14

Further, the book is written to be **application-agnostic**. You won't learn how to use any of the packaged ICM software packages from reading this book. I have seen most of the offerings in the marketplace, and have worked closely with some of them, but anything specific I say about any vendor's product will likely be out of date by the time you read this. I'm writing with the assumption that most of the products approach the ICM problem in roughly similar ways – just with different strengths and weaknesses and different user interfaces, processing and interaction models. And I'm assuming that all of them will get the "right" answer if configured properly. So this isn't a buyer's guide to ICM software, and nor is it a user manual. It's just a way to let you do a better job of specifying or building a system using whatever tools are available.

I make a lot of pronouncements. If you will recall something I said a few paragraphs ago, however, no two ICM practitioners agree on anything or use the same words when describing ICM. So how come I'm laying down the law as though I have some Cosmic Conduit to the Objective Truth about ICM? Well, because I do, of course – pay no attention to those other folks. But the real reason is, I want to raise discussions if they help us get to a more rational standard. Sometimes knowing that there's a differing opinion out there about something can make you re-evaluate your own perspective. So feel free to disagree with some of my more arrogant statements, tell me I'm a moron if we meet at some ICM industry hootenanny, but maybe they'll help you test your own ideas and come to a more refined understanding.

I tell a lot of anecdotes about projects I have had the luck to be part of to illustrate points. Some of them might sound like I'm trying to be funny, but on my honor, such as it is, each one is true. I have changed enough of the details to make identifying the companies as hard as possible because, hey, I'd like to keep working in the industry and some of the people who did these things are still my friends. But the stories are all things I have seen with my very own eyes in my work in the ICM industry. Maybe some of you will recognize yourselves...

So... enjoy the 14-hour flight!

CHAPTER TWO – WHAT ARE WE ACTUALLY TALKING ABOUT?

Variable Compensation

Variable compensation is the practice of paying employees and agents different amounts to reflect their different levels of performance for the work they do. Variable pay can be in the form of withholding a percentage of pay pending a passing score on specific metrics, or it can be in the form of rewarding above and beyond the regular level of pay for exceptional work. Or it can be a combination of the two.

"Pay" is made up of varying proportions of base salary and variable earnings. Variable compensation is often described using **pay-mix** ratios of base salary to variable pay for acceptable performance – 50:50, 70:30 or 90:10, for example. The ratios generally total 100 (or 100%), but they don't have to. The idea is that the payee – the person being paid variably, and yes, I know this is a circular definition – will want to work harder or better to earn the variable piece, and ideally, any **upside** as well.[1] In simple terms, it's a bribe to convince them to do what we want them to.

Variable compensation is often, but not invariably, used to reward or motivate sales performance. Sales performance has a high value to a company, and is (theoretically) easy to measure, so it lends itself to this practice. A significant amount of this book will be aimed at companies implementing ICM to pay their sales force. But variable pay can be used for anything that can be measured: call center agent **Pay-for-Performance** (**P4P**) is an increasingly common example of that.

ICM vs SPM

ICM – Incentive Compensation Management – refers to the systems and practices supporting the payment of variable compensation by companies to their sales force, agents, or other entities whose performance against desired metrics can help the company be more successful. The "I" in ICM – **incentive** – is the key word. The foundation of ICM rests on the idea that a company can reward good behavior – often in a monetary way – on the part of the payees to cause them to do more of the good behavior, and perhaps do less of other bad behaviors. Ideally, this results in greater sales, efficiency, quality, or customer satisfaction for the company – enough greater that it makes up for the costs of administering and paying the incentives.

SPM – Sales Performance Management – refers to a broader set of concepts and systems that provide visibility into and improvement to the selling process for a company. SPM often encompasses ICM, and indeed, many people use the terms interchangeably or treat ICM as a subset of SPM. But I would argue that they should be treated as separate concepts. SPM will often use ICM as one of the tools to improve sales performance, and some SPM practices feed into and inform ICM, but not all ICM is related to selling, and not all SPM is about incentives.

The obvious disconnect is where ICM is used for incenting and rewarding employees for measurable work they do – agents in a call center, for example, or quality of services provided by support organizations – who never sell

---

[1] Upside is variable pay above the standard or norm that should reward outstanding work. Plans without upside cease motivating good behavior the moment the minimum acceptable level of achievement has been attained, which is generally not a good thing, though that depends on your business model and what you're trying to achieve.

to customers at all. And there are aspects of a complete SPM model that do not touch on compensation, such as sales coaching and planning.

My view is that the two disciplines overlap but are not the same, and I think the distinction between them can sometimes be a bit hazy:

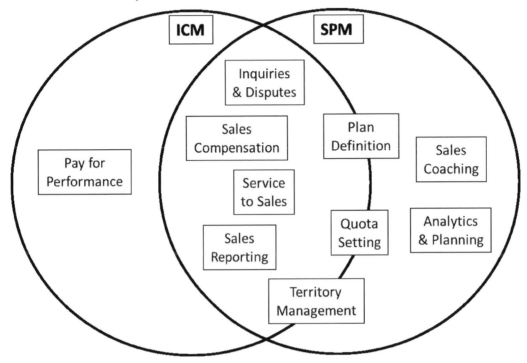

Figure 2 - ICM vs. SPM

For example, I tend to think of plan definition, quota setting, and territory management as ICM functions, but not everyone would agree and I can certainly see their point. ICM cannot succeed without those functions (at least, not in companies that have a selling model for which they are relevant), but they could be seen as feeds to ICM, rather than as core ICM.

To be clear, this book will focus primarily on ICM, particularly large-scale, enterprise ICM. It will also cover some of the gray areas where ICM and SPM overlap, but will not address SPM-specific concepts and practices in depth.

How is it supposed to Work?

In an ideal world, incentive compensation is all about aligning tactics – the behavior of employees, agents, channel partners, and others – to the company's strategy by using rewards (and sometimes financial punishment) based on performance against goals. So ideally, a company knows what it wants to do and to achieve, it has measureable targets to indicate progress towards those goals, and it conveys the goals and associated rewards to the people and entities who can influence progress with the work they do.

There is an unspoken bargain underlying the practice of incentive compensation. By putting the payee on a comp plan, we are telling them that they will make more money by achieving high performance on the things we're measuring, which in turn will make the company successful. The performance against defined metrics is supposed to tie directly to what the company needs. But turn that idea over, and you will see how the stereotypical "sales guy" looks at the situation. To a sales rep, there is an implication that ***anything they do to*** *make their commission checks bigger is okay,* or even commendable, because the plan only rewards them for good behaviors. This can have **unintended consequences**, many of which we will discuss later in the book.

A well designed and communicated compensation plan should make it obvious to the plan participants exactly what is expected of them and exactly what they must do to achieve greater rewards. Their attainment against the targets and goals should be measured regularly and communicated to these people and entities to give them the excitement of knowing that they are doing well and will be rewarded handsomely. If they are not doing well, their performance reports should provide the reminder that they need to do better if they would like to see more in the check come payday.

There is a diagram that has made the rounds of the ICM space in various configurations over the years that explains how companies should run the process of variable comp. This is one form of it:

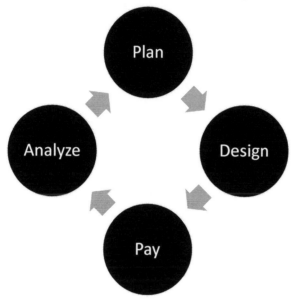

Figure 3 - The Cycle of Variable Compensation

I've seen this diagram built with anywhere from three to six bubbles, but the main point it makes is that you need to:

- Know what you want to accomplish
- Come up with a program to make it happen
- Put that program into place and let it run
- Figure out what went wrong and what went right – sometimes at the end of the plan period, sometimes during the plan period, and use that knowledge in your next round of planning

Incentive Compensation Management systems should (ideally) support the "Pay" and "Analyze" bubbles. The other bubbles are functions that take place outside of the ICM system, though they might be considered core SPM.

Due to the nature of how different companies operate in different industries, with different goals and being in different parts of the abstract life-cycle of the company, industry, and product, there is no such thing as the perfect compensation plan that can be implemented everywhere (with minor tweaks, of course) that will do what every company needs it to do. Even what they want to measure and optimize is unique to every company, and certainly the data they have to support incentive comp is different. There are **best practices** that should be considered, and we'll describe them in detail in the **BEST PRACTICES IN INCENTIVE COMPENSATION** section, but a best practice for me in my current situation might well be a worst practice for you in yours. Like standards, the nice thing about best practices is that you have so many to choose from.[2]

Compensation plans are almost invariably 'company confidential' because they represent a company's response to conditions in its marketplace. They hold an interesting mirror up to a company by showing what is important to the company, and often, by showing where the company's problems are in their sales process. The stereotypical comp plan is two pages of metrics and goals, and 15 pages of legalese and terms and conditions. The tweaks and turns in a comp plan are there because someone found an issue that needed to be addressed and codified in the plan. And the issues in my company are different from the issues at yours.

Incentive Compensation Management systems are designed and built with broad sets of functionality to support as much of the variability inherent in variable compensation as possible. But if your company has any complexity at all (which is why you might be considering implementing a new system and why you might be reading this book), you will likely find gaps in every ICM system ever sold. It's not that the system is bad: it's that there will almost certainly be that one bizarre thing your company does that no one has ever asked for before, and the system might not have a convenient way to do it. We call this "the **Weirdness**", and we'll discuss it more as we go along. That doesn't mean no system will work for you: it just means that the project team might need to get creative.

What is the Logic of ICM?

While every packaged or custom ICM system is different, they mostly adhere to a fairly logical flow to support the way comp plans are written and administered in most companies:

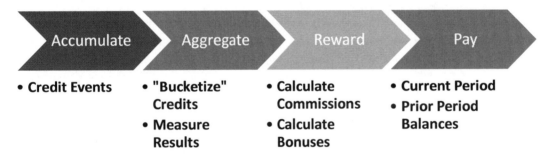

Figure 4 - ICM Logical Flow

There can be more or fewer bells and whistles, more or fewer discreet stages, stopping points along the way or not, but this general approach solves the bulk of incentive comp calculations. We'll explore all of this in greater detail later in the book, but here is a simple explanation of what each chunk in the picture means.

ACCUMULATE STAGE

Incentive comp is about comparing actual performance against expectations, and in ICM, performance is generally based on business events that are caused or created by the payee. Those business events are very often sales transactions or orders, though they could be customer satisfaction scores, calls answered, a record of activities performed or miles driven, or anything else that can be sourced as unique events and ascribed to a payee in the system. We generically call these events "**transactions**", and that's how I will refer to them in this book.

---

[2] "The nice thing about standards is that you have so many to choose from." David Wetherall; Andrew S. Tanenbaum, (2011). Computer networks. Upper Saddle River, NJ: Pearson Prentice Hall (2001)

A transaction tells us that something happened, and it has interesting attributes that tell us what, when, to whom, where, what it was worth, and whatever else we think is important to track. In the simplest case, it also tells us who did it – which payee should receive **credit** for the event – but of course, not everything is simple. But regardless of the complexity, the first thing we need to do is to determine that *this event* should be tied to *this payee* (or *these payees*). That tie between a payee and a transaction is usually called a **credit** in ICM – it reflects the results of the **crediting** process. An ICM credit is not the same as the credit given to a customer as a refund, though you might give a payee credit for a credit event. Sorry.

It is very important to note that *a credit is different from a transaction*. A credit joins to a specific transaction, but it is its own thing and has a life of its own separate from the transaction to which it is tied. A credit has a value that might or might not be the value of the transaction: two reps might have been involved in making a deal happen, so they might **split** the credit – each get half credit for the deal. And in the ICM universe, the company might actually credit each of them 75% of the deal, or 100%/100%, or 30%/30%. That's a company policy, and while you might think it's crazy (or not), it is a perfectly valid thing to do if it fits the comp plan terms and conditions.

If the transaction doesn't tell us who to credit, how do we know? We generally have to look at the various attributes on the transaction – maybe customer name, or where it is to be shipped, or the product, or the sales channel, or anything else – and compare those values to the list of things the payee is supposed to get credit for. The payee's list is called, generically, a **territory**. A territory takes many forms, but a territory definition along the lines of "Widgets or Rugalators sold in Western Iowa to Retail Outlets through the Reseller Channel" would be recognizable to most sales reps. In this case we have a product dimension, a customer dimension, a geographical dimension, and a sales channel dimension. Territories can have more or fewer dimensions. We will discuss territories in agonizing depth later on.

In the insurance world, there are (or should be) systems that explicitly track which agent is servicing which policies. This is a step removed from the "rep's name on the transaction" that we ICM implementers love, but matching transactions to the relevant servicing agents, then stamping their names on the transaction on its way into the ICM system, is a standard approach to ICM implementations in the insurance vertical.

In addition to the payee who caused the business event to happen, others might be credited as well. Almost invariably the payee's boss, and the boss's boss, will be paid for the payee's performance, and the usual route to accomplishing this is to give them their own credits for the transaction. This is often called **rollup**, and we'll discuss that idea in depth. In addition to the managerial hierarchy, there might be other people rewarded based on their roles in the company and in the sale (we'll refer to this as **overlay**), and each of them will also get credit for the same transactions. This can be some of the most complicated processing an ICM system performs.

To reiterate, the most important lesson to be learned here is, the transaction is different from the credit. The credit is a join between a transaction and a payee, and if a transaction is changed for whatever reason, the credits generated for that transaction (their existence and their values) will likely change because of it.

AGGREGATE STAGE

Having credited the load of transactions to the appropriate payees, what next? We measure them. We can add up the total revenue amount for them, or the number of units sold, or the number of orders. More interestingly, we might want to separate the credits into separate metrics – a Widget Metric and a Rugalator Metric, for example. We do that by either looking through the credits to attributes (like ProductID or ShipToState) on the underlying transactions they represent, or we might have an ICM system that puts attributes on the credits themselves. But however the system is architected, we need the ability to throw the credits into different buckets for separate aggregations.[3]

Most ICM products will allow you to refer to the value of a specific metric, and to aggregate those values intelligently at later stages in the calculation process. The system will usually allow you to get month-to-date, quarter-to-date, year-to-date, rolling months, or other periodic sums of values. So when we refer to a payee's Widget Metric, we are actually referring to either the current period or aggregated values of that metric. I use the convention of Metric.period (e.g., WidgetMetric.month or RugalatorMetric.year) to refer to the single or aggregated values of the credits in a payee's given metric.[4]

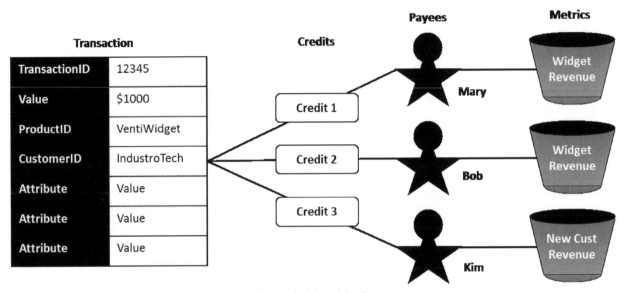

Figure 5 - One Transaction, Many Credits to Many Payees for Many Metrics

REWARD STAGE

So we have tied payees to events in the form of credits, and measured those credits in the form of metrics or buckets or what have you, then what's next? We calculate rewards based on how well the payee has done.

"How well the payee has done" could be absolute and flat: "We pay $2 for every Widget sold, and we pay 5% of all Rugalator revenue – no matter what." Or the reward could be based on attainment against a predefined level of performance we expect the sales rep or manager to achieve. This predefined level is often called a **quota**, or sometimes a **target** or a **goal**. Or all three interchangeably, sometimes in the same sentence spoken by the same person.[5] The actual performance against quota is called **attainment** (by me, if not by everyone else). Attainment equals actual performance divided by quota. If my quota is 100 Widgets, and I've actually sold 35 Widgets, I am at 35% attainment against quota.

Whether flat or attainment-based, we have the compensation plan to tell us how much the payee has earned for the results she has achieved. The plan should be explicit about what every percent of attainment, unit, dollar,

---

[3] This process is often called "bucketizing". Spellcheck programs and English majors hate this.

[4] The bucket analogy is not an exact one, by the way. You can only throw a rock into one bucket at a time, but a credit can contribute to multiple metrics. I might have a sales order that generates a single credit that contributes to both my Widget Revenue Metric, but also my New Customer Metric, because I sold a Widget to a customer who has never bought a Widget from us before. It's the same credit for the same transaction, but it's counted twice for compensation purposes. This is perfectly legit.

[5] In this book I'm going to call it **quota**, unless I forget and call it a target. Or a goal.

Euro, new customer, percent of customer satisfaction, or whatever else the metric is, is worth.

And now, I will hereby lay down the law on some compensation language. There is no universally (in comp) agreed upon definition of the words **commission** and **bonus**. This is odd considering how fundamental they are to the compensation domain. So I will cut the knot and end the confusion. You're welcome.

- A **commission** is the amount earned as a factor of the level of performance. Each incremental unit of performance results in incremental earnings.

  A commission is like a hillside: each additional step you take takes you higher (or lower) on the slope.
- A **bonus** is a yes/no decision on earnings based on rules or conditions written into the plan. For performance below that necessary to meet the bonus condition (like, maybe, the payee's quota?), there is no bonus. For performance above the condition, there is no additional bonus amount.

  A bonus is like a cliff. Before you step off, you are still where you were. After you step off, you are falling, but no amount of additional steps will make you fall further.

Perhaps this tasteful drawing will help clarify the difference:

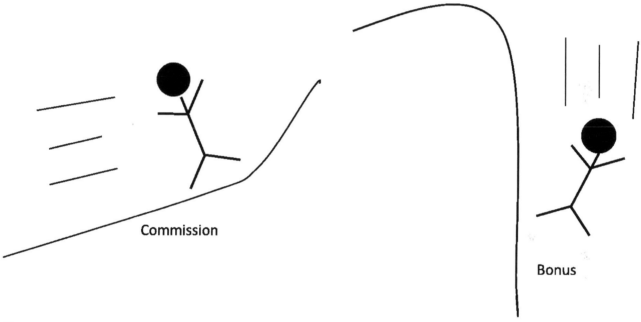

Figure 6 - Commissions vs Bonuses

Or maybe not. Of course, this being incentive comp, there are gray areas. Some commission plans require you meet a certain minimum level of performance before you start collecting commissions, but from that point forward, they behave like regular commissions. And some bonuses might be written as, if you exceed quota, or if your manager likes you, you get a bonus of 1% of your revenue for the year. That's very commission-like, but it still has the cliff of whether you hit your quota (or whether your manager likes you). But for the purposes of this book, consider commissions to be a slope, with earnings calculated as a factor of performance, and a bonus to be a cliff, with earnings based on meeting a specific condition in the plan. This will be on the test.

Sometimes the amount to pay is not explicitly stated. We might need to do some math or perform some lookups to tease the rate out. Most ICM systems will allow you to bring these intermediate values you've calculated to the surface for reporting and for later calculations. For example, if my commission rate is my target variable earnings divided by my quota,[6] the ICM system will probably allow me to do that math and then later, refer to that value

---

[6] Which, actually, it is – this is the foundational formula for base commission rates.

in calculations and reports. What are my **target variable earnings**? Target earnings are the value of commissions and bonuses I will earn if I hit *exactly* 100% of my quota – to the penny. More on this later in the book.

The Reward Stage of the ICM calculation process, then, is the place where we look at the values in your various buckets, apply rules and conditions to them, and generate the incentives we have agreed to pay you based on your compensation plan.

PAY STAGE

There is usually quite a bit of logic associated with the payment chunk of the ICM process. This is because this stage is where money changes hands, and folks on both sides of that interaction care deeply about it.

In its simplest form, we look at what you've earned this period, tell payroll or accounts payable how much that is, and they write you a check for that amount. In the real world it's a little harder because of the unfortunately common practice of rerunning the calculations for a period that's already been paid. That happens a lot for more or less good reasons, and it is important that we remember what we've already paid so we don't end up overpaying or underpaying the payees.

Every ICM system is different, but in general, each of the prior stages of the ICM process generates dynamic or fluid results. Add a transaction, change a territory or quota, even change a plan, and the results of the Accumulate, Aggregate, and Reward Stages will change to reflect what the calculations look like today. There usually is no permanent record of what the calculation looked like yesterday.

But the Payment Stage is different. Every payment to a payee is (generally) written in stone. Only in this way we can be sure that, if we recalculate and come up with a different answer, we will pay only the difference between the previous calculation and today's calculation. That additional payment amount will be added to the payment for the next open period in most ICM systems.

That difference might well be a negative amount, by the way. Most companies don't send bills to their sales reps if an order they sold **debooks** (i.e., the order is cancelled by the buyer) later, so the **delta** (the difference between payments) is generally withheld out of future earnings for the next open, unpaid period. Just more complexity in the Payment Stage, in other words.

Many ICM systems have the concept of **trial** payments and **posted** payments built in. A trial payment allows the Comp Team to generate a file or report of the payment amounts so they see how much will be paid if they hit the "post" button, but the payments are not yet written in stone at that point. This allows the team to get approvals from the CFO or VP of Sales, catch errors, become insanely jealous about how much the reps make, or whatever other functions are built around the payment process. When everyone is ready, the trial payments are posted (i.e., "written in stone"), and a file is sent to the Payroll or Accounts Payable system. Posted payments are saved and referenced in future payment processes. Once payments are posted, then any new payments in the period will generate positive or negative deltas, rather than a payment for the total amount of earnings for the period.

Why is ICM hard?

Or is it? Why would anyone need to build or use a jillion dollar software package just to figure out how much to pay people for doing their jobs? This is the Big Question, and the foundation of this book.

From a marketing perspective, I should probably tell you that ICM is fun-'n'-easy. But I hope you're realistic enough to know that's a fib. So yes, ICM really is that hard. I have spent most of my career making career limiting moves because I don't buy into the marketing message, and I think it does a disservice to customers to let them think their project will be a walk in the park. It might be, but that is the exception, and it's not something to plan on. I plan on it being hard, then try to come up with ways to make it easier.

There are lots of reasons why ICM is hard, but I think the reasons come down to these, and in roughly this order of impact:

- Bad data
- Bad processes
- Organizational issues
- Comp plan complexity

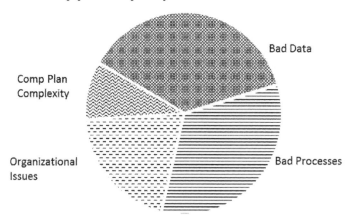

Figure 7 – Relative Project Impact of Complicating ICM Factors

Let's address each in turn.

BAD DATA

Let's begin with this: ICM is an incredibly data-dependent application, and it is dependent on more different source systems than just about any other application in the enterprise. Most systems in a company handle a single kind of data and then become the source of truth for the rest of the company for questions on the data they create and manage. For instance, HR creates and manages data about the people in the company, and the HR system is where you go to find out about employees. Sales Order Management owns the data about what the company has sold, and aside from possibly validating that the product sold is actually a product the company makes, it owns everything to do with creating order and transaction data.

ICM, on the other hand, is (generally) the source of truth for incentive comp results. To calculate them, though, it needs HR data and Sales Order Management data for sure, plus financial data, product data, customer data, shipment data, compliance data, customer satisfaction data, or any other source data used in comp calculations. Sometimes there are multiple upstream systems for the same kind of data – transaction data, for instance – and those systems might not model their data in the same way or mean the same things when they refer to a specific value.

And sometimes, the same event or object might be in two different systems but in such a way that they cannot be reconciled. Insurance carriers and brokers have this problem all the time. Prior to a merger, the same independent agents might have been selling for two carriers. After the carriers merge, it might well be impossible to determine that J. H. Smith for Carrier A is the same as John Henderson Smith for Carrier B without a human being looking at each one manually and making a guess.

And just try to reconcile sales information across the many systems that touch it, each of which looks at the data from a different perspective, and each of which uses different unique identifiers:

$1M in the Sales Order Management System

$1.3M in the CRM System
(I over-forecasted this one because they beat me up
for a discount to sign this quarter)

$780K in the Fulfillment System
(the SpaceWidgets are out of stock – sorry)

$390K in the Accounts Payable System
(this customer gets billed for 50% on shipping,
50% on formal acceptance)

The $1M Order from
Amalgamated Corp.

Figure 8 - One Event, Many Systematic Representations

So ICM, which is dependent on data from all of these systems, has a much tougher integration problem than most systems from which it draws data. Determining which data is needed,[7] what it means, and designing around its weaknesses, are generally significant parts of any ICM project.

The best data – your favorite data – the data you live and breathe by – is "bad" for ICM purposes when it doesn't adequately support commission and bonus calculations. What makes data "bad" for ICM? The answer to that includes data that is:

- Inaccurate
- Untimely
- Incomplete
- Unstable

Inaccurate data ought to be a no-brainer. You have to trust that the data you use to calculate and pay commissions is true or else you shouldn't be using it to generate real checks for real money. Why would any data in an enterprise be inaccurate? Don't you own and control your systems? Answer: no, not always. Data being fed to the ICM system might be coming from a reporting system that takes (presumably good) source data, but then applies logic, filters, or math to it. That's how the company wants to report on it, but it doesn't mean we can trust it to pay on it.

Or the inaccurate data might come from a system that was cobbled together from various others after corporate mergers, and the various systems don't agree on what certain values in certain fields mean. We'd always love to get pristine data from the original source system, but corporate politics might prevent that from happening. So we calculate and pay the best we can based on what we think we know, but we know that the results might well be wrong.

---

[7] Yes, I know "data" is a plural noun, so this sentence ought to read "Determining which data are needed". But I will generally be referring to data as a class or concept, not as many separate atomic 'datums', and will therefore typically say "data (class, single) is" rather than "data (objects, plural) are". It flows better. My insincere apologies if that offends anyone.

Incidentally, what exactly is "accuracy"? I'd like to believe in objective truth, but systematically, data is accurate if we all agree it's accurate, regardless of whether it maps directly and elegantly to anything real in the outside world. I've had customers tell me that the data from the system we're integrating with for the new ICM system? Yeah, that data isn't accurate, exactly, but it's what everyone in the company uses, so that's what we are going to pay on. So it is accurate as far as ICM is concerned, and we trust it from that perspective, but it isn't "true".

Untimely data is data that isn't available when you need it. We might need to pay commissions by the last day of the month after the business took place, but we don't get the transaction feed from our sales channel until the 15th of the month after that – not an uncommon scenario in Manufacturing and High Tech, by the way. So we pay our incentives for a given month twice: once without the channel data, then corrected a month later with the channel data. This makes the first payment, by definition and predictably, wrong. Reporting, accruals, trust in the system – all are compromised because the channel data is untimely. But it may be unavoidable.

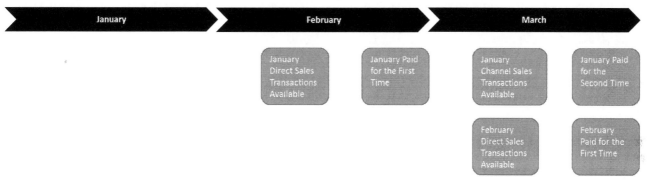

Figure 9 - Untimely Transaction Data

Incomplete data is data that doesn't include all the values you need to process it. It could be as easy as the data feed not being configured to include a particular field that is necessary for accurate incentive comp processing. That should be easy to fix. Except that it's sometimes practically impossible to get the change to the feed processed without a two-year-long IT project that is approved only after a cost-benefit analysis conducted by an independent department.

Sometimes plans need to apply logic to data about the values in your feed that aren't included in the feed itself. We might have sales territories for which we need to know the ship-to address for a customer, and all we have on the transaction itself is the customer name without any address information. Thus the transaction data is incomplete for our purposes until we join the transactions to the customer tracking system to pull out the additional address data we need. It's not that the raw transaction data is inaccurate; it's just that the source system that feeds it to us doesn't care about or track the value we need in order to pay compensation.

Unstable data is data that is known to change over time. It's quite possible that the data we receive is accurate, timely, and complete based on what we know now, but business decisions might change over time that would cause the calculations we perform to be wrong later. This is often the case with quotas. We might calculate commissions based on sales performance against quotas or targets. If the company is having a particularly good or particularly bad year, it is not uncommon to change quotas mid-year – and to make the changes retroactive back to the start of the year. Those quota changes can have an impact on commission calculations going back many months, depending on how the plans are written and when the change is made. So while the data was "true" as of when we used it the first time, now the truth has changed, and the results based on the first truth need to be recalculated against the second one.

This is something we need to design for as thoughtfully as possible. Reprocessing results from prior, already paid periods is generally easy from a software perspective – the math is the math. But from a reporting perspective, and from the perspective of the payees' trust in the system and even their motivation to sell, this is a red flag.

BAD PROCESSES

Bad processes are processes, policies and procedures that run counter to the efficient operation of the business. I believe there are two types of bad processes:

- Actively harmful practices that have become codified as business-as-usual processes; and
- Actively good practices that aren't followed because the business chooses not to.

An example of the first might a comp plan that incents payees **not** to sell – I'll be describing several of these later in the book.[8] They are usually pretty subtle, but sales reps might do the math and realize that they'll make more money by holding a deal back until the next quarter or next year because they have either already hit a payment cap, or because they realize they won't get past a threshold this quarter. Where sales reps have any control over when deals will be signed, they will often do something counterproductive (from the perspective of the author of the comp plan) that will hurt company performance now because it will help their commission check later. We call these unintended consequences, and I savor them like fine wine whenever I find new ones.

An example of the second might be an incentive like President's Club, which is designed to reward the most successful sales reps with an all-expenses-paid trip in February to someplace warm and luxurious. Only reps who have sold more than 110% of their quota are invited. Except… this rep at 98% of quota called to complain so the VP told us we had to invite him too, since he's a good guy and it was just bad luck he missed hitting quota this year, wasn't his fault, really. Good policy – reward the best reps. Bad process – allowing anyone who whines loudly enough to go. It cheapens it for the people who earned it, and it makes the Sales Ops team look like bad guys because they tried to follow the policy until they were overruled.

Most often, bad processes come down to making exceptions to policies and rules. Exceptions are bad for ICM, both systematically and in the broader sense of incentive programs. Sometimes exceptions have to be made (and designed for) where it is known that something cannot be measured by the system due to bad data or other factors that can't be written into the comp plans. And sometimes, business situations arise that mean that extraordinary measures must be taken to make the system fairer to the payees.

But for some customers, it often seems that exceptions are the rule, not the exception. Where this is the case, the rules written into the comp plans become meaningless because the reps know that they might be overridden, making actual performance against metrics less important than a payee's ability to talk his or her manager into making another exception "just this once".

We'll talk more about process failures later in the book. What's important, from our point of view, is that bad processes make your ICM program less effective as a whole.

ORGANIZATIONAL ISSUES

The best, most efficient operations occur when all the constituents of a business process and the systems that support it work in partnership with each other for the greater good. And there are companies where this happens, and projects for these companies are a joy to work on. But, sadly, there are many where it doesn't.

The business side – Sales, Sales Ops, and Compensation – is often in an adversarial relationship with the technical side – IT and the peripheral system owners. As an outsider, I sometimes perceive that one side is in the right, and sometimes I believe it's the other – neither business nor IT always have the moral high ground. But where there

---

[8] Hey! Did you know "incent" isn't actually a verb? My apologies, but we'll be using it as one since there isn't a better way to express the concept. I guess "motivate" would work, but I like the whiff of bribery that comes with "incent".

are fundamental disagreements between the sides about what the system should do, that's a project that is in trouble.

I was working on requirements for a project once for a Financial Services company. After one discovery workshop session, the IT director took me aside in the hallway to tell me, "Don't worry about what the comp people tell you. I'll give you the **real** system requirements." Sometimes I dream that I'll be allowed to ignore one side or the other, but in this case, I actually thought the business folks were being perfectly reasonable in what they were asking for. But it spotlighted the difficulties we'd be facing on the project: the business and IT folks weren't on the same side.

Figure 10 - Too Much Time Spent Looking for Clip Art

Sometimes the battle isn't between business and IT; sometimes it's between Sales Ops and Sales (or HR, or Finance). And some companies just allow it to become a free-for-all. For our purposes, what matters most is that, in the event of a dysfunctional compensation ecosystem, *the comp folks always lose the battle*. They may have comp plan verbiage, policies, company rules, even the law on their side, but if they don't get the support of the rest of the company, they will not succeed. Further, they will generally be blamed for all the problems the company has experienced getting incentives paid.

Where the organizational problems are knotty enough, no amount of software in the world will make ICM work for that company. But I try not to say that out loud when I'm working for an ICM software vendor. And sometimes we can use the system implementation project as a lever to help get the organization on track.

COMPENSATION PLAN COMPLEXITY

Most ICM products will handle most types of compensation plan complexity reasonably well. Non-linear rates, thresholds, conditions – all that stuff is part of the bread and butter of comp plans and of ICM systems.

But there are classes of comp plan design issues that can be, essentially, insurmountable in software. And many of those challenges seem, on the surface, to be perfectly rational. It's only when you try to code and test them that you realize that the math just doesn't make sense. We'll discuss these at length further on, but generally speaking, where the order of transaction processing can impact the output of the system, then the plan is flawed. In other words, in a given plan period, if a rep would be paid more if Transaction 1 arrives before Transaction 2 than she or he would be paid if Transaction 2 arrived before Transaction 1, then you have a plan that will be impossible to test, and worse, will lead to reps "gaming" the system and disputing every commission amount. It's just a math problem inherent in the comp plan logic – it's not a failure of the ICM software.

As an example of this, consider George:

COMP PLAN:
Pay $1000 per Widget until Payee exceeds Rugalator Quota.
Then pay $2000 per Widget for every Widget sold after that.

It's October 1st.
George has sold 98 Rugalators against a Rugalator Quota of 100.

It's October 10th.
Blue, Inc. agrees to buy 5 Widgets from George.
If George sends in that paperwork, he will receive $5000.
But George is negotiating a deal with LimeGreen LLC
for some Rugalators. It makes him forgetful.

It's October 29th.
LimeGreen LLC buys 3 Rugalators from George.
George sends in the paperwork.

It's October 31st.
George "remembers" he has the Blue Inc. Widget Order.
George sends in the paperwork and receives $10,000.
Same order, but by holding it, George pockets an extra $5000.
Bad George! B-A-A-D-D-D GEORGE!!!

Figure 11 - George is a Naughty Sales Rep

But more importantly, even if the plan math works and the ICM system has all the data it needs to calculate accurate results, a plan that's too complex will be a distraction from selling for the payees. It should be possible to explain to the reps exactly how they're being paid in 25-words-or-less, and it should be obvious from the explanation exactly what the company wants and expects from the payees. If there are too many conditions, exceptions, gates, thresholds, non-linear rates, and nit-picky details, the reps won't understand their plans. Or they might understand their plans, but just not in the way the plans were written, leading to disputes at best, and unintended consequences at worst.

Again, that's not an ICM software problem, but it is an SPM problem and it's something that diminishes the return on investment from the comp program.

Time – the Hidden Challenge of ICM

Bad data, bad processes, organizational issues, and plan complexity are challenges in and of themselves, but the real problems that they contribute to are all about **time**. By time, I am referring to the common practice of recalculating and re-paying incentive comp for a given period numerous times throughout the year.

Reprocessing prior periods isn't a problem addressed by most systems in a company. It's not clear what "reprocessing February" in an HR system would even mean. Financial systems generally try very hard not to do it. If you go back and restate prior results in most financial systems, that's considered a *Very Bad Thing*, and Wall Street and the regulators sometimes take notice of it. But it's a common practice in incentive compensation. And the reasons why it happens keep coming back to bad data and bad processes, which I believe I might have mentioned previously.

Most ICM applications are very good at the mechanical aspects of recalculation. Change the data in some way, go back and rerun, and the application will create new results that reflect the new data. And the ICM software will generally be pretty good about paying or recovering only the delta payment amount out of future earnings. So where's the problem?

There are actually a couple of problems. One is about reporting. Okay, I earned $100 in January. I got the report at the beginning of February, got the check, and everything was fine. Now it's April, and I see that I've got an extra $5 in my check, and my report says something about a balance from January. Great, I'm happy, but why did it change?

And then in July, I see that I *owe $15 back*, with another entry for January. *Say what the huh?!?*

Figure 12 - Impact of Retroactive Processing

It's usually pretty easy to figure out what changed when there are new or adjusted transactions. But a retroactive change to some other data that supports the compensation process – say, a quota or a territory change, or a change to some status that's used in the condition check of a bonus – those are hard to find and report on. It's partly how the data is stored in the ICM system, partly about the way systems process rules, but it can also be about plan complexity, unstable data, or an exception made behind the scenes. Whatever the reason for the changed results, the main outcome is that the payees stop trusting the system and start doing their own accounting to be sure they're not being cheated out of money they feel should be going to them. [9]

The other problem presented by reprocessing prior periods is a purely operational one. Software is not magic and results are not generated instantaneously. We get spoiled by the desktop applications we use – make a change to a cell in a spreadsheet and it updates everything lickety split. But if you have a system processing millions of transactions for thousands of payees, that takes time – sometimes several hours, depending on variables like hardware size, plan complexity, and system architecture.

If you want to go back and reprocess the results for several months, you might need several of those several-hour processing blocks to make it happen, and sometimes there aren't enough hours in the night to pull that off. I worked with a customer who reprocessed every monthly period every night for the entire year – a lot of transactions for a lot of payees. They complained bitterly about how long it took. As the vendor, we complained bitterly that they did it in the first place. We had not specified enough hardware to enable them to do that when we were selling to them, which was before we knew that this was something they felt they needed to do. It never even occurred to us to ask them about it.

Could they have avoided it by changing a process or six to make it unnecessary to recalculate every night? I believe so, had they chosen to, and I believe they eventually did make some process changes. But with so much churn in their prior period calculations and payments, did their payees really feel that the system was paying

---

[9] This is called "**shadow accounting**" in the ICM / SPM biz. There's reason to believe it actually lowers your revenue if the reps spend too much time doing it.

them accurately? I'm doubtful.

On most projects, one of the first questions I ask is whether the customer recalculates prior, paid periods. And almost always I hear, "No. Not really. Well, occasionally, but only for special circumstances. Actually, we usually reprocess three prior periods every month. Unless we need to go back further. Yeah, okay, *we do it all the time*. We're so ashamed." But even if the customer stops at 'no', I still assume and plan on 'yes', because they always do.

For whatever reason a company might choose to recalculate their incentives in later periods, recalculation absolutely must be planned for, designed for, and tested for. And that can make an otherwise rational system suddenly seem far more complex than anticipated.

The Weirdness – It's a Technical Term

If it isn't one thing, it's another. Virtually every large and complex ICM project uncovers something that makes experienced consultants shake their heads, take a deep breath, and say, "Alrighty then!" For want of a better term, I call it the "Weirdness".

Sometimes we can guess what the Weirdness might be during the sales process or during the project kickoff, but often we don't find it until we are deep into the process of gathering system requirements. Some customers flaunt their Weirdness. For them, it's a source of pride that they have a problem that cannot be solved in Earthly software. Others seem genuinely unaware that this thing they've been doing for years is Weird. But it's that process, policy, or procedure that cannot be described without the SME stumbling over it and apparently contradicting everything we have heard before (or whatever was just agreed to two minutes ago).

Often the Weirdness is in service to a comp plan strategy that makes perfect sense – except that the available data doesn't support it in an elegant way. Or it might have been based on an exception made for one payee seven years ago that HR said had to be made for all payees forever after in the interests of fairness. Or it's a strange reporting requirement that apparently is the opposite of the comp requirements. It often has to do with some of the temporal issues we discussed in the last section. It could be anything; if I could tell you what it was here, it wouldn't be Weird, would it?

The point is, you wouldn't be thinking about maybe implementing an ICM system if ICM processing were easy for your company. There are lots of hard things about ICM built into the domain. Most off-the-shelf ICM systems handle the normal hard stuff with their eyes closed and a hand tied behind their backs. Ah, but the Weirdness… That's where we need to get creative to make the system work.

Figure 13 – Discovering the Weirdness.

Bad Data

- Inaccurate
- Untimely
- Incomplete
- Unstable

Bad Processes

- Bad processes codified
- Good processes ignored

Organizational Issues

- IT vs. Business
- Everyone vs. Comp

Comp Plan Complexity

- Overly complex
- Incomprehensible

Time

- Reprocessing periods often

The Weirdness

- Ahhh, the Weirdness

Figure 14 - Why is ICM Hard?

CHAPTER THREE – ADMINISTERING VARIABLE COMPENSATION

Variable comp, and ICM in particular, is an application without a fixed home in the world. By this I mean, it's not necessarily a Sales application, or a Sales Ops application, or a Finance application, or an HR application – it might be any one of them. In companies with lots of business units, it might be a Sales Finance function for one business unit, and an HR function for another. In insurance, it's sometimes a Marketing function: they are paying the people who take their products to market. It can live anywhere, which is one of the things that drive ICM software sales people crazy. They never know who might be interested in talking to them, so figuring out where a potential buyer sits can be time consuming.

Wherever it lives, ICM is often administered by a team of specialists. For the purposes of this book, we'll refer to this team as the Compensation Department, or more informally, the Comp Team.

How is it Done Today?

There is a broad spectrum of more or less formal ICM solutions in the business world. ICM operations can be handled in method ranging anywhere from:

- Completely manually, to
- Using spreadsheets, to
- Using an internally or custom developed "application", to
- Using a packaged application

Which method is best? They all are, depending on a company's unique circumstances.

MANUAL PROCESSING

If you have small number of reps generating a small number of transactions with simple metrics and comp plans, then manually is great. A human being looks at every order, applies local knowledge, maybe makes a phone call to the sales manager to verify, and says, "This rep just got $xx for this order. It'll go out in the next pay run." The admin might enter the results into a spreadsheet for tracking, but the spreadsheet might not even be doing the calculation. In the event of a query or dispute, a phone call takes care of the problem. Sales reports can be an email to the rep with a copy to the manager.

SPREADSHEETS

Growth is the name of the game, and when a function that used to be done in someone's head grows a little too unwieldy, technology enters the fray. Spreadsheets are wonderful tools that have grown into something amazingly versatile and powerful. ICM vendors will tell you all the problems with them, but for the small- to mid-sized company, it's hard to beat the flexibility, simplicity, and most of all, the low-cost of using spreadsheets.

Spreadsheets will handle very complex logic,[10] and a skilled spreadsheet jockey can program new comp plan logic in hours, rather than days or weeks if the plans change suddenly. Spreadsheets can be their own

---

[10] Here's a deep dark ICM industry secret: spreadsheets will often handle more complex logic than packaged ICM applications can. That's not necessarily a slam on the packaged apps. If you need that much logic to pay your people, your plans are almost certainly too complex.

compensation reports for the payees – the numbers you want to communicate are all right there, and the layout can even help explain the comp plan logic to the person seeing the report in a way that a report out of a system might not.

So what are the downsides to spreadsheets the ICM vendors will warn you about? First and foremost, spreadsheets are **error-prone**. They are programmed by knowledgeable and skilled people, but everyone makes mistakes, and it's difficult to test a spreadsheet. And it is far too easy to overtype a cell thinking you are changing a value, when in fact you have just destroyed a formula.

I saw this on a project several years ago – an admin had overtyped a single cell in the middle of a large compensation worksheet, so in one cell, a complex formula with dependencies all over the worksheet was turned into the hardwired value "17". That spreadsheet was copied and reused every month for several months afterwards with the mistake buried in it. It wasn't until we were trying to validate results from the new ICM system and couldn't get one set of numbers to tie out that the mistake was discovered. At that point, the Comp Team had to go back and figure out how many payments were wrong because of it, and the answer was "lots". It's easier to rigorously test an ICM system than a mass of spreadsheets.

Spreadsheets are **not auditable**. A change to a spreadsheet doesn't give you a paper-trail to figure out who made the change, what was changed, and when was it made. In the land of Sarbanes-Oxley, where auditable processes are king, this can be worrisome. It's awfully hard to have confidence in the rock-solidity of your numbers when anyone with a laptop can accidentally or fraudulently tamper with the system that handles one of the major expenses of your company. Packaged ICM applications usually have auditing built in.

Spreadsheets are **not scalable**. Spreadsheet software will allow virtually unlimited rows and columns and worksheets, but that does not make them infinitely useful after a certain size. There comes a point in a company's life when the spreadsheets hold you back. The comp plan complexity is too great, there are too many exceptions, finding the right row and column for the reference value you need is too cumbersome, or you have too many reps and transactions – whatever reason, you will know when you have gone beyond what spreadsheets want to do for you.

HOMEGROWN OR CUSTOM APPLICATIONS

By this I am referring to any system built to a single company's specification, whether by internal IT resources or by an outside consulting firm. The advantage to this kind of system is that it is tailored to the problem it will be addressing, and that is not a trivial thing. It can be made to look like anything you want it to, and you can arrange for it to do practically anything you can think of. Some homegrown systems handle amazingly complex calculations and processes because they are explicitly designed to. And the best part is, you know who built the system, so if anything goes wrong, you know who to yell at. That's sometimes a comfort.

How are they developed? At some point, the Sales VP or CFO will approach the CIO and say, "You know, we've outgrown spreadsheets. Can we build something a little more bulletproof to manage the sales comp? Our plans are easy – I mean, we're doing them on laptops now, right?" The CIO will pass the problem off to the IT honcho and say, "Make it so." Because really, how hard can it be? Just grab data out of the Sales Order Management system, plug in a few formulas, badda bing, job done, no one gets hurt, move on to the next thing.

So the IT guy has a meeting to get system requirements from the Comp Team and starts having the "Why is ICM Hard?" discussion. Uh oh, looks like we might need two or three meetings for this requirements gathering phase. Six weeks later, neither side is happy with the other. The IT people think the Comp Team is making stuff up just to mess with their heads, and the Comp Team thinks the IT side are too lazy and inflexible and they won't support the company's business operations. The IT group eventually nails down enough requirements to build a system that will manage the comp plans in place today because they've been given a deadline and they need to deliver something.

Okay, so that's a little unfair, but not by much. If you haven't dealt with ICM systematically before, it isn't always clear what the requirements mean, and from there, what variables must be built into the system to make it work now and next year. There are a lot of homegrown applications out there, whether built internally or by a consulting company. They may be big and powerful and perform like champs, but the nearly universal complaint about them is that they are inflexible and unresponsive to changes in the business. They are nearly always built to manage incentives exactly as they are done at a point in time. Over time, the one-off application might grow and expand its functionality, but if its foundation isn't built with flexibility in mind, it will eventually be limiting to the Comp Team.

One other issue I have seen with home-made systems is that they tend to become very monolithic. Everything from loading data, to calculations, to reports – the entire process gets embedded into the system. This makes it incredibly complex. And when that guy who designed it a decade ago leaves the company, it can turn a request for a simple change to the system into a two-year project. I have been in the position of trying to integrate a new ICM system – essentially, the calculation engine – into an ecosystem that would still have the legacy, homebrew system in place to provide other functionality. We were told that there was no way to turn off the commission calculation in the old system – they couldn't shut that functionality off, and once they brought data into the system, it was going to do what it was going to do and there was no stopping it.

Can you tell I've spent a lot of time working with ICM system vendors? During the ICM sales cycle, there always came a time when we get into the discussion of "build versus buy" with the customer. Why should they spend a bazillion bucks on our system when they have a perfectly good IT department sitting there with nothing better to do than to build it themselves? It was nearly a universal case that if the CIO has ever tried to build an ICM system before, we always got a recommendation for "buy" decision. If the CIO hasn't, then the recommendation was sometimes to build it internally.

PACKAGED APPLICATIONS

A packaged application doesn't fit as neatly as a well-tailored internal application. It can't, because it is built for the entire ICM universe, not just for a particular customer. But the flip side of that coin is that it is built for flexibility – it was built for the entire universe. But the downside of that is, it was built based on the common practices and customer requirements that the vendor has seen and rolled into the product. If you have that weird double-overhand half-gainer with a twist (unless you are holding a pair of jacks or better) in your comp plan or process, and the vendor has never been asked to accomplish anything like that before (and probably would have said 'no' if they had been asked), that won't be in the application you buy. But conversely, if you ask for the double-overhand half-gainer, and another customer does, and another, the function stands a chance of being incorporated into the product. No guarantee, but it's possible.

Which leads to another advantage of the packaged solution: it does change and grow over time. The vendors have entire Engineering departments whose job it is to improve the application, whether in terms of functionality, performance, ease of use, aesthetics, or any other desirable quality. You are theoretically just an upgrade away from a product that might suit your needs better afterwards than it does today.

But note – most ICM vendors have, at some point in their histories, created new versions of the application that did not have upgrade paths from the prior versions. Time and technology march on. When the technology has evolved to the extent that there is more benefit from rebuilding the product than from improving it, vendors do have to make the agonizing decision about whether to take the leap. This can be a tremendous expense for customers on the old version – essentially, they must reimplement, rather than upgrade, and the vendors are keenly aware of the unhappiness they will cause in their customer-base if they re-architect. Something for you to consider in the decision process.[11]

This book is aimed primarily for companies operating at the upper end of the spreadsheet method through companies using home-built and packaged applications. If you are in the sweet spot of spreadsheets, or if you are still doing compensation manually, there may be big chunks of this book that don't apply to you. The chapters on comp theory and best practices might still be useful, but the systematic stuff might not.

Who Does ICM?

Stereotypically, outsiders tend to think of the Compensation Department as being divided between "business" and "IT". The business folks are the ones who deal with the payees, comp plans, and the results generated by the system as they relate to the humans and companies being paid. They deal with the queries and disputes, and are generally the ones who understand how the payees are getting their money.

The IT staff are the ones who deal with the systems that support the business. They keep the lights blinking, and they make sure data is flowing in and out. They do performance tuning on the hardware, software, and networks.

Sometimes all of this is done by one person, and sometimes it's a team of dozens on each side. Some business staff are very savvy about the systems they use and interface to, and often the IT folks understand the comp plan logic inside out. But regardless of the makeup of the team, this logical breakdown makes sense of the kinds of functions that must be performed to get the commission and bonus checks out on time.

Let's explore the different functions that make up ICM in a large company – say, ConGlomCo, Inc., the world's scrappiest Widget and Rugalator[12] manufacturing company.

THE COMP LEAD

Let's call ConGlomCo's Comp Lead "Tammy"[13] for the sake of making her more human for you. Tammy could be of any gender and be named anything ("Tommy"?), but Tammy is where we will start and someone we will often come back to. I'm going to go weirdly deep into who Tammy (sometimes) is because this role is so central to the ICM function and the ICM project, and it's important to have a sense of what this job entails. I promise the descriptions of the other roles will be far less cosmic and psychological, but I hope you'll bear with me on this one.

Tammy the Comp Lead could have any title from Comp Admin to Comp Analyst to Comp Manager to Director of Comp, depending on how titles work at ConGlomCo and how big the group is. Tammy is the person who 'gets it' with respect to how incentive compensation is paid at ConGlomCo. She may not manage the Comp Department, but she runs the day-to-day operations. She knows the comp plans inside out, knows the systems well enough to know exactly what she can get out of them and what she can't, knows the history, and knows where the bodies are buried. Sometimes Tammy knows exactly how much every payee is going to be paid this

---

[11] A SaaS solution might help you avoid that problem, incidentally. The SaaS vendors are responsible for managing software upgrades themselves, so they may be better able to head off the orphan code line problem.

[12] I hope you will take the idea of Widgets and Rugalators in stride as representing whatever it is that a multi-product company sells. I understand that your company doesn't sell Widgets. Or Rugalators either, come to think of it.

[13] Why "Tammy"? I worked for a system vendor in the early days of ICM. The Comp Leads for three of our first five customers were Tami, Tammi, and Tammy, and I've met others with that name and in that role since. Coincidence? You make the call, but I think not. At any rate, our Tammy is a composite of many people, some of whom were named Tammy. It's kind of a tribute to some people who taught me a lot.

month even before the transactions arrive and the system processes (no kidding – I've seen it).

Tammy could well be the most cynical person in the company. She has spent years making commissions and bonuses happen despite the lousy data, unstable systems, and the awful processes she is forced to follow. She has been there longer than the VP of Sales, and she was there before the previous one too. She despises all sales people with a passion that burns white hot, and sometimes she lets it show, but she would throw herself on a grenade to be sure they get paid accurately and on time.

Despite that, she is too often perceived as the enemy by the sales reps, some of whom have cars that are worth more than Tammy's annual salary. And she is only the enemy until they need an exception handled – then they sweet talk her and tell her she's the greatest and, "We couldn't do it without *YOU*, Tammy!" Tammy is not fooled; Tammy was not born yesterday. Sometimes, in some companies, Tammy is invited to President's Club; usually she is not.

Tammy has infinite responsibilities and practically no authority. She often doesn't go home until after midnight for days at a time at quarter- and year-end. Her only job satisfaction, and it's not much to cling to, is that she knows that if she gets hit by a bus, ConGlomCo will come to a screeching halt. There's no one who else who can make sure the sales reps get their commissions, and there's no way those lazy overpaid jerks will sell anything unless we bribe them to.

I'm spending a lot of time on hypothetical Tammy's personality, and of course it's a ridiculous generalization to say that everyone in this position works, thinks and feels the way I've described. Except…

Except that I've met this person numerous times on numerous projects over the years, and I have developed a tremendous respect for her (or him). She is frequently fighting an uphill battle against overwhelming odds, and she is often the most underappreciated person in the company. The fact that ConGlomCo is doing an ICM implementation means that they have finally realized that the current system (or lack thereof) is broken, and any failures to pay incentives over the years might not have been Tammy's fault, though she might have gotten the blame for them when they happened.

Note to companies: if you don't have Tammy on the payroll, you probably should find her. The trouble is, it can take years for someone to become Tammy.

And here's a hint for any of you consultants doing your first ICM implementations: do not disregard Tammy or devalue what she has to tell you because you think she's not as technically savvy as you are. That's possibly true, but Tammy knows everything you need to know to make the new system work. Sometime Tammy gets caught up in how things were done in the old system, and sometimes she insists that a million exceptions be built into the new system because that's how it works now, but there's a reason for that.

Remember, she is smart enough to know that the old system and old processes were rotten; but *she never had the authority to change them*. And unless someone with "VP" after their name comes along and changes the processes especially for this project, *Tammy doesn't have the authority to define requirements for the new ICM as anything other than the way things are done today*. We never want to build the old system in new software, and she doesn't want us to, but the Comp Lead is not authorized to tell you to do it "smarter", even if she would dearly love to. We'll talk about this problem in more detail a little later.

Okay, enough about Tammy for the moment. Let's discuss other roles involved in administering variable compensation.

COMP ADMINS

There may be many others in the Comp Department who assist Tammy. Comp Admins or Comp Analysts is a broad title for the people who work on the business side to maintain data, validate results, answer queries and disputes from the payees, and perform other tasks pertaining to incentive comp. Sometimes they have specialized tasks, while others might be jacks-of-all-trades in the department.

How many of them should there be? That's a tough question, and one that gets asked often. It all comes down to the complexity of the comp plans and the quality of the systems and processes supporting them. If the plans pay a flat $2 per Widget sold and 5% of Rugalator revenue, and the data feeds are accurate, complete and timely? You can get by with far fewer Comp Admins. If the data is lousy and the plans are incomprehensible? You can't get enough. The benchmarks are widely scattered because it's hard to make apples-to-apples comparisons. I have seen ratios for payees-to-admins of anywhere from around 30:1 to 200:1 in the high-tech space, which tends to be a high-touch kind of model.

This leads to an important point. When making the case for building a new ICM system, eliminating staff isn't really a factor in the return on investment story. Sure, if your systems are really awful (or non-existent) today and if you require infinite hand-holding to get the payroll runs out, then yes, you might be able to eliminate or retool some of the staff. But compensation is a hands-on endeavor, and you won't be able to build a system that runs itself and automates every aspect of paying your sales force.

Further, and cynically, the admin staff isn't that expensive. It's a lot cheaper to add a couple of admins and give them computers than it is to implement ICM software. The ROI is not about admin costs. *The ROI is eliminating payment errors* (which are always on the overpayment side), *improved data for reporting and analytics, greater system stability and performance, and greater flexibility in comp plan management*. But eliminating an admin or two won't pay for the new system.

THE COMP PLAN DESIGNER

The Comp Plan Designer is generally not in the Comp Department. Usually she is in a finance role of some sort. The common practice is that, sometime early in the fourth quarter, corporate will determine the revenue target for the upcoming year. The various execs, but primarily the Sales VP, will spring into action to find a way to deliver that number. This involves organizing and fine tuning the sales model, tweaking the sales channels, considering the probable impact of new and obsolete products, and devising compensation plans that will lead the sales force to applying their best efforts to selling exactly what the company needs them to sell. This is where the Comp Plan Designer comes in.

The Comp Plan Designer could start from a blank sheet to build the comp plans for the upcoming year from scratch. More likely and more ideally, though, she will take into account the sales organization and sales roles currently in place, the data available to the ICM system, and current plan structures and metrics. This makes sense because comp plans that require nonexistent data will very likely fail. At the same time, she doesn't want to be limited to just tweaking what's already there – she needs room for flexibility and creativity to address changing market conditions. The right answer is a balance between the "as-is" state (known-good because they're paying on it now) and a better "to-be" state.

Ideally, the Comp Plan Designer is consulting with Tammy, Sales Management, IT, and Finance throughout the process to assure a smooth transition from this year's to next year's plans. And by early in the final month of the last quarter the Comp Plan Designer will deliver to Tammy the new plans for configuration into the ICM system. Tammy and her crew will figure out how to translate the plans into system-ese, build them out and test them in a sandbox environment, gather any extra data elements that might be needed, and be ready to roll out with the new plans in production by the end of the first month of the first quarter when checks need to go out.

That's the ideal scenario. The common scenario is that by the end of the last quarter it has become obvious that the new plans won't be approved in time, so Tammy is told to "just pay draws for the first month, okay?" How much should the draws be? Okay, fine, we'll do that. In a good year, the plans have been approved by the last week of the first quarter, and Tammy and her staff work all weekend to slam them into the production ICM system, push the "process" button, and cover their ears hoping nothing explodes.

In too many companies, Tammy and IT will not have been consulted throughout this process. That leads to the stomach-churning moment when she realizes that the new plans cannot be configured in the current system with the data available. In a rational company that would lead to taking the plans back to the drawing board. In an irrational company (i.e., all of them), Tammy is told to "just make it happen, m'kay?" And amazingly enough, she sometimes finds a way, but it will be heavily manual and involve creating and codifying a lot of bad processes to manage it. Those new bad processes will then become permanent system requirements moving forward. The odds are slim that anyone will allocate budget to getting a data feed that supports the new plans for the Comp Department from a new source system, so they'll scrounge the data from reports or out of thin air.

Many companies don't get their plans sent out until halfway through the year. This is demoralizing for the Comp Department and leaves the sales force without guidance about what they should be doing. They mostly just work to last year's metrics plus whatever rumors they might have picked up, and they hope the metrics won't change significantly this year. A good friend of mine got his comp plan on – literally – the last day of the quarter and discovered that instead of being paid on revenue, he was being paid on profitability. Too often optimizing one of those metrics minimizes the other, and that was the case for him. For several months he had been pushing for the wrong thing from a commission and a company strategy perspective.

I don't want to sound like I'm blaming the Comp Plan Designer for these process breakdowns. There are usually lots of people with their fingers in the pie. Someone needs a part of the plan tweaked for this group, that group won't accept this plan because it results in a pay cut, this Sales Manager won't give up his territories to that one, etc. They say a camel is a horse designed by a committee, and the wreckage of the Comp Plan Designer's formerly neat and elegant plans that is eventually shoehorned into place can be a classic case of the Comp Committee "helping" the process along.

SYSTEM ADMINISTRATORS

We've been discussing the business side so far, but there are a lot of technical resources who must support ICM processes as well. There's a group we usually just call "IT" – "Information Technology", but that's not very precise. In that group are System Administrators who own the hardware and software that on which the comp operations run. They procure, maintain and tune the database and calculation servers. They keep the network backbone linking the systems up to spec. They make sure the data feeds into and out of the ICM system are processed properly. They keep the report servers up, and are generally responsible for generating new reports and queries as needed. This is the group that keeps the lights blinking, in other words.

Sometimes there is a dedicated team of IT staff assigned to the ICM systems, with others brought in as needed in special circumstances. This works best, in general, because after a short while, they and the business side of the team can begin to get into a rhythm of working together and start to speak something approaching the same language. Sometimes the IT staff are assigned to the ICM system on a part-time basis, in addition to being allocated to other systems as well. This is still pretty good – they get continuity of knowledge and experience.

The worst case is when IT and the business side are completely segregated from each other. Given the distributed nature of IT and systems today, this can easily happen. When this is the case, the two sides are more likely to have an adversarial relationship. In that situation, again, the ICM business team usually loses the battles. They need a lot of attention to keep the system operational, and anything less than whole-hearted support causes roadblocks.

OTHER CONSTITUENTS: SALES MANAGEMENT

Sales Management is everyone from sales managers (the bosses of the individual sales reps) on up through the organization to the people who actually define the sales process. Up to a certain level, it is not uncommon for some of these people to be payees in the system – managers, directors, and VPs who direct the sales force and are rewarded for the success of their people. Aside from their own commission and bonus checks, these people need reports and analytics from the system to enable them to have greater clarity into what is really happening among their subordinates.

OTHER CONSTITUENTS: FINANCE

There is a nebulous class of people who are interested in reports and analytics from the ICM system at a more corporate level than Sales Management. They tend to be pretty demanding about what they want from the system in terms of data and dimensions of data. Since the project team often only meets them for one hour during that one reporting requirements workshop and then never sees them again, we tend to regard them as shy and skittish creatures who rarely come into the light.

But make no mistake, these are the people who really get the most return on investment from a new ICM system. With a better ICM system, they can finally get good, scrubbed data[14] to use to analyze trends, forecast revenue and expenses, and respond to market conditions. So it is up to the project team to design a solution that will provide the level of analytics these folks need.

OTHER CONSTITUENTS: PERIPHERAL SYSTEMS OWNERS

There are many systems upstream of the ICM system – the sources of data used to calculate and pay incentives. And there are a few downstream systems as well – systems that receive data from the ICM system. A change to any of these systems has impacts on everything downstream, so it is important to view the enterprise IT ecosystem as a unified whole when looking at changes to data, processes, or plans. It is good to have periodic meetings between representatives of each of these systems to be sure that this tiny insignificant barely noticeable little tweak I'm considering making to my process won't drive the company to a systematic meltdown (see **APPENDIX TWO**). There is often an **Enterprise Architect** whose job it is to keep track of all of a company's system interactions and make sure no one steps on anyone else's toes, but I've seen Enterprise Architects throw up their hands in disgust when it comes to ICM.

One reason for this is that ICM, by its nature, a moving target. It must be reconfigured regularly to meet changes in the marketplace. Most systems in a company are "set it and forget it" – once you have configured them to suit your operational needs, they pretty much stay that way until further notice. But you are constantly rewriting compensation logic over the life of the ICM system.[15] A new metric on a single comp plan can mean new data feeds in and new data out, so other systems must at least be aware of what the Comp Department is up to, and in a happy world, they contribute to it.

---

[14] "Scrubbed data" – data that has been validated for accuracy every month by every sales person in the company. The sales folks tend to be the most motivated QA department in existence where sales data is concerned.
[15] That is, you do if your ICM system is flexible enough to allow it. If not, that might be one reason you're considering investing in a different system (or ought to).

CHAPTER FOUR – WHAT DO ICM SYSTEMS DO?

Having discussed what ICM is and having met the people who use, care for, and care about it, let's talk about what the system does and how it supports the incentive compensation management process. An ICM system calculates and pays incentives to people, companies, and other entities for performance against predefined metrics. Most off-the-shelf ICM systems have a few bits of functionality in common that allow them to do this.

Data

At a minimum, ICM systems must store and maintain – systematically or manually – data about the payees and about the events that are used to track the payees' performance against metrics. Inevitably, there will be other kinds of data needed as well. We commonly divide these types of data into three categories: reference data, transaction data, and plan data.

A note on style: I will be using Object.Attribute (or System.Object.Attribute) to refer to representations of data in a company's systems. By this I mean, I might refer to HR.Employee.JobTitle to describe the attribute (the Job Title) of a kind of object (the Employee) stored in a system (the HR system). If I leave out the system reference, I'm most likely referring to the data in the ICM system. How that data is stored in your company is, of course, specific to the system and your company, so my reference here will be to the logical or "business name" of the object and attribute – the way human beings might refer to it.

DATE-EFFECTIVITY OF DATA

There's a very important concept about that way data is stored in systems that will inform our discussions moving forward. That is the idea of **"date effective"** storage of data (also called **"temporal"**, **"historical"**, or even **"stateful"**, for which I apologize). What this means is that I have a new record in the system representing every change to every object – whatever the object is – and each record has a from-date and a to-date to allow me to see what this object looked like at a specific moment in time. For example:

- Mary Jones was hired as a Sales Rep working for Sara Smith on May 15, 2011
- Mary Jones married and changed her name to Mary Johnson on July 17, 2012
- Mary Johnson's manager changed to Bob Lee on October 1, 2012
- Mary Johnson became Sales Manager reporting to Janet Holmes on January 1, 2014

With date-effectivity, I can ask, "Who was this employee on December 1, 2011?" and know that she was Mary Jones working for Sara Smith at that moment in time. Without date-effectivity, all I know is what Mary Johnson looks like today – there is no historical **state** stored for her. It's shocking to me how many HR systems do not store data date-effectively. This is often call a data "snapshot" – our only view into the data is the snapshot of what the world looks like right this moment.

The reason this matters to us? Remember how I told you that it's a common practice to rerun incentive calculations for prior periods? An important prerequisite to doing that well is that *the system must process against what the world looked like in the prior period*, not necessarily what it looks like today.[16] HR systems

---

[16] Or what we say the world looked like in the prior period – *today's version of the prior period*. If someone's quota was $1M in January, but today in September I say the quota was $2M *retroactive to January*, then we must reprocess January using the $2M number. If I say the quota was $2M *retroactive to July*, then when we reprocess

don't "reprocess", so maintaining the historical record isn't that interesting to them, and from a data management perspective, it's more efficient not to. But ICM systems have to know what the world looked like on a given date, and this imposes interesting challenges to data maintenance and loads.

This also leads to one very odd data scenario that happens to be common in ICM – *date-effectivity of date-effective or period-based data.* By this I mean, you might have monthly quotas or targets. The payee's quota, year-to-date, might well be the sum of monthly quotas, year-to-date. But, based on more or less valid business reasons, those quotas might change during the plan year. They might change from that date forward, or they might be changed retroactively – sometimes back to the start of the plan year, requiring a recalculation of the prior periods.

In this case, then, you would have the January version of the January quota and the January version of the February quota, and you would have the February version of the January quota and the February version of the February quota, etc. This starts getting into the idea of multi-dimensional time, and it's the first step towards making heads explode.

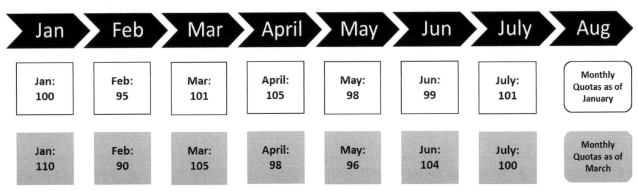

Figure 15 - Date-effectivity of Date-effective Data – the March version of January, and the January version of March

The second step to making heads explode is realizing that we are processing the January financial period in the middle of February in real time, and possibly paying it in a March paycheck. So when I ask what the value of a given object in "February" is, you have several different ways you might answer that question. Drawing time lines on a white board and pointing at the chunks you mean is sometimes the only way to be sure we're all discussing the same time slice called "February". I worked on a project once that eventually worked out to have seven different definitions of the word "hour". It was no wonder that no two project staff could ever agree on anything and that the system had flames coming out of it when it tried to go live.

Incidentally, most ICM systems do allow reference data to be tracked date-effectively, even if the sources systems feeding ICM do not. But that can impose a data integration challenge once the project begins.

REFERENCE DATA: PAYEES

Reference data is the data that provides the context for incentive processing. The most basic and universal form of reference data in ICM is **payee** data. Payees are the people and entities for whom we track performance and calculate and pay incentives. The payee is generally the level at which the system processes.

Payee data for employees of a company often comes into ICM as a feed from the HR system, but there is often a lot of work performed to transform that feed to make it work for ICM. For one thing, the HR data must be filtered to find the employees who are actually being paid by the system, which is typically a minority of a company's staff. If the Employee.JobTitle is specific enough, that's a great filter to use, but sometimes it's more

---

January, we must use the $1M quota in our calculations.

complicated than that.

Payees can be modeled in a variety of different ways. The **"single object"** model is to have a row in the system that represents our entire knowledge of the payee (Mary, in this case). Everything we know about Mary is stored as an attribute (think "columns") on Mary's (single) record. These might include her manager's name, her job title, her hire date, her favorite color, whatever we care about and can get our hands on systematically.

Payee Attribute	Value
Name	Mary Johnson
Job	Sales Rep – St. Paul
Manager	Bob Lee
Hire Data	May 15, 2011
Salary	$90,000
Quota	$1,000,000
Termination Date	- - -

Figure 16 - The Single-Object Payee Model

The single object model is the simplest one to and understand, but it can be very limiting. It maps most neatly to how HR departments view their data, but it doesn't fully solve the ICM problem because it assumes all payees only have one job at a time. And often, HR systems that track payees in a single object don't seem to care about the history of the payee (see our date-effectivity discussion above). They don't track the state of the data across time. So when I look at Mary's record, I see what she looks like today, but I might not be able to tell what she looked like yesterday or last week or last year – information that could impact her commissions and bonuses.

Therefore, for companies that do not store payee data date-effectively, the usual data integration approach is to get a snapshot – a feed of all possibly relevant payee records – from HR on a periodic basis (daily is good). Then either the customer feeding the data, or the ICM implementers building the systematic data feed, must compare that snapshot to all the equivalent records in the system today. Most will be unchanged – people don't change jobs every 5 minutes, after all. But some number of records will have changed in some more or less significant way. If the change is one that ICM cares about, the existing record will be end-dated and a new record reflecting the change will be created. This enables us to say, "Yesterday the payee looked like *that*; today the payee looks like *this.*

New records obviously must be created where we don't see that payee on this snapshot in the system today. It probably means we've got a new hire, or an existing employee who has recently taken a selling role, and whose job title now means that she or he is eligible to become a payee in the ICM system.

The more challenging one is when *a record in the ICM system is not in the snapshot of data we get from HR one day*. That usually means that the payee has been terminated or has changed jobs. There might be rules in the plans that care about why a payee has become inactive, but if all we get is "active" records from HR for people on a specific list of job titles on comp plans, that missing knowledge is a gap that must be filled.

To do this kind of data transformation from snapshots, we must have a reliable unique ID – a physical or logical database **key** - to work with to join the HR data with the ICM data. Payee.Name is not a good one. Notice that Mary Jones changed to Mary Johnson at some point in her career here at ConGlomCo. TaxID is the next obvious candidate, but that's actually kind of illegal – it's confidential information. So we end up using whatever the HR system gives us as the unique ID, but often Mary herself won't even know her HR ID. Figuring out which payee is on the other end of the phone can be an annoying challenge for the Comp Admins in large companies with five sales reps named Mary Johnson.

Having disparaged the single-object payee model, let's consider an alternative. The "**double-object**" payee model tracks not only the person (or company) being paid, but also that payee's job. The usual approach is to have a table for the payees, and one for the jobs, and the job record includes a field to track which payee is holding the job now. Why does this model help us?

Payee Attribute	Value
Name	Mary Johnson
Manager	Bob Lee
Hire Date	May 15, 2011
Salary	$90,000
Termination Date	- - -

Job Attribute	Value
Job	Sales Rep – St. Paul
Title	Sales Representative
Org Manager	Sales Director – Great Lakes
End Date	- - -
Payee Name	Mary Johnson
Quota	$1,000,000

Figure 17 – The Double-Object Payee Model

The job a person does is different from the person himself or herself. Mary was a Sales Rep for two and a half years, and then she became the Sales Manager – Great Lakes. If she sticks around, she might become the Sales Director – Eastern US. More interestingly, she might have been Sales Rep – Minneapolis, but also been in an acting or temporary role as Sales Rep – St. Paul when the person holding that job went on leave to follow her dream of joining the rodeo.

From an ICM perspective, Mary might well have been paid for performance in both of those jobs simultaneously but separately, depending on the company's policies and practices. So a single record representing Mary doesn't tell us enough – we need to know and track Mary as a sales rep in Minneapolis and Mary as a sales rep in St. Paul. The double object model allows us to track Mary doing multiple jobs in parallel, and it also allows us to do interesting analytics on performance for a position across time and across the payees holding it.

Of course, there are disadvantages with the double object payee model. The most annoying is that you have to come up with a unique job name for every payee, even if they are call center agents and don't have a uniquely identifiable job ("Third Desk from the Left in the Fourth Row"?). You often end up creating goofy names like "Northeast Sales Rep 5". It works a lot better at the management level, as the "District Manager – Northeast" is probably a meaningful job name, and once Larry leaves the job, Carey will take it over. But for the individual contributors in the sales group or the call center, finding a job name is a challenge.

I'm going to get a little philosophical here to help explain why another model makes the most sense.[17] Mary is different from Larry – the payees absolutely must be treated separately. The "Sales Rep – Minneapolis" job is different from the "Sales Rep – St. Paul" job. The might report to different managers, or have other attributes that are different than just the name. So it makes sense to track them separately, too.

When you dig deeper, Mary doing the "Sales Rep – St. Paul" job is different from Larry doing the "Sales Rep – St. Paul" job. Mary might have a different quota as the St. Paul Rep than Larry had: Mary's quota is $1,000,000 per year, while Larry's annual quota was $850,000. There might be different target earnings or commission rates as well. So that quota doesn't really belong to Mary or Larry – Mary's quota as District Manager is $10,000,000. And the quota doesn't belong to the "Sales Rep – St. Paul" job, since it was different for Mary and Larry. It belongs to the **engagement** of Mary (or Larry) doing the "Sales Rep – St. Paul" job. The *engagement is a meaningful object in its own right, and it has attributes of its own that are different from the payee or the job to which they are assigned*.

So you can probably guess that I think of the payee – job – engagement model as the **three-object payee**, and I think it is the most complete and flexible approach to modeling the data. This is handled by having a table for payees, a table for jobs, and a table for engagements, which refers to this payee doing this job during this time frame. Each table has the attributes for its unique object.

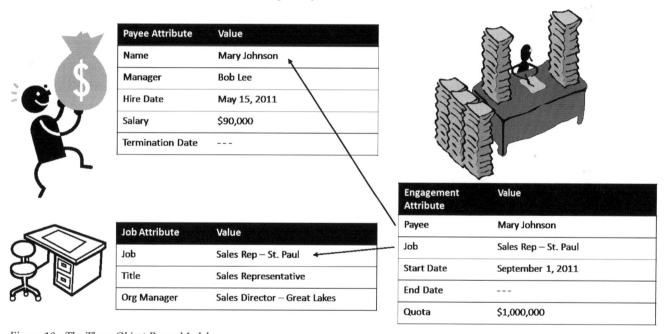

Figure 18 - The Three-Object Payee Model

It has the same major disadvantages as the double object model – you need to make up job names for each payee, for one. And if you have a simple compensation environment where people have well-defined and straight-forward jobs that don't change often, then it might be overkill. But if you have a complex environment – and the fact that you're reading this section after all I have done to make you throw the book away long before indicates that maybe you do – then the three object model is the only one that handles all the Weirdness of payees doing

---

[17] Now would be an excellent time for you to go and get a cup of coffee while I get this out of my system.

jobs in essentially random ways.[18] If you are an insurance carrier paying independent agents, it is the only way to be sure you won't have to jump through some pretty wicked hoops to get the system to calculate separate metrics per instance of the payee properly. (See APPENDIX THREE)

REFERENCE DATA: PAYEE HIERARCHIES

A natural extension of the payee is where exactly that payee sits in the organization, since that can have an impact on how the payee is compensated, who might receive compensation based on what that payee has done, and who cares about it enough to want to read reports on the subject. There are several **hierarchies** in play in ICM, and we'll explore them here.

The **HR Hierarchy** is the one that tells us who a payee's boss is, and in turn, whom that payee might manage. The HR department will generally track the Manager ID of a given employee, and that is our usual source of data for this. This is generally a one-to-many relationship – one manager (or "parent") to one or several subordinates (or "children). This stands to reason – most of us have one manager who has the authority to pat us on the back or fire us, and our one manager often has many subordinates.

The **Reporting Hierarchy** is often exactly the same as the HR Hierarchy, but it doesn't need to be. It just says who has the authority to see reports on my performance and incentive pay. That would usually be my manager, but if the company is convoluted enough in the way it manages its people, it would certainly be possible to have a different day-to-day manager than the person identified by the HR system. Most ICM applications have a built-in report security mechanism that will use the Reporting Hierarchy to determine who can drill down to see a payee's performance and pay. Again, this is generally a one-to-many relationship, but there are situations where it becomes a many-to-many relationship (many parents (or superiors) for each child, and many children (or subordinates) for each parent).

Rollup or **Overlay Hierarchies** are used to give sales credit to payees other than the one who actually got the deal signed. It might be to the sales rep's boss (or bosses), or to anyone else who could be said to contribute to the sale. Therefore, these can go from nearly anybody to nearly anyone, sometimes lots of nearly anyones. Maybe a picture will help muddy the waters a bit:

---

[18] By "random", I mean compensation activities that aren't intuitively obvious to an outsider who doesn't know your business processes. The actual payees might be acting in a clear and focused manner, but the fact that they might be holding three engagements simultaneously was most likely unpredictable for the implementation team on the first day.

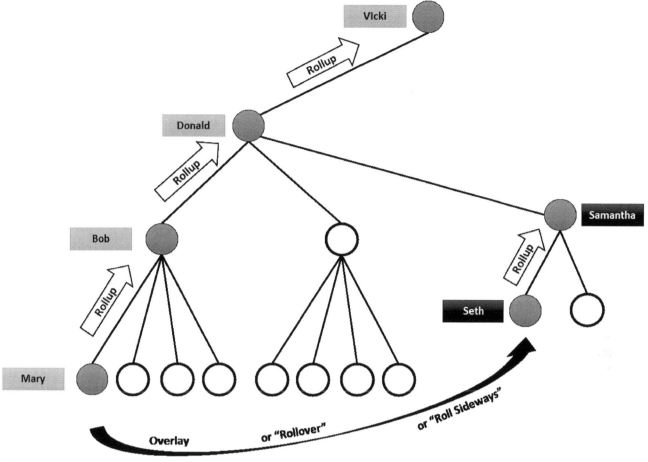

Figure 19 - Sales Hierarchies

Mary reports to Bob the Sales Manager, who reports to Donald the Director, who in turn reports to Vicki the VP of Sales. This relationship would likely come from the HR department. The nice thing in this case is that it also represents the business pretty well. Since it reflects the report security we want, we can use the HR Hierarchy for our Reporting Hierarchy as well.

Now, Mary is a Sales Rep, and she is compensated for everything she sells. Bob, her boss, is a Sales Manager, and commonly, he is compensated for everything Mary and her three peers sell. The way we tend to think about that in ICM is that we "roll" sales credit from Mary (and her peers) to Bob.[19] Then Bob rolls to Donald, and Donald rolls to Vicki. That might be done in various ways in an ICM system, but however it happens, we might want to call the relationship between Mary and Bob a **"Rollup"** relationship, and the vast web of rollup relationships throughout the company might be called the Rollup Hierarchy.

So if everyone rolls to their bosses, why do we need any other kind of hierarchy or relationship? Well, it might happen that Mary's sales credits are also used to compensate Seth the Presales Engineer over there on the right. Seth supports Mary and her peers, so whatever is sold in Bob's sales district is also credited to Seth so that he can get paid for his work. Mary does not work for Seth – Seth doesn't even work for Bob. Because they have no real

---

[19] To tie back to my previous rant about how we model payees, I'd like to point out that, while I'm saying Mary rolls to Bob, I really mean that Mary's Sales Rep job rolls to Bob's Sales Manager's job. If Mary or Bob leaves, someone else will fill those positions and the rollup will likely stay the same. But it's easier to illustrate it this way.

relationship with each other, we cannot just use the Reporting or HR hierarchy to roll Mary's credits to Seth. So we need another kind of relationship.[20] Let's think of that as an "**Overlay**" relationship: Seth is "overlaid" onto Bob's district.

We might call it an Overlay, we might refer to it as "**Rollover**", "**Roll Sideways**", even "**Roll Down**" depending on how we define it and how we draw the picture of the organization. But the point is, because sales crediting is often far more complex than just rolling up to the boss, we need to think about how credits will be moved in the ICM system.

One thing that makes this a challenge from an implementation perspective is that the complex overlay relationships are very seldom stored in a system from which the ICM system can pull data in a nice orderly feed. It lives entirely in the heads and spreadsheets of Tammy and her team. In fact, the new ICM system will likely become the system of record for, and likely the only consumer of, the company's overlay relationships.

Oh, and another reason we likely don't want to define roll relationships using the HR or Reporting relationships? Seth rolls his credits to his boss, Samantha the Sales Engineering Manager. Great – that's still the HR Relationship, right (once you get it to Seth, I mean)? Yes, but Samantha also reports to Donald the Director. If you roll Samantha's credits to Donald, he might be double dipping on Mary's sales, depending on how the ICM system handles rolled credits. Mary rolls credit for the SpiffyCon order to Bob, who rolls it to Donald. Mary also rolls credit for the SpiffyCon order to Seth, who rolls it to Samantha, who rolls it to Donald. Oops – this might be a problem. That's why I didn't show a rollup relationship between Samantha and Donald in the illustration.

Every system works differently, so this scenario might not automatically result in double counting credits. And some companies actually want to double count – they set Donald's quota twice as high (or his commission rate half as high) because they take that into account. The point is, though, you have to think about it and you have to design either the system configuration, your business processes, or both, with this possibility in mind.

REFERENCE DATA: PRODUCTS

A common practice in variable compensation is to pay for sales of different products differently. In the Telco world, for instance, contracts are where the money is, so that's often the major component of the comp plan. Handsets? They'll pay more or less, depending on whether it's the new must-have product or a phone near the end of its sellable life. Accessories? They'll pay a little, but it's not something they want the sales folk to be concentrating on. So the comp plan tells us that these categories of products are important, and the Product ID on the transaction enables us to make decisions about how the person selling will be paid.

But the Product ID on the transaction might be in the form of "X19-J4(b)", since that's how the product might be represented in the order entry system. Is that a 24-month contract renewal, a zippy new smart phone, or a black leather case? I don't have any idea – do you? But until I figure it out, I don't know how much to pay the sales associate who took the order.

To that end, then, we often need a table of Products in ICM, and usually that table is hierarchical – it's a tree, rather than a list. The interesting thing about products is that the Manufacturing or Sales Order Management view of products might be different from the way the Comp Department looks at them. They all agree that an "X19-J4(b)" exists as a product, and they all probably agree that it's a spiffy Bluetooth headset – the black one, not the silver one – but we might disagree whether that makes it an Accessory or a Handset. You might have a strong opinion about it (of COURSE it's an accessory – any idiot knows that!), but if the comp plan is written to

---

[20] We need to conceptualize a different relationship in our heads, even if we don't need one systematically. All ICM systems manage crediting relationships in their own unique way, but the concept is real, even if the representation in the various systems is different.

include it with Handsets for commissioning purposes, then ICM needs to treat it as a Handset.

[*WARNING*: Heavy-duty philosophical rambling commencing.] One thing that is interesting about hierarchies or trees is that the leaves – the lowest level, the actual products themselves – are real, but everything above them is just organization that we humans impose on them.[21] It makes it easier for us to think about them or group them. But that order that seems so logical to us is really just an accident, and other orderings might work equally as well. Where ICM is concerned, it's all about what makes it most convenient for the comp process, but that can change year by year as the company changes the way they take their products to market.

Many years ago I worked with a sport clothing manufacturing company on an ICM project. They had six different ways of organizing their products, and all were used in determining compensation. One tree structure was based on which sport the product was used for. Another tree was based on what body part the product went on, and there were four others as well. The same pair of soccer shoes appeared in all six different trees, and a sale for the pair of soccer shoes was interesting to many different sales reps – maybe one who was responsible for soccer-related apparel or another who was responsible for footwear. So which was the "real" product tree? They all were.

Back to the example I gave above about the X19-J4(b) unit above – the categorization doesn't have to be "right" in any way other than the Compensation Department telling us it's right based on how the comp plans were written. To give a silly example, if your company sells animals, where would you put porpoises? Well, according to the science boffins, they are mammals and that's where they belong. But our company is going to call them fish and categorize them that way because the fish sales rep is responsible for selling them and is compensated for revenue that relates to them. And don't get me started on where we categorize bats! Objective truth is a very tenuous concept here in the ICM world.

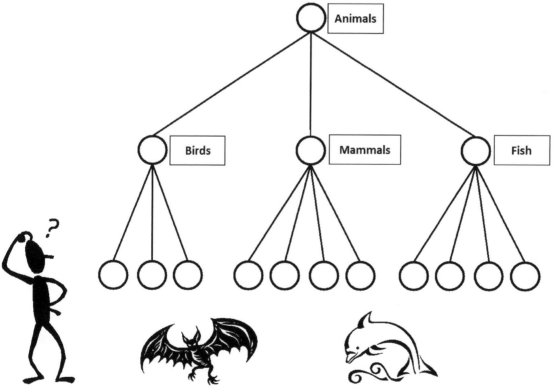

Figure 20 - Categorization of Ambiguous Members

---

[21] Whoa – is it time for another cup of coffee already?

So enough of this philosophical theoretical mumbo jumbo – where do I find the data and how do I represent it in my ICM system? Darn good question. Some companies do have a "product master" buried in some Finance Department system somewhere, and that is often the primary source. But remember, just because Finance says a porpoise is a mammal doesn't mean that the Comp Department wants to see it on the mammal branch of the Product tree. It sometimes happens that the product master maps to sales comp, but it's not a safe assumption that it always will. And the product master will nearly always show a single version of the tree, while there might well be others. At the end of the day, the source for your Product table might just be a spreadsheet the Comp Team manages manually and then uploads into ICM. Most ICM systems insist on a one-to-many parent-to-child relationship in this table because the confusion caused by both the fish sales rep and the mammal sales rep thinking porpoises belong to them and getting credit for the same order might be unacceptable. But companies do the darnedest things, so maybe that is supposed to happen according to the comp plan.

REFERENCE DATA: GEOGRAPHY

Geography is often a key dimension of data in the definition of sales territories. We will explore territories further in a later chapter, but for now, let's just think of a territory as the "space" in which a sales rep conducts his business – sales reps often call it their **"patch"**. Not every industry uses sales territories, but many do, so it's worth exploring the ways in which they can be defined.

Mention the word "territory" to someone new to ICM, and one of the first things that will come to that person's mind will be something to do with geography. "Territory" just sounds like it has to do with the physical places where a sales rep would sell, so geography must be how we define it. And sometimes we do: it is often a part of a territory definition, even if it isn't the entire definition. Products, customers, sales channels, industries and other dimensions make up territories as well, but location is often a significant part.

So how do we define location? What value on which field on a transaction can I look at to know this transaction qualifies as Central New York State, Bay Area, or Midwest? It turns out that's hard. Well actually, the answer is easy, but the implementation of the answer is hard, especially in the US. The way to think about this is to imagine that you are on your first day on the job of paying incentive compensation, and all you know is what's in the Territory Cookbook they gave you and what you can see on the transaction. And your sense of geography is weak, so you can't just look at an address and know what it is near. ICM systems don't know anything that they haven't been told explicitly, so for the purposes of this example, neither can you.

The Territory Cookbook might make the name of the state part of the territory definition, but Rhode Island is tiny and Alaska is huge, so that's not usually granular or detailed enough. City name is good, but there are lots of towns called Springfield in the US, so you probably want to make that the combination of City and State. And there are often towns outside the city limits that are included in the territory, too. Look at Los Angeles and all the small towns that comprise it, and it becomes clear that if I'm the Greater Los Angeles sales rep, I might want more than just "City = Los Angeles" as my territory definition.

As much as we try to avoid it, it most often seems to come down to postal codes, called ZIP Codes[22] here in the US. In many parts of the world, the postal code actually tells you something. In Germany, the first digit of the postal code refers to a major city, and the rest of the numbers have to do with areas in or around that city. But in the US, postal codes are only broadly logical, but in the actual implementation, they are somewhat random. Postal Code numbers are the identifiers of a post office, and they are placed for the convenience of the Postal Service, not for people trying to figure out what a city looks like from a data perspective.

A metropolitan area might have a list of postal codes that don't fall into a well-defined range – there will be gaps

---

[22] It turns out ZIP Code ("Zone Improvement Plan") is a trademark of the US Postal Service, so I will just refer to them generically as postal codes.

and orphan numbers due to a given post office being located nearby, but possibly even in the next state. We can't just say that "postal codes 12345 to 12543 = BigCityVille". In the event, the ranges might be:

- "12345
- OR 12347 – 12396
- OR 12399 – 12484
- OR 12486 – 12512
- OR 12533 – 12543

-- equal BigCityVille".

That's a lot to keep track of in your Territory Cookbook, and none of it is intuitive. Throw in the ZIP+4 concept and it's especially evil from a data maintenance perspective. But as bad as it is, there's not much choice in the matter. So quite often, a sales rep's territory will be defined in the Territory Cookbook as "Product X AND Postal Codes between XXX and YYY (plus exceptions)".

In our Product data discussion, we discussed how the hierarchy or tree is just something we construct for our convenience in dealing with lots of fine-grained data. Geography is one of those category hierarchies where we have to make decisions about where we will put something, not by any objective truth, but for the purposes of paying incentive compensation. So again, we can slice and dice and categorize our geography structures any way we choose.

The US is often divided at the highest level between East and West. Or sometimes, North and South. Or maybe, East, Central, West and South. Or occasionally, Northwest, Southwest, Northeast, and Southeast. Or… Or… Or… Or… So what does it mean when I say the Sales Director gets credit for all sales in the East? It means whatever the geography tree structure the Comp Team gave you tells you it means. That spreadsheet is probably all you have to go on, since geographical data, especially the structure of it, is seldom stored in any system. And the definition will change with next year's plans.

REFERENCE DATA: CUSTOMERS

The two most common reasons we would want to store customer data are:

- When a territory definition is a list of "named accounts" to which the sales rep is assigned; or
- When we need to look at a Customer ID on a transaction, then go to the Customer reference data table to find the address for a geography-based territory, or for any other kind of data stored there but not on the transaction.

Implementation teams generally really like having named accounts in the territory definition. It's usually pretty easy data to store and access, depending on the ICM system, and it means that sales crediting – often one of the hardest jobs in ICM – can be accomplished much more easily with a fairly simple lookup.

The second case – where the Customer ID on the transaction is only the first step on the path to sales crediting – is common, and it adds a little extra complexity to the task of assigning the right transactions to the right sales reps. The good news about it, though, is that the customer reference data is usually pretty reliable and easy to source from either the CRM system or even Accounts Receivable.

OTHER REFERENCE DATA

As discussed, comp plans can be written to measure and reward anything for which you have data. Sales territories can be complex, multi-dimensional views of the business as well. So while products, geography, and customers are the bread and butter dimensions of territory definition, they are not the only ones. Sales Channel, data source (which sale order system provided the data might tell us something about how the transaction was sold), event type (new contracts versus contract renewals, for example) – all might be part of a payee's or group of payees' territory definitions, and we need to have that data in the ICM system.

As the Comp Team, you need to know what other kinds of data are needed to credit and pay incentives, and it's a good idea to know where it comes from before the project starts. As implementers, you need to know to ask. Some of that data might be available in a system, but never lose sight of the fact that if there is a user interface screen where it can be entered and maintained, that's a good solution for categories with small numbers of members. Not everything has to be loaded by way of a feed.

PLAN DATA

Variables

In most ICM systems, we try to write the compensation plan logic as generically as we can so that the same plan can be used by as many payees or groups of payees as possible. This means we don't have to write a plan per payee, which is hard to maintain and is a lot of work besides. The way we accomplish this is to leave placeholders in the rules and formulas that call values that are specific to the payee or a group of payees. The plan logic might be, essentially, "If the payee exceeds his or her Annual Quota Variable, then give the payee his or her Annual Bonus Amount Variable. When the system processes for Mary, it calls out for her unique Quota and Bonus Amount values, and then it calls out for Larry's variables when it is processing his plan.

These variables can include the quotas and territories we have already looked at, but also plan component weightings, target earnings, bonus amounts, commission rates, lookup tables, eligibility flags (e.g., 'yes' or 'no'), and various other values that might be associated to payees, roles, job titles, or comp plans. I usually classify these kinds of data as **plan data**, though technically it is all a form of reference data. It's just reference data that has a few special kinds of behavior.

Quotas, rates, factors, targets, scores, amounts – all are **numeric values**. Some of these values may be absolute – they are what they are, and are timeless. IQ or Shoe Size[23] are values like this. But other values, like quota or bonus amount, might be tied to time periods. A plan might call for the quota to be specified for the year, or for each month, and the bonus amount to be specified at the quarter level, or even the month level. As I've mentioned once or eighteen times already, every ICM system does everything differently, so each will store and call this data in a different way. For purposes of this book, however, when there is a numeric value that is tied to a specific plan period, I will usually refer to it as Variable.period (e.g., "WidgetQuota.year", or "RugalatorBonusAmount.quarter". Where the value is not period specific, I will just describe it as "Payee.variable", e.g., "Payee.IQ".

Other kinds of values might be **text values** – perhaps a General Ledger code for where this payee's business should be accounted for, or even a territory code that might be matched to something on a transaction. Not every ICM system has places to put text variables that can be called by the plan. Then it becomes a matter of finding a payee or job attribute to hang it on.

The implementation team must look for the most efficient ways to store and retrieve this data given the system architecture and the plan requirements pertaining to the customer. And some of the constraints go back to how payees are stored in the application. If the application data model does not have, or cannot be extended to have, specific data objects to represent periodic named values like quotas or weight factors, or text values, then the values tend to be stored on the payee record.

---

[23] Just as "Widgets" and "Rugalators" are an abstract way to represent a company's products, we sometimes use "Shoe Size" or "IQ" as shorthand for any value that might be an attribute of a payee or a plan variable. I've never actually seen a customer base incentive comp on IQ or shoe size. Yet.

Which part of the payee record? If you have a three object model (see Figure 18 - The Three-Object Payee Model) the engagement is usually the place to go for plan variables. If you only have two objects – payees and jobs – then you need to decide whether the value you are storing is really tied to the payee, or whether it is actually tied to the job. Shoe Size or IQ? Definitely the payee. "Eligible for Bonus" flag? That's a bit more of a gray area. The critical thing is to try to find reasons why your design is wrong – say, one payee holds two jobs, so putting the value on the payee instead of the job would possibly fail.

Tables

Many ICM applications have functionality to support **Lookup Tables** and **Rate Tables**. This can provide a lot of flexibility. A Lookup Table allows the plan logic to pass in one or many values from the payee or the transaction to pull back a single return value, typically a number. In insurance, the commission rate might be based on a multi-dimensional lookup involving the type of product, the contract ID, the age of the policy, the age of the insured, the state where it was sold, the payee's status, and maybe other things besides. In the complex matrix of dimensions, a single rate of "17%" might be returned for the combination being fed. This saves writing a lot of complex logic.

A Rate Table (often called a stepping rate table, or a tiered rate table) is generally based on revenue for the plan period against quota, but it allows rates to vary based on different levels of attainment. A rate table might look something like this:

Tier	Low	High	Commission Rate
1		<= 75%	2%
2	> 75%	<= 100%	3%
3	> 100%		4%

Figure 21 - Rate Table Example

It doesn't look like much, but what it's saying is this: for all revenue up to 75% of the quota value for the quota period (e.g., the year for annual quotas, or the quarter for quarterly quotas), the payee earns 2% in commissions. For the incremental revenue over 75% of quota attainment, the payee earns 3% commission. For all revenue above the quota value, the payee earns 4%. So if a payee has a quota of $1,000,000, and in the plan period has sold $1,100,000, the payoff would be:

- $750,000 * 2% = $15,000, plus –
- $250,000 * 3% = $7,500, plus –
- $100,000 * 4% = $4,000, for a total of –
- $26,500 (= $15,000 + $7,500 + $4,000)

You can write formulas like this pretty easily in a spreadsheet, so why spend so much effort on this? There are two reasons why this is harder than it looks. First of all, while the annual quota and the annual revenue lend themselves to this calculation pretty easily (heck – I kept track of the math in the paragraph above in my head), in many cases the commissions are earned and paid monthly. So the application has to keep track of where on the attainment scale the payee is coming into the month, how much is sold this month, and then calculate just the incremental value for the month.

And the second reason why it's more complex than it looks is because, in many businesses, revenue can go away. Customers might cancel orders that the payee sold a month or two ago, and now we have to subtract revenue attainment. Or worse, maybe the business is never debooked at all, but we raise the payee's quota retroactively. Instead of coming into the month at 83% of quota, based on the quota she had before the change, Mary's quota might be raised and now she's coming in at 57% attainment – she might actually owe commissions back to the company. That's the kind of thing that makes the sales reps hate Tammy, but it's really not her fault.

Those formulas could still be written in a spreadsheet by an ambitious comp admin, but the point is, they are long and ugly. If the ICM application can handle this for you automagically, so much the better. And another "incidentally" – I plugged in numeric values in the rate table example. But often, the rates and sometimes even the attainment ranges are based on other variables. And sometimes they are formulas based on variables. The most fundamental compensation formula is this one:

- **Component Base Commission Rate** = ((Payee.TargetIncentiveEarnings * ComponentWeight) / Quota)

Single Component Commission Rate Calculation

Let's use a simple example to explain this one. On a plan with a single metric and a single kind of reward for it (let's say there is no bonus, just commissions), the Component Weight would be 100%. So if Mary's Target Incentive Earnings (the variable piece of her annual earnings as written into her comp plan) is $50,000, and her annual quota is $1,000,000, then her Base Commission Rate would be:

- $50,000 / 1,000,000 = 5%

If you turn that formula over, and ask how much Mary would earn if she sold exactly $1,000,000 worth – to the penny – of Widgets, you would see:

- $1,000,000 * 5% = $50,000

So the Base Commission Rate equals the commission rate it would take to get a payee to *exactly* their Target Incentive Earnings if they sell *exactly* their quota amount. The rest of the rate table might reference some factor of her Base Commission Rate in each of the "Commission Rate" boxes in the rate table above. This is a long explanation for the kind of functionality we hope to find out-of-the-box in the ICM application we are using – we want the rate table to keep track of attainment, and we want it to allow us to plug in formulas instead of having to hard wire the values.

Three Component Commission Rate Calculation

So that example was way too easy – let's make it harder. Larry has two metrics on his plan – a Widget Revenue Commission and a Rugalator Revenue Commission. The Widget Revenue Commission on his plan is weighted 60%, and the Rugalator is weighted 30%. So if we do the math –

What? Wait – where's the last 10%? Oh yeah, that's the bonus he gets for hitting both quotas. Two metrics, but three components. Did I forget to mention that?

So yeah, anyway, he has the same Target Incentive Earnings as Mary - $50,000. His Widget Quota is $1,200K, while his Rugalator Quota is $750K. So his Base Commission Rate for Widgets would be:

- (($50,000 * 60%) / $1,200K) = 2.5%
  (I had to use the calculator for this one)

His Rugalator Base Commission Rate would be:

- (($50,000 * 30%) / $750K) = 2%.

And of course his Annual Bonus Amount (not rate) would be:

- ($50,000 * 10%) = $5000

Threshold Commission Rate Calculation

What? Still not hard enough? Alrighty then, but don't say I didn't warn you. Remember Mary and her $50K Target Incentive Earnings, her $1M Widget Quota, and her single metric, single component plan? Yeah, well actually Mary has a **threshold** built into her rate table. That means she doesn't collect any commissions until she has sold enough to pay the cost of having her do business – her salary, her laptop, her cubicle, etc. She has to earn a bunch back before she sees any commissions. So her rate table looks like this:

Tier	Low	High	Commission Rate
1		<= 50%	0%
2	> 50%	<= 100%	Base Rate * 200%
3	> 100%		Base Rate * 300%

Figure 22 - Threshold Example

Why "Base Rate * 200%"? Because she doesn't get any of her Target Incentive Earnings for the first 50% of her quota that she sells – (Tier 1). That means she has to earn all of her Target Incentive Earnings for only half of her quota (Tier 2). That changes the math to:

- Tier 2 Commission Rate =
  ($50,000 / ($1,000K * 50%) =
  ($50,000 / $500,000) = 10%

And her Accelerated Commission Rate (Tier 3) is 15%, which is one of the funny things about thresholds. You might have it in mind to pay Mary 5% under quota, and 7.5% over quota, but once you put that threshold in, that means *her perceived commission rate would drop once she hit quota:*

Tier	Low	High	Commission Rate
1		<= 50%	0%
2	> 50%	<= 100%	Base Rate * 200%
3	> 100%		*Base Rate * 150%*

Figure 23 - Threshold Anomaly

She would be earning 5% under quota (eventually) and 7.5% over quota with this rate table, but I bet she would feel somewhat disincented for doing her job. Her commission rate would drop from 10% (at Tier 2) to 7.5% (at Tier 3). But while you could explain the math until you were blue in the face, there would almost certainly be some grumbling. And fair's fair – you are making her take all the risk, commission-wise, for the first 50% of quota, so you have to pay a little something extra for the bits over quota. But the amount extra you have to pay would seem to be much higher if you put the threshold in. The right answer might be "Base Rate * 200%" for both Tier 2 and Tier 3, but even that would leave a slight bad taste just from looking at the rate table. Darn these humans and their darn psychologies!

Territories

We have touched on aspects of Territories in the Crediting section and in the Reference Data sections above. We know that a sales rep is responsible for, sells into, and gets credit for transactions that match his or her Sales Territory. If we write Crediting logic in a generalized way, we would want to say "If Transaction.Attributes (products, customers, sales channels, geography, whatever other dimensions you've got) match SalesRep.Territory (from the Territory Cookbook), then give Credit for the Transaction".

So here's the problem: I was kinda pulling your leg.[24] There is no such thing as a Territory Cookbook. There is every individual company's implementation of Territories, but there is no universal way to describe them, and no universal way to store them for or in an ICM system. Like so many things, Territories are hard (and I am NOT whining – *I'm NOT!*).

Let's look at a visual representation of a complex (but not ridiculously so) Sales Territory. This payee gets credit for all Consumer grade Widgets (except the Model X19 Widget) sold through the Direct Sales Channel in the Western US or in Michigan:

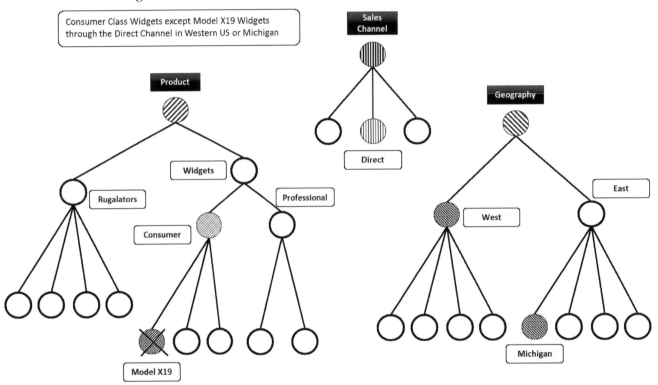

Figure 24 - Complex Sales Territory Visualization

To understand what the payee will get credit for, we have to take hierarchies into consideration (if I specify a higher level node, I assume it includes everything below it), and we have to find a way to include things that you would expect to be excluded (Michigan doesn't feel like it belongs here), or exclude things you would expect to be included (why doesn't the rep get X19 Widgets? I dunno - maybe there are specialized reps who sell those).

Maybe it seems like I am piling on the complexity here, but there are many sales territories in the real world that look far worse. And remember – this is just one sales rep's Territory. You might have 1000 reps with Territories that are more or less as bad as this one. And while I am showing category trees with only a few members each, there could be literally hundreds or thousands of leaves and branches in a given tree.

Territories are plan variables just like quotas, rates, true/false flags, etc. There are ways you could figure out how to represent Territories like this in rows on a spreadsheet, but there is no getting past the fact that maintaining the mythical Territory Cookbook is a big job.

This would be an ideal time for me to tell you the best way to do it, but I must let you down here. There *is* no good way to do it, in any product, for any customer. There are tools that can simplify and manage aspects of this, but the complex Territory definition with lots of AND's, OR's, and NOT's, is something I have not seen in any

---

[24] I'm such a scamp!

packaged, best-of-breed territory product. This is one of the hardest parts of a hard domain. The person who solves this problem in a way that can feed ICM systems would be a benefactor to mankind and would earn the thanks of a grateful nation. I'd do it for you, but I'm a little busy right now.

TRANSACTION DATA

Okay, you cry, you're killin' us with all this reference data. Give us something we can sink our teeth into. Give us the transactions we're going to use to compensate people! Alrighty then – off we go to the transaction system to suck some data into ICM.

So where exactly *is* the transaction system? The usual place to look is something we generically call the Sales Order Management system, but it could really be in any number of systems in the company. It might come from a third party vendor in the form of a flat file of reseller information. It might be a bunch of call center data about calls answered and customer satisfaction scores. It might be in a few rows in a spreadsheet the admin uploads to the system every few days. In ICM terms, transactions are any data that we use to measure and reward payees. While that is often sales data, it doesn't have to be.

What does a transaction look like? The Sales Order Management system owner will probably show you a file format that has 185 fields on it, all with cryptic three-letter-acronyms for column names, and you'll be told to take what you need. So what do you need?

I would argue that the transaction wants to be made up of the minimum set of data that can provide:

- Data for accurate Crediting
- A value or values to be used in measurement (even if the value is 1 or 0)
- Categorization data for aggregation into all appropriate buckets
- Reporting data to allow research into disputes and queries
- Sales reporting for the payees.

Anything else is either gravy, or it is actively harmful, depending on your outlook. My outlook is that it approaches harmfulness. This is a hot-button issue for me, and I'll go into it in excruciating depth in the Data Integration Challenges section (don't say you weren't warned). But suffice it to say, if there is no direct need identified for any given attribute, then I don't want it in the ICM system.

Therefore, when defining transaction data requirements (and reference data requirements too), I generally use a matrix to determine, for a given attribute, whether it is needed for:

- Crediting
- Compensation
- Reporting
- Research

I go over this sheet with the customer and have them tell me how they will use the data. If there is no checkmark in any of those boxes, it takes a lot to convince me that the attribute belongs in the feed to ICM. "But we might need it!" is not an answer. Now, I do try to temper my principles with common sense. If a company pays on revenue, but has profitability information available on the transaction data in the current system, I can easily believe that someday they might choose to compensate based on that instead or as well – this *is* a variable compensation system we're talking about. So that's a field I'm okay bringing into the ICM system. But Payee.IQ or Shoe Size? When is that last time anyone really needed to know that? Be honest! So out it goes.

One creative use of Transaction data in ICM is to bring a single variable value into the system for the payees. If there's no logical place to put their Customer Satisfaction score in the ICM data model, a Transaction can be a good way to bring it into the system. It doesn't get aggregated or used over time. It might be something needed to know whether the payee is eligible for compensation this month. If you can't arrange a feed to do it any other way, a transaction is a potential solution. It doesn't come out of any of the usual systems – it might be a spreadsheet that gets uploaded by the Comp Admins – but it introduces data associated with individual payees in a generally tidy way.

Compensation Plans

COMPONENTS & RULES

Comp Plans, Comp Components, and Comp Rules are where the heavy lifting in ICM happens. They are the complex calculations that make up payees' variable pay. A definition is called for here, since this is another foundational aspect of ICM on which no two people can agree on meanings. From this point forward, then, let's treat these terms this way:

- A **Compensation Plan** is the complete contract between the payer and the payee that contains all of the metric definitions, incentive logic, formulas and conditions pertaining to variable compensation for a specific Payee Engagement (see **FIGURE 18 - THE THREE-OBJECT PAYEE MODEL**);
- A **Compensation Component** is a subset of a Comp Plan. It is the end-to-end logic for a metric and its associated incentives. A Comp Plan might have one or many Comp Components;
- **Compensation Rules** make up the Component. Rules include crediting logic, conditions and formulas that provide the logic of the calculation.

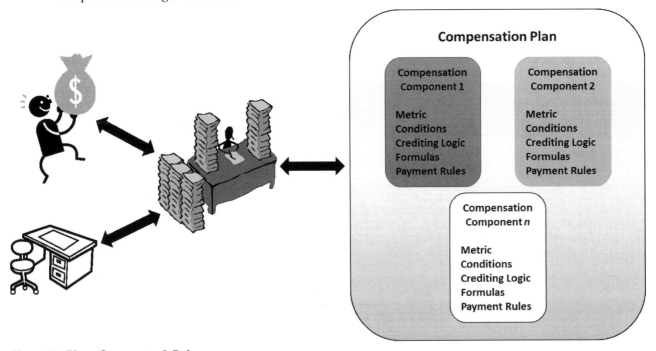

Figure 25 - Plans, Components & Rules

Logically, Plans should be tied to the Engagement, as the same payee doing a different job in parallel ("Sales Rep – Minneapolis" and acting "District Sales Manager – Great Lakes District", for example) could well be on separate plans. I believe this definition ties most neatly with the way most (but by no means all) customers communicate their Comp Plans to their payees. There are usually a couple of pages describing the metrics and calculations by which the payees will be rewarded for them, plus many pages of rules describing what qualifies as revenue (or whatever the metric is based on), eligibility, recovery, exceptions, and other legalese about how the plan will be administered. But the single document they hand over to the payee is often called the Comp Plan, regardless of how complex the definition is.

ICM systems all manage Comp Plans and Components differently, and customers use the terms differently, so this leads to a lot of confusion and *"But your sales guy said!"* conversations on projects. For example, customers often ask, "Can a payee be on multiple plans in your system?" Are they asking about multiple Plans, or do they really mean Components? And do they mean at the same time, or across time? Vendors tend to answer that question in a way that assumes that the product's architecture is the one that the customer wants, so one way or another, the answer will be 'yes'. It just may not be the 'yes' that answers the question being asked.

Conversely, every ICM vendor and implementer asks every customer, "How many Comp Plans do you have for your payees?" That's an impossible question to answer without knowing how the vendor's system models Plans, Components, and Rules. The real question they are asking is, "How much discreet logic must we write to pay your payees, assuming the use of variables like territories, quotas, and rate tables?" Some customers think of a plan as distinct if there are different quotas or other variables, while other customers consider several components mixed and matched as a single Plan. Customers never know how to answer that question, and neither do the vendors until after they have performed a complete requirements definition project phase, but it is critical to the implementers' estimates for the project effort and duration. So the vendor will make a more-or-less informed guess and estimate based on that.

As stated earlier, no ICM system implementer wants to write a Comp Plan per payee, and no customer should ever want to have to maintain that either. So a significant amount of time will normally be taken during the Requirements and Design Phases finding the best way to reuse Plans and Components to map to the ICM system's representation of the business logic that goes into paying incentives.

PLAN ASSIGNMENT

Most ICM systems will allow you to assign payees to plans in an intelligent and dynamic way. This means that you don't have to explicitly assign each of your 5000 payees to a plan one at a time. Sometimes the assignment might be based on something like "Payee.JobTitle", but of course it's often more complicated than that. The point of bringing this up is that the project team and the Comp Team need to be clear on exactly how we know Mary is on the Sales Rep Comp Plan, while Larry is on the Account Rep Comp Plan, and then come up with a mechanism that works to manage it.

Reporting

Some of the greatest value-add of a new ICM system, especially in a sales environment, is improved reporting for the payees and the folks trying to make sense of revenue and expenses. A thoughtfully designed ICM implementation can bring a tremendous amount of data to the surface for payee reporting, administrative reports, and financial analysis. When describing compensation requirements, it is important to also address reporting requirements at the same time. It should not be an afterthought, as the way the Plans are written can radically impact the data available for reporting on the other end.

Another question vendors ask customers is, "How many reports will you want?" And there is never an answer that meets each side's needs, because how the customers report today might well be different from the way they will report after the system is implemented. And further, they probably don't agree on what a report actually is. So the answer always comes back as either "6" or "175".[25] This makes estimating really ugly, so again, the vendors will usually just make a random guess and bid based on that.

---

[25] Literally – always. It will always be one of those two numbers. Count on it. The real answer will be 35.

Therefore, and as a service to both vendors and customers, I would like to make a distinction between the various means of getting data out of the ICM system, because I believe it can help clarify requirements and design. Regardless of how the ICM system handles reporting, I think there are four ways to look at the questions we can ask of it:

- Reports
- Analytics
- Queries via the User Interface
- Feeds to Downstream Systems (including reporting systems)

Of course, these distinctions are somewhat artificial, and there is a lot of gray area between them, but for purposes of defining requirements, they can sometimes help. Let's examine each type.

REPORTS

For purposes of our discussion, let's assume a report is a prebuilt query against the data in the ICM system that returns a (more or less) formatted electronic or paper response. The report is something that might be run once a day, or once a year, but think of it as something that has an existence in the operational life of the Comp Department. A report often has a name. Reports can often have drill-down navigation to other reports – from summary level data to detailed data. A report might have filters or other variables in the way it returns data, but essentially, it is a canned question of the data in the system. It might have graphics, but a report is generally a snapshot of the state of the world.

The use of filters and variables also muddies the waters with respect to how many reports the customer needs. I have often dealt with the requirement for, "The Rolling 30 Days of Revenue report, the Rolling 45 Days of Revenue report, the Rolling 60 Days of Revenue report – so that's three reports right there, right?" Well, no, that's actually one report, and the system should prompt you for the number of days' revenue you want when you run it. And that's the same idea behind a Widget Revenue report and a Rugalator Revenue report. If they have the same basic logic, just add a filter to specify the product when you run the report.

A flavor of reporting is operational reports – reports about the status, health and well-being of the ICM system and processes around it. It might include last compensation calculation process, performance against system SLAs, adherence to workflow SLAs, last payment file generated, and for how much – stuff that the operations staff need, but that mostly doesn't go to the payees.

There will always be Weirdness and exceptions when the ICM implementation team is there doing the work, but assume in a modern system that there will be reuse and flexibility in the reporting functionality. Ask, but assume.

ANALYTICS

I look at analytics as the more ad hoc queries of the data in order to enable better visibility into trends, ranking, multi-dimensional comparisons, operational red flags, and other questions that enable better decision making about the business. Analytic reports can be scheduled and prebuilt too, but generally they have a smaller, more specialized audience than the audience for reporting. They are about slicing and dicing data, rather than just laying it out. Often analytics reports will have charts and graphs to show their information visually. Often analytic reports can drill down to the detail underneath as well.

QUERIES ON THE USER INTERFACE

Most ICM systems have pretty good built-in access to the data in the system, especially for the administrative users. And Tammy and her senior people are notoriously good at teasing data out of the system when they have the tools to do it. So if the VP of Sales wants to know how the Director – Northeast is doing this year compared to last year, Tammy can find the data by way of the user interface (UI). This is base functionality of most ICM applications – the ability to go in and ask targeted questions of the data in the system.

Coming from a world where there isn't comprehensive access to incentive comp data, though, many times customers will submit requirements for "reports" to enable the users to get answers to these ad-hoc questions that could be answered by way of the UI. It is important to ask for access to the data for the kinds of questions the Comp Team are asked for every day, but the fact that it might be available without building a formal report should always be considered.

FEEDS TO DOWNSTREAM SYSTEMS

Most likely there will be separate requirements gathering workshops where scheduled, bullet-proof feeds from ICM to downstream systems will be discussed. For the most part, we don't need to think of that as a reporting requirement. But if the ICM system is feeding an enterprise data warehouse, the distinction gets blurry.

Further, I was on a project where we were getting to the bottom of the "we need 175 reports" requirement. One "report" we were told was needed was, essentially, a list of every sales transaction for the month or quarter. This was for a large customer, so the report would return millions of rows. We asked who read it and how it was used. We were told that two analysts used the data for some mysterious financial purpose, and that every month they took the report, downloaded it to a .csv file,[26] and then they would munge the data to their hearts' content. So how about treating that as a feed to their reporting database instead? Yeah, that could work too.

Reports generally take some effort, call for some formatting, get displayed on a screen, and have a cost associated with building them and maintaining them. A feed of data to a downstream system isn't free, but it tends to be a little cheaper to build and maintain, and it can eliminate the steps necessary to convert the report into the kind of data the analysts want in the first place.

Again, some of the distinctions between these kinds of data presentation are a bit fuzzy, but when trying to define requirements for a system, they might help focus both sides of the project on what actually needs to be delivered.

Workflows

A tool being built into a lot of ICM applications is workflow management. This allows processes to be codified, routed, tracked, and reported. The most common workflows in ICM are for payee disputes ("Hey! Where's my money?!?") and for payment approvals – making sure the VP of Sales and the CFO know how much people are being paid before they approve the checks being generated.

We'll talk about them in more detail later.

---

[26] CSV – comma separated values. A file format that can be opened in spreadsheets or database tables.

Reference Data

- Payees
- Categories (Products, Geography, Customers, Etc.)
- Other Foundational Data

Plan Data

- Variables
- Tables
- Territories

Transaction Data

- Sales Orders
- External Feeds
- Other Metrics

Comp Plans

- Components & Rules
- Plan Assignments

Reports

- Canned Reports
- Analytics
- Queries
- Feeds

Workflows

- Payee Queries & Disputes
- Payment Approval
- Others?

Figure 26 - The Inventory of ICM System Configuration Stuff

CHAPTER FIVE – PLANNING FOR YOUR ICM PROJECT

I have been very careful to describe the complexity of ICM systems and processes early in order to make this chapter make more sense. By touching on the various things that make projects hard, I hope to prepare you for a view into how a project works – both ideally and actually.

Every customer is different, every vendor is different, and every project is different. We know this. But there are common areas of risk that everyone should be aware of before starting a project. We want to sail past the avoidable problems so we can focus on solving the real problems. This chapter will be directed mostly towards the customer – the buyer of the ICM system – but both sides of the relationship should be able to learn something from it.

The Waterfall Methodology

By far the most common project methodology in the ICM world is called the "waterfall" methodology. There can be more or fewer phases, but these are representative:

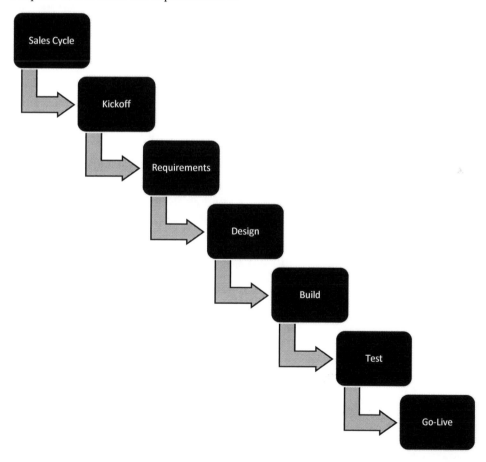

In the waterfall methodology, each project phase has specific deliverables. In theory, work on one phase cannot begin until the prior phase is completed to the satisfaction of both sides. In practice, it often does. There is usually a bit of overlap between phases just because it would be crazy not to start thinking about where you are going in advance. We will describe them all in excruciating detail in the following sections.

The Project Team

If you decide to go ahead with an ICM project, who are the likely players?

THE CUSTOMER SIDE

We have met Tammy and the **Comp Team** back in the "**WHO DOES ICM**" section. They play a tremendous role in the success of the project. Depending on the size of the team and other operational considerations, the entire Comp Team is unlikely to be fully involved for the duration of the project, but everyone will probably need to attend at least a few meetings where their areas of expertise are discussed. The usual approach is for Tammy and a few, representative, somewhat senior people to be the most active on the project, with others brought is as needed. A similar idea is used on the IT side of the house. A handful of the most knowledgeable and involved technical staff will attend, with others brought in when their expertise is required.

While their presence is critical, there can sometimes be a dark side to the Comp Team being a cornerstone of the project. Remember how I mentioned that Tammy is often and unfairly the most underappreciated person in the company? Tammy has been telling people this job is hard and that she has had an uphill fight to get the commission paid for years. Now we're finally going to install a new system, and someone might put it into Tammy's head that the entire process will be automated, with the strong implication that her job is going to be at risk. This does not exactly incent Tammy and the team to give whole-hearted support to the project.

Without a willingness on both sides to meet each other more than hallway, the project will not be successful – it's as simple as that. If Tammy holds back, or neglects to give a valuable piece of information, or only discusses the happy path instead of the real path, then the system will be built without the complexity it will need to handle incentive comp at the company. And this will come out during testing when the system won't get the same results for the same data as the legacy comp system did.

I want to stress, I have only seen this happen a few times, and absolutely not on the majority of projects. But it is a key success factor that Tammy and her team feel like partners in this process, not as victims of it, because they will still be equally important in the management of compensation when the system goes live. Their knowledge and experience will not be replaced by the software. And until it goes live, they will have two full-time jobs – their regular day jobs, and the implementation project.

Therefore, *it is critical that the Comp Team be involved in the project from the beginning*, from planning through presales through implementation. Do not call her one day and say, "We're installing some comp software called iCompPlus. You have to be on the project. Make it successful." It's a recipe for resentment, half-hearted support, and withheld information.

Other than the Comp Team, there are other players we need to identify as well. One is the **Executive Sponsor**. The Executive Sponsor is the person with the title and the budget to make the project happen. We all agree that there needs to be new ICM software installed, but who owns it and who is feeling enough pain with the old system to buy it? That would be the Exec Sponsor. Some Exec Sponsors remain actively involved for the duration of the implementation. Sadly, many do not. Having someone with the will and authority to make tough decisions when roadblocks appear is invaluable.

One of the project success predictors I developed early on in the wild, wooly days of ICM had to do with the rank of the person who would lose a job if the project failed. If it was VP or higher, then I knew we would have the involvement needed to keep all the moving parts moving on the customer side. Director? That introduced risk. Tammy or a manager-level person? That was a huge red flag. An ICM project usually has so many cross-department interactions and dependencies that someone high up has to be concerned and caring to break logjams that come up when the project staff have different agendas. Far be it from me to be pessimistic, but a huge, complex project with tentacles reaching throughout the organization, but with no executive support, isn't going to work.

The **Program Management Office** – the **PMO**[27] – is something we almost never used to see, but now we very often do. The theory behind it is that the team running **BAU** – **"business as usual"** –operations might not have the vocabulary, the techniques, or the rigor to run a project. Projects do require different skills and muscles than operations do to be performed well. So the PMO is full of people who do projects across the enterprise – maybe ICM this week, General Ledger next month, and CRM next year. **Project Managers** (**PMs** – we will hear about them a lot) are the bread and butter of the PMO, but there are various other specialists brought in as well. These can include:

- **Communications Specialists** to help market and explain what is being done:
- **Training Specialists** to put together user and end-user tutorials so that people can hit the ground running on Day One after go-live;
- **Governance Specialists** who make sure the standards and rules established by corporate are being adhered to with respect to proper documentation and achievement of project milestones;
- **Enterprise Architects** – sometimes they live in the PMO instead of the IT infrastructure.

The PMO can be more or less powerful. They sometimes merely provide support to projects, but in other organizations, they have the power of life and death over the projects they oversee. Ideally they fall somewhere in between (that is, ideally from an implementation guy's perspective). It's important that standards be maintained on a project, but as I might have mentioned, ICM projects often have different problems than other kinds of IT projects. Sometimes a rigid adherence to a specific methodology that doesn't map neatly to the ICM problem can detract from the effectiveness of the project team as a whole.

The PMO or the IT group might also provide a **Test Lead**. This person is responsible for directing the customer side testing, including the creation of the test strategy. The Test Lead's job begins early in the **Requirements Phase** – it doesn't begin the day the system is configured and made available for testing.

And let us not forget the various contributors to the procurement process. Comp is in flames. Tammy convinces her bosses that the world can't go on like this, they agree to shop for a system, maybe an SI is brought in to help with the evaluation. RFIs and demos are performed (more on this later) and eventually TotalBigIncent is selected as the ICM vendor of choice. Then **Procurement** steps in.

A sales rep's job is to sell for the best price. Procurement's job is to buy for the best price. Funny how the same words – "best price" – can have diametrically opposite meanings. The Procurement person's job is not to find a way to "yes"; it is to make the sale difficult for the vendor and good for the customer's bottom line. If they can make the vendor's sales rep cry in a meeting, they have won.[28]

I'm not a software sales guy so my interest in this part of the process is only intellectual, not part of my core being. The one thing I would suggest as a consideration is this: a billion dollar company can absorb a worse deal than a small company can, and a lot of the ICM vendors are small companies. If you insist on a 99% discount, the small company might be in a position where they need to make the deal on those terms. But they might also be in

---

[27] Sometimes "Project Management Office" instead of "Program Management Office". Programs are multiple related projects. And sometimes the "O" is for "Organization". I love standardization, and hope to eventually see some someday.

[28] And better yet, make the vendor's VP of Sales cry – *that's the best!* Or at least, that's how I hear the story from the software sales folks I've worked with. Take it with a grain of salt.

the position that they won't survive many more years if they don't bring in a little revenue at some point, great customer logos on their corporate sales presentation notwithstanding. Now, I am not suggesting that the procurement people roll over for the vendor sales people – I always think it's a good idea to make sales people cry occasionally, and it gives the Procurement folks a lot of job satisfaction. But do bear in mind, the company you're beating up might not be around to support their product if they don't make at least a few bucks along the way. Just sayin'.

Part of the procurement team is the dreaded **Legal** staff. You've agreed to buy the TotalBigIncent product, you've beaten them up for a 98% discount and taken the shoes out of their children's mouths, and now Legal steps into the smoking wreckage to argue over contract terms. This is where project start dates really get delayed. One side submits a contract for the software and services, the other side squawks over the terms and conditions and sends back "**redlines**", and back and forth it goes. This can take weeks, or even longer. It's not just an intellectual exercise, by the way. The T&Cs matter – they can affect whether one side or the other can recognize revenue or whether they will be unprotected in the event of bad things happening with the project or the software.

Procurement is something that happens before the project starts, so it might well seem irrelevant for the purposes of this book. The only reason I'm wasting so much space on it is because of project scheduling. During the sales cycle, dates for the project to complete are proposed, usually with the stated proviso that the project commence at a certain point as well. If the commencement is too far delayed, and it's always later than even the customer team thinks it will be, the end date must, inevitably, slip. This concept is pretty easy to grasp, but in the event, it sometimes becomes murky.

I worked on a project several years ago that began in early November. During the negotiations back in the prior May and June, the customer and the vendor all agreed that in principle, there was no reason why the software couldn't go live in March of the following year. But Purchasing and Legal delayed the contract signing (with help from the vendor's team as well, of course) until nearly half a year later. On project Day One, we put together an aggressive but somewhat realistic schedule that called for go-live in July or August. And the IT director said, "No. Your sales person said we'd go live on March 1. So we will. And no, there will be no project scope cut." As far as I know, they didn't go live on March 1 of the coming year. Or, for that matter, on March 1 of the year after. The shocking conclusion: unrealistic project leadership often leads to failed projects.

THE IMPLEMENTER SIDE

The implementation team, whether from the vendor, a Systems Integrator, or even the customer side, often consists of the following roles:

- The **Project** (or **Program**) **Manager** – the **PM**. This is the person responsible for keeping the implementation staff on track and managing project scope and budget.
  Interestingly, many customers try to limit the vendor PM role or eliminate it entirely. In my experience, it just increases the distractions for the project staff when the customer succeeds. Someone outside of the day-to-day project work has to be the conduit between the teams. If the vendor is responsible for delivering the project on time and on budget, someone other than the consultants needs to have that as their primary focus. It might not need to be a full-time position, but it can't be much less than half-time if there is any project complexity at all.
- **Compensation Consultants**. Comp consultants – sometimes called **Business Analysts** or **Functional Analysts** – are responsible for understanding the business requirements and for configuring the application to support them. This can be a technical role, but some applications have a fairly business-user-friendly front end that allows non-techies like me to manage them. Often the comp consultants lead the Requirements and Design Phases because the business functionality of the system necessarily drives the data integration, reporting, and process activities.

- **Data Integration (DI) Consultants**. These are the people responsible for importing data from source systems, and sending data to the downstream systems, including performing such transformations and enrichments as the data needs in order to support compensation calculations. On some projects, this is the most complex task. But not on all projects.
- **Reporting Consultants**. Sometimes this is handled by the DI consultants, but if the application has a separate reporting piece, especially one that uses third-party reporting tools, then a specialist (or several) might be needed to get the best out of it.
- **Technical Consultants**. These folks deal with the systematic aspects of the solution, whether installing the software, managing network functionality, performing DBA (Database Administration) tasks, or any other "keep the lights blinking" functions.
- **Organizational Change Management (OCM) Consultants**. These people are concerned with how the Comp Team's and payees' jobs will be impacted by the implementation of a new system. Training is clearly part of this. Business consulting about better future-state or to-be-state policies and procedures can also be part of an OCM engagement. There is tremendous value in having this work performed as part of the project, but once it's time to map the vendor's product and services to the customer's budget, this is invariably the first thing cut. Over time, I would like to see this become a core part of the project plan, but even vendors propose cutting this function first when they are trying to bring the price down.

Note – the roles might be performed by one person each, or several. And one person might have one role, or several. This is a logical breakdown, not a staffing plan.

Other vendor-side roles include the **Account Manager** – often the sales rep who sold the system to the customer, the vendor's **Executive Sponsor** – the high-level person responsible for maintaining the strategic relationship between the two companies, and something relatively new in the industry – the **Customer Success** group. The Customer Success role can be as tactical as managing the customer reference pool as an aid to the sales community, or it can be a very strategic function with proactive engagement with the customer community to be sure that the customers feel that they have a voice in the future of the vendors company and on the product roadmap.

Finally, another group to get to know is the vendor's **Tech Support** organization. They typically do not get involved until the project team hands off to the customer on project go-live. Again, not a slam on any ICM vendor's application, but given the complexity of the problem and the sheer mass of the software, all of which was written by fallible human beings, issues do arise. Sometimes they are not software issues, by the way. There might be data issues that make things fall over. Or the implementation team didn't catch an edge case in their requirements, design, and testing, that suddenly wrong results, or no results, are popping out of the system. Tech Support is where the problem solving starts, but they might not be able to give you an answer if the problem exists outside of the software.

THE STEERING COMMITTEE

One of the most important creations in an ICM implementation project is the **Steering Committee**, often shortened to "**SteerCo**". This is a group consisting of managerial level cross-functional customer and vendor staff, plus exec sponsors from both sides. The SteerCo keeps an eye on project progress and eliminates roadblocks across departments to keep the project from stalling. Where there are conflicts on the project, the conflicts are escalated to the SteerCo for resolution.

The SteerCo should meet no less often than monthly, and more is better, but the specific cadence of their meetings will be dependent on the project and the culture. But if the SteerCo only meets at the start of the project to kick it off, and at the end of the project to claim credit for its success, then they aren't really steering, are they? And unless the project goes ridiculously smoothly, there might not be a lot of success to claim credit for. An active

Steering Committee is a boon to the teams – they really do need interest and involvement.

PROJECT CONTINUITY

Ideally, the project team that starts the project is the same team that finishes it. This holds for both the customer and vendor side. But ICM projects can be long and the world is not an ideal place. Over time, employees get promoted, get sick, retire, leave to take other jobs, or do any of those other things that make human beings so hard to manage and plan around. What can you do? People are just ornery.

With the complexity of a customer's ICM requirements and especially the Weirdness they bring to compensation operations, trying to bring a new person up to speed on the problem being solved is exceptionally challenging. But it is a fact of project life, and that's part of the contingency vendors (and customers) should bring to the table when planning the project.

If a vendor swaps staff in and out of the project as often as they change their socks, you have a right to complain, and should. But key people will sometimes need to leave. One reason they have become key people is by being good at their jobs, and good people have an expectation that there might be a promotion to middle management waiting for them if they do well. That promotion might well come in the middle of your project.

The Sales Cycle

The first place a project can fail is during the acquisition of the software and services. No – let me rephrase that. A great project starts with a thoughtful, realistic, and well-managed **Acquisition Phase**. There – much better.

I'm going to feed into an unpleasant stereotype or two here, but I'm doing it to provide some clarity into how projects can get derailed before they begin. An ideal project is a partnership between the customer and the vendor, and I have had the very great pleasure of working on projects like that. But never forget: the vendor's job is to sell the product.

The vendor (whether for software, services, or both) *is not looking for ways to convince the customer not to buy their product.* Quite the opposite, in fact. So if the vendor's sales rep, who is compensated to say "yes", can find a way to say "yes", then "yes" is what you will hear. And if the customer asks the question in such a way as to allow interpretation, then any interpretation that can lead to a "yes" is the one that will be applied. If you work in Sales Comp, this should be obvious to you. You are paying sales reps whose job it is to find a way to "yes", and you pay more to the ones who do it better. Please keep this in mind during the sales cycle. It colors every conversation.

ROI – THE RETURN ON INVESTMENT OF THE ICM PROJECT

I stated earlier that the ROI of an ICM project is *not the ability to lay off or repurpose your compensation staff*. ICM will always be a high-touch business process, and you need knowledgeable comp staff to support that. And when you look at the total cost of the software and the project, and compare that to the cost of the staff administering incentive comp for your company, it will take an awfully long time to repay the cost of the project even if you could eliminate staff.

The real ROI is about error reduction, visibility and compliance.

Error Reduction

Before I throw some math at you, I need to point out one fairly obvious (on careful reflection) fact about errors in variable compensation. I'm going to call it **Ol' Unka DK's Only Law of Incentive Calculation Errors**:

- Errors in variable compensation are *always in the payee's favor.*

If you *underpay* them, they *will* report it to you so you can fix them.

If you *overpay* them, they *might* report it to you.

Maybe I'm reinforcing an unfair stereotype about sales people. Nah – I'm not. This is just human nature, and besides, I've witnessed this kind of behavior for years. So when we talk about errors, those are an *expense* for the company. They don't wash out.

So here are a few ideas and numbers that have been thrown around in the industry for years, and then we'll look at how a new ICM system will benefit you.

- A Manufacturing / High Tech company will often pay in the neighborhood of *15% of revenue in commissions and bonuses.* For a $1B company, this is *$150M.*
- Error rate benchmarks I have seen reported for variable compensation fall in the 10% - 15% range. So let's just say 5% to be conservative. Remembering that errors equal overpayments, *5% of $150M is $7.5M in overpayments.*
- Let's agree that the new system only eliminates half of the errors, though I think it's safe to say the results will be far better than that. *You have just saved $3.75M per year in overpayments of commissions and bonuses by implementing the new system* if you have a $1B company. That probably pays for the project in the first year, with profitability coming thereafter.

Visibility

But wait – there's more! There is a positive hit to the top line as well! Or at least, we in the ICM industry think, hope and say there is.

- A figure commonly tossed around in the ICM world is that payees spend *four hours a week* (10% of their work week) performing **"shadow accounting"** – checking the results of the ICM system or function because they don't trust what comes out of it. I don't really buy that number myself, so let's just call it *two hours a week,* or 5% of their time.
- If they trust the system to be accurate, *and only eliminate half of their shadow accounting time,* that's still one hour, or 2.5% more selling time in a 40-hour week.
- I don't think I'd buy a 2.5% increase in sales based on 2.5% more selling time, but what if we just call it a 1% increase? For the $1B company, that's an *annual increase of $10M in revenue.*

And here's a crazy idea. What if incentive comp actually does change the payees' behavior (for the better, I mean)? What if it actually works?[29] A new system that allows you to create and modify plans to respond better to market conditions, and a system that will give the payees better visibility into their own activities, will likely increase the payees' motivation and ability to sell. It's difficult to put numbers on this, but if incentive comp works (and I have to think it does), then there could well be further increases in the top line to be had as well.

Now, has anyone ever validated these numbers? Well, yes, sort of. Some vendors have worked with customers to try to create hard-number ROI statements, but every company is different and has different problems, so what works for one customer might not pertain to you. Take any of this with a raised eyebrow. Error reduction is important, and we strongly believe it happens, but it's difficult to be sure unless you run two systems in parallel for a year, which never happens.

Compliance

Most spreadsheet-based incentive comp operations cannot be audited: they don't have a bulletproof mechanism built in to show that the system is complying with company policies and procedures. Most enterprise ICM applications have that right out of the box. Sarbanes-Oxley is not the boogeymen it used to be in the past, but it's

---

[29] Nah, don't be ridiculous.

still real. Companies still buy ICM systems due to failed audits.

ICM reporting is another selling point, especially in highly regulated financial services industries. Sometimes it's difficult to get that COBOL system that was written in the late-70s to generate the reports you are on the hook to deliver tomorrow. ICM applications are generally easier to mine regulatory data from.

Hosted or SaaS Operational Savings

There is one further ROI number that is actually pretty easy to generate, and that is the system savings – hardware, third-party software, and maintenance staff – that will be realized if you let the vendor **host** your solution or provide it in a **SaaS** – **Software-as-a-Service** – model. The amount you save is obviously based on how much it would cost you to do it yourself and what the vendor will charge, but that's math you can probably do without too much effort, and I bet the vendor would be happy to help you do it. Vendors like it, it could save you some money, what's not to love?

THE RFI / RFP

In my time working for various ICM system vendors, I have worked on more RFIs and RFPs[30] than you can shake a stick at. Generally I have done it as the representative of the services delivery side, so my agenda has always been to be as realistic as possible, short of having the sales rep knock my teeth down my throat because, *"You can't say that to the customer! They'll never buy from us if you do!"* But since I will be the one who has to make the solution work, I really don't want to go into it promising something I cannot deliver.

I have become a bit of a connoisseur of bad RFIs, because generally, they all are. The two primary mistakes I see in most of them are:

- They are too fine-grained, and/or;
- They present the problem in the form of a solution – which might not be the right one

I think there is a perception that if the question is detailed enough, then there is no place for the vendor to hide. In fact, it works the other way. If I get a question asking, "Can your solution process one million transactions per night?" the answer is, "Well sure it can!" And under my breath, I'm thinking, ["Given enough hardware, of course."] The next question will be, "Can your solution reprocess prior periods?" Sez me, "You bet it can! [Given enough time]".

Now, those two questions individually can be resolved to a "yes". However, if they are read together, the answer might well turn into, "Um, yeah, maybe…" And the more finely grained the questions in that vein, the worse the combined answer will likely become. Let me remind you: it's not the sales rep's job to explain to the customer that, while each individual answer is "yes", the overall answer when you combine these five questions together is, "Are you *nuts?!?* No system can do that!"

Often these questions are in a workbook that will be uploaded to a proposal management system. This seems like a great idea, except that if the solution is complex enough, counting "yes" answers on the spreadsheets is not necessarily going to get you to a reliable score. And as I've mentioned, ICM is more than complex enough to invalidate any weak methodology.

So here's a hint: no professional sales rep with a working pulse will willingly send out an RFI response with

---

[30] **"Request for Information"**, and **"Requests for Proposal"**. These are the formal documents customers require vendors to fill out to describe their solution and what it will cost. They are often in the form of workbooks with a dozen tabs and 100 detailed questions per tab. Each question has a possible "Fully Meets"/"Partially Meets"/"Does not Meet" response, often with a comments section. They are brutal, and they are generally made worse by the short deadlines the customers give for their completion. But hey, I'm not bitter.

anything less than a "fully meets requirements" on every question. They will move mountains to find ways to interpret the questions to make sure that happens. So you get RFIs from five vendors, count the "fully meets" responses, and lo and behold – their products all do 100% of everything you want! Wow – what are the odds of that happening? So you are really no further ahead.

Often the questions in the RFI include terminology and functionality that clearly is based on a specific vendor's architecture. This can happen when that vendor's sales rep has a great relationship with the customer and "helps" them with their RFI. Or an SI (a Systems Integrator – a consulting company) has been retained to do the vendor evaluation, but already has a preferred vendor. They have to invite the other big names in for due diligence in the buying process, but there's one they are really pulling for. When the other vendors see the question, "Does your solution use a Topspin-Overhand-Slam function to manage sales crediting?" we all know that this project was wired up for ICM-o-Tron Solutions and they are the ones to beat.

Again, there are a couple of problems that come out of this. One is, we might not have a "Topspin-Overhand-Slam" function in our application, but we get to exactly the same place in a very different way. So the technically correct answer is "no", because we don't use that functionality. But a "yes" is a defensible answer, since we can do what is being asked for. So, are we lying if we say "yes"? You tell me.

More importantly, though, we know that we are facing an uphill battle in this sales effort because the RFI was written to ICM-o-Tron's specification. And all's fair in love and software sales, so an even more liberal interpretation than usual will be brought to bear on any question that might indicate a gap in our product.

So is there a better way? Yes, but it is time and resource intensive.

- Inventory and analyze the complex challenges your company faces in its compensation operations;
- Document the problems in the form of scenarios with enough detail to show the edge conditions, and ask the vendor to explain *how the solution will address the challenge* in enough detail to know what is configured via the UI, what is managed by way of data loading, and what requires customization or pre- or post-processing. In other words, not *"can you?"*, but rather *"how will you?"*
- Have a committee of knowledgeable people from across the organization (business and IT) read the responses;
- Invite each vendor in to have frank discussions about the ones on which you have questions or concerns.

There's a lot of homework to be done, and it takes a lot longer than making each vendor fill in a "yes" on the top question and then "copy-down" to all the other questions on the sheet for loading into your proposal management system. And it requires realistic expectations on the part of the customer, and this is key.

THE DEMO

There are, essentially, three different levels of product demonstrations vendors can perform to show their software's capabilities. In order of complexity and effort, they consist of:

- The Generic Demo
- The Custom or Targeted Demo
- The Proof of Concept

There is a lot of gray area between them, as you might imagine. The **generic demo** is the simplest. Most of the vendors create a small sample company or two and implement them in their application to show the product's base functionality. Many of the applications will allow the name of the fake companies to be replaced with the names and logos of the prospect company (that's you) to make it seem a little warmer and fuzzier. But the data and plans are very vanilla, nothing juicy and interesting. This is a demo that they should be able to show you in a week or two if you're in a rush, but they would generally prefer a little more time if they can get it. For a first meeting, this should be fine. If you like the vendor and they like you, then you can realistically go on to the next level.

The **custom** or **targeted demo** is a much more complex affair. The vendor's SEs[31] will use what they have learned about your company from the sales meetings you have held so far, plus your website, plus any documentation you have sent, to try to show you exactly what your company might look like in their application. They'll use real data if they have it, or make up the best data they can to eliminate any anomalies that can make an overly literal customer say, *"But we don't sell Widgets"* during the demo. They might actually run transactions through the system to show results being calculated, though everyone hates to have to do that.

Custom demos do not write themselves. They are very time consuming to build. No ICM vendor has unlimited resources to build them, so most vendors have to pick and choose where to apply their resources. The vendors will generally try to limit custom demos to customers who have shown at least a moderate inclination to buy the product. If the SEs are already tied up working on another custom demo, it might be a month before they could have a second one completed. When the rep calls the SEs and says, "Great news! GigundaTech wants a custom demo a week from Friday!" this is not necessarily a source of universal joy.

As a plea for sanity, please understand that you are asking for, essentially, a (lightweight) version of a complete year-long implementation in a week or two when you spring that on the vendors. Should you ask? Sure, but don't be offended when they try to limit what they can build and show you in the allotted time. No one is trying to hide anything from you; they just don't have the ability to whip up something that fast.

The most difficult form of demo is the **proof of concept**. That's when the customer sends over a jillion rows of data, every comp plan, all of their reference data, every report, and says, "Okay, build our system, run the data, run the reports, and show us the results. Oh, and make it run fast." As you might expect, this is a significant challenge to any vendor. Just getting hold of the hardware to run a full production instance is not a trivial or inexpensive prospect. Then getting the time to understand what they're seeing – there is never a read-me file to explain what the data actually means – and coming up with a way to express the plans in the software is a several week effort.

The vendors will ask for a limit in the scope of what they will build. They will ask for a significant amount of time with your SMEs to explain everything they're seeing. And they might well ask you to pay a fee for the amount of work being done – sometimes with the expectation that the fee will be applied to the software sale or project services fees should you decide to buy the product. For these reasons, a proof of concept is not something to enter into lightly. It should be proof of a strong commitment from both sides of the vendor-client relationship. And it should not be rushed, regardless of when you want the system to go live.

THE REFERENCE CHECK

When the customer has narrowed down the list of potential vendors, commonly they ask for a reference call (or several) with customers *exactly like themselves* who have used (and loved) the ICM application. It's a fair thing to ask for, but the problem is, there are not thousands of customers out there for the vendors to choose from. So they have to try to pick a customer from the same industry, or with the same data volumes, or just anyone they can call who will say nice things about them. And honestly, every ICM project will have had some hiccups, so the vendor call is fraught with tension on the part of the sales rep setting it up. They usually try to get both sides to agree to only ask (or answer) questions within a set of boundaries.

Industry and data volumes aside, the real predictor of success is the project planning and well-set expectations the customer brings to the project, and the quality of the implementation team doing the work.

---

[31] Sales Engineers – the presales technical folks who support sales reps. They do the demos and answer the technical questions while the suave, silver-tongued sales rep does the selling and gets all the credit.

REALISTIC EXPECTATIONS

You might well have bad data, bad processes, bad organizational interactions, or complex plans – they may be contributing causes for your purchase of ICM software. These will make the project harder, no matter what the vendor says about how complete its ICM solution is. So describe what the vendor will have to address in your scenarios, not just "Can your solution add a column of numbers and get a 95% accurate answer?" If the comp challenges are great enough to require a new system, do not just assume that any off-the-shelf software package will fully meet your requirements. They might, but they probably won't. Not fully meeting the requirement in the RFI (nor a custom demo) does not mean your project will fail if you choose this solution – it just means there might need to be a creative approach to making it succeed. So be realistic. The project is where your implementation succeeds, not in the software.

One creative approach, or perhaps a realistic expectation I increasingly bring to every ICM project, is that there will be some pre- or post-processing built into whatever solution we build. It's a nearly universal fact of life on any large or complex project. Even if the product can be made to twist itself around corners to solve a particularly edgy edge case, it might not be the right answer to do it that way in the production system. So given the need for data manipulation to make your data work for the ICM system or to solve the incentive compensation problem, you need to be receptive to having the conversation about **preprocessing**. Having the vendor explain to you that they won't be showing you this requirement in the product because they would expect to do some data transformation during the import to manage that piece of the puzzle should not be a disqualifier.

If it seems like the vendor is suggesting burying complex logic in the preprocessor, then by all means, pull the cord and stop that train until they come up with an explanation that satisfies you. But if it's just a matter of pulling attributes from System A and slapping them on the transaction based on CustomerID, for example? That's not really logic, that's just a data lookup based on data that should be readily available. So don't rule it out if the vendor points out that possibility as part of the solution. Remember, preprocessing is not (exactly…) the same as customization.

And the most important realistic expectation is about the time it takes to complete a project. My all-time favorite sales effort for an ICM vendor ever was for a customer who had a large and complex problem that needed a large and complex solution. I had been asked by our sales folks to come up with a project estimate – how many consultants for how long – so we could give an implementation services bid. I came up with something in the low-seven-figures – far north of a million dollars, for about 16 months' worth of effort. The sales guy infarcted, as I suspected he would, and a team of managers got together to bring the number down. They massaged the numbers and came in at appreciably less than a million for maybe 10 or 12 months' worth.

We presented it to the customer, who said, "It doesn't look like you understand the problem. This project will be long and hard for these reasons. These are the constraints. These are the challenges. And this is how much time we have allocated for it. Now go back and do it again." When we came back with a number in the high-seven-figures – far closer to ten million dollars for many phases over many years – the customer told us, "Okay, that's too much, but at least you're bidding on the real project, not just telling us what you think we want to hear." We eventually got the deal – but for an amount in the mid-seven-figures. The customer had hard negotiators, but realistic ones.

So this customer was smart enough to know that the low-cost solution wasn't the right one. Many others would have snapped up the deal we were proposing, then been unhappy when we started hitting them with change requests for the additional project scope we had not bid on in the first place.

And finally, *please do not punish the vendor for being honest with you*. Ask why you got the answer you didn't like – there may be something hiding in those bushes that the vendor sees and responds to that you might not have recognized as a problem. Or maybe they were trying to answer what you were really asking, not just what was in the RFI. A "bad" answer should be a trigger for a good conversation, not an automatic disqualifier.

A related concept is to apply the smell-test to anything you are told. Not all vendors lie, but truth can be a very slippery commodity. Do not listen with happy ears and believe things that you should doubt. I also participated in a far worse sales effort during which we were given a whomping huge pile of data – unrealistically large, given their actual operational requirements – to run a performance benchmark against, which was very close to a POC as described above. It would be our system versus the enemy's system.

We loaded the data, got a little bit creative in how to process it, ran the process, tuned it, reran it, and came back with a run time of around eight hours. Our competitors came back with a run time of less than an hour. We were patting ourselves on the back because we knew there was no way a savvy IT person would believe the sub-one-hour answer. An object-oriented language based system running rules and calculations just does not perform like that on the sheer volume of data we were asked to process. So we knew the customer would have no choice but to choose us.

But they kept telling us that our competitors were eight-to-ten times faster than we were, and unless we could get our times down, we were out of it. So we went nuts tuning and getting creative about how we processed, and even so, we lost the deal. I do not believe the customer ever actually asked to see our competitor's system run, and they never asked the competitor to run it, change values or rule conditions, and run it again to show that the system was actually calculating. They had only the vendor's word that the system ran that fast. I am not sure it ever did run that fast in production, but I wasn't there so I can't say for sure.

FIXED PRICE VS. TIME & MATERIALS

After choosing the software package, the customer then wants the vendor or a Systems Integrator, or both, to install and configure it. And nearly invariably, having the vendor bid the project on a **fixed price** basis is proposed. In other words, the vendor comes up with the total fees for the entire project, and that amount will be paid on the satisfactory completion of specific project milestones. The opposite of fixed price is **time and materials**, or **T&M** – the vendor charges by the hour for all hours worked.

It's not hard to see why fixed price appeals to customers. They know in advance what the project will cost, and they can budget for it. And if the milestones are not completed to their satisfaction, there is no outlay until the work is done.

And it's also not hard to see why vendors hate fixed price (I had a boss who called it "the 'F' word") and prefer to work on T&M projects. On a fixed price contract, the vendor assumes all of the risk. If the project runs long, the work still must be done, but it can't be charged for. There are revenue recognition issues that come with it – from an accounting standpoint, it is sometimes quite a big exposure for the vendor, especially if they are a publicly traded company.

There are some enterprise applications that can be safely bid fixed price. Anything with clearly delineated functionality, clear cut integration requirements, and minimal choices that must be made about how it will be used is a great candidate for that. But those products typically have very short implementation projects, while ICM projects are often long. At least, the medium-to-large, medium-to-high complexity ICM projects are.

The way customers limit risk on T&M projects is to define SOWs (Statements of Work), with a price tag, for either the whole or portions of the project, and then only write purchase orders to cover the scope of the SOW. This means that they haven't left a blank check for the vendor to use up – there is an upper limit on what they have committed to pay for.

And the way vendors limit their risk on fixed price projects is to estimate the project duration very conservatively, assuming the worst on every variable, then they tack on an additional 25% to 30% in "**contingency**". They also try to tightly define the scope of the project, and if the customer project team takes too long to shake hands in the morning, the vendors whip out a CR (Change Request) for additional time and money. For this reason, the project manager will be accused of "nickel and diming" the customer. Don't blame the PM – that's the most important part of the job on a fixed price contract.

I come from the vendor side, so understand that my glasses are not exactly rose-colored with respect to fixed price contracts. Take it for what it's worth, but there are two main reasons I don't like them. One is based on the premise of this entire book – namely, ICM is hard and Weird. And there are a million things that we don't even agree on the names of, so when I try to determine the scope of a project for a fixed price bid, I don't know what your answers to my questions mean. Are you answering what I meant by those words, or were you answering what you meant by them? Are you answering based on your wacky data and processes, or are you answering based on the functionality I am responsible for? My experience tells me that this project will most likely take about this long [holding hands a couple of feet apart]. But I don't know for sure, and I've been surprised by projects that just... never... ... ended... ... ...

Figure 27 - Month 34 of the Never-Ending Project

The other reason, and this might even be more important, is because fixed price contracts make partnership between the vendor and the customer nearly impossible. If I see a problem that might not be in scope, but will absolutely make the system better if I solve it, I want to solve it. If I'm working T&M, there is less exposure if I do. Maybe I've already found a simpler, cheaper way to do some other part of the project (which I would not tell you about if it were fixed price, by the way). Either way, there should probably be a CR reflecting that the scope has changed, but I might feel that I can afford to throw the unforeseen problem into the mix if the project is going well otherwise.

But I totally get why customers want fixed price contracts – they'd be insane not to try to limit their risk. That said, I have seen a compromise solution used recently that I like. The compromise is to do a T&M Requirements Phase for the project, with one deliverable being a fixed price bid for the rest of the project. By the end of discovery, we should have a pretty good idea of how complex the project will be, how many plans will be built, how clean the data is, how responsive or unresponsive the customer is,[32] and most of the other variables that lengthen (or very occasionally, shorten) the project. At that point, the vendor can give a fixed price bid with a clearly defined scope and a reasonable degree of confidence. But this I can promise you: ***there will still be 30% contingency tacked onto the estimate.***

---

[32] This matters. If I'm waiting for signoff on a requirements document and I have allocated three days for the signature process, but the customer takes two weeks, I've got a lot of expense building up keeping the team together that I cannot charge for.

THE VENDOR EVALUATION ENGAGEMENT

As alluded to in the **RFI / RFP** section, an increasingly common practice in the ICM world is to bring in outside help in the vendor selection process. It's generally one I agree with. The reason it makes sense is, most people have not done an ICM project – there just haven't been that many of them in the history of the industry. And far fewer people have done two or more, so customer in-house experience in the selection of ICM vendors is necessarily limited. Bringing in either a big SI or a small boutique consulting company to walk you through the process and help you avoid pitfalls can only be a good thing.

The consultants will likely want to do enough requirements discovery to understand your major problems, and they should help you craft your RFI so that it actually answers the questions you should have about vendor capabilities. They'll help you evaluate the responses, and will guide you through the second round, when you will invite in the candidate vendors to give a targeted demo of their product as it relates to your requirements. The consulting company will help you understand what you saw, and they'll help you apply the smell test to the answers you have been given. This is valuable stuff.

Are there negatives? Yes, but not significantly negatively enough to reject the idea out of hand. Some SIs have better (or worse) relationships with different ICM application vendors, which could affect their objectivity. There is always the awkwardness around whether the SI could or should be invited to participate in the implementation, and again, that could impact their objectivity with respect to the selection. And of course, these engagements aren't cheap, but if they save you a ton of time later (and time does equal money, especially on big IT projects), then they are most likely worth the money.

THE WORST POSITION TO BE IN OF ALL

And what, finally, was the strangest sales effort I have participated in? I have had to persuade my employers to walk away from deals on a few occasions because I knew we were not a good fit. That almost never ends well – the sales people just hate doing that and the word goes around that I am not a team player. In one case, our CEO, after beating up the sales guys and me for making him walk away, got on the phone with the buyer to tell him we were withdrawing our names from consideration since we were not a good fit for what they needed. *And the buyer refused to take "no" for an answer!* He was screaming at our CEO that, darn it, we HAD to sell to him and this was unacceptable! We tried to explain to him that this wasn't just a new sales tactic – we really could not solve his compensation problems and we already knew the project would fail. He didn't care. His current compensation system was so awful that he was desperate to buy something – *anything* – even though we told him explicitly that it would not work.

Of course, it didn't escape the CEO's and the sales rep's attention that we could have charged any amount we wanted and the customer would have paid it. But no, we walked away. I didn't get invited to join the fellas for lunch very often for a while after that.

I am not exactly sure what the lesson to draw from this is. Other than, maybe, don't ever put yourself in this position as a customer.

Project Preparation & Kickoff

PROJECT READINESS CONSULTING

A relatively new service being offered in the ICM industry is **Project Readiness Consulting**. The big SIs and the smaller boutique consulting firms have started making this a standard offering, and even some ICM vendors have begun to propose it to their newly signed customers. The idea is that, if this is your company's first ICM project, or the first one in a long time, then there are things you might not know you need to prepare for to get the best out of the implementation and the system. And the time to learn this is before the project kicks off, not during or after the project.

A Project Readiness Assessment is designed to answer the question of whether the customer is adequately prepared to make the project as successful as possible. This is most certain when a clear vision of project goals is in place. The assessment team will try to determine:

- What is the project vision?
  - Why is the system being implemented?
  - What is the proposed ROI?
  - What are the current pain points the project is supposed to mitigate?
  - Are there clear success criteria established?
    What metrics will be used to measure that?
- Is the project team identified and assembled?
  - And is it the right team?
    Hint: **Subject Matter Experts (SMEs)** who have never been part of the Comp Team are not the right people to drive the project. You need the folks who really know how compensation is administered for this.
  - Is there time and budget to train them on the new system?
- Have the system requirements been assembled?
  - For compensation?
  - For data integration?
  - For reporting?
  - Do all parties agree that these are the real requirements?
- Have the ground rules of the project been defined?
  - How will the project team be able to do their current day jobs and still participate in the project?
  - Will the project be a collaborative build?
    Or is the vendor expected to deliver a "turn-key" system with no hands on involvement from the customer team? (More on this in the BUILD PHASE section)
  - Is there Project Governance in place?
  - In the event of a conflict, who has decision-making authority?
- Has the ideal future state been defined with respect to operational processes?
  - Have bad processes been identified, and better ones proposed to replace them?
  - Have communication and training plans been put in place to allow a smooth transition to the new system when it goes live?

A Readiness Assessment can be a half-day long, or a couple of weeks, or even longer. It won't be any more successful than the customer's prep and the vendor's diligence allow. Trying to gather and sort all of the threads of a 2-year project in a single three-hour meeting will probably not give much clarity or certainty.

I participated in a one-day Readiness Assessment once. Among other things, we asked, "Have you defined all the compensation plan requirements?" The answer was the Comp Team lead smacking a big stack of paper and telling us it was all right here. We wrote a glowing Readiness Report, then showed up a few weeks later to do the project. And no, actually, that was just a big stack of new, old, and obsolete comp plan printouts in no discernable order. No one had ever sat down and sorted through them to see which ones were still applicable. We complained that the team wasn't ready. The customer pointed out that the Readiness Assessment they had just paid for had said everything was great. We clearly should have dug deeper, but in the time allotted, we couldn't. The assessment was only as good as the time and effort put into it – by both sides.

PROJECT MECHANICS: LOCATION

Where is everyone going to sit? And by that I don't even mean just which room has been reserved. I mean, in what city? Will the project be performed onsite at the customer's facilities? And if so, in one location or several? Or will the teams be remote?

In the early days of ICM, nearly every project was conducted onsite at the customer's offices for almost the entire project duration. ICM consultants could confidently expect to be on 100% travel for as long as they were in the business. I always suspected the reason was that customers didn't trust the consultants to be working the hours they were billing and wanted to see them actually putting in the time, but there were other reasons, too. The ability to work remotely with online meetings was not as robust as it is today, for one thing.

That paradigm is changing pretty radically these days. Travel is expensive and a lot of customers don't want to pay for it. Network access is becoming seamless – we no longer have to be in the building with the servers to be able to work on the system. And telecommuting is cheap, available, and powerful. Now the percent of travel becomes part of the negotiation about the project time and duration, and the trend is toward zero, even if it won't get all the way there.

With all that being said, however, I still feel that there are project phases that cannot be performed effectively in any way other than in person, face-to-face, onsite. Requirements discovery is the main one. We will talk about this is more detail in the **REQUIREMENTS PHASE** section, but the ability to draw a picture on the whiteboard, have the SME come over and make a subtle correction to it, and then to see the nods of agreement (or the reluctant nod that's almost a headshake) is priceless. That level of communication does not happen on a conference call. The hallway conversation is often the one where that clarifying detail that changes the entire understanding of a problem is nailed down.

So if we agree that some degree of actual human interaction is necessary, how do you configure the workspace for the team? If the customer has multiple facilities, and IT is located in one while the business operations staff are located in another, should we divide up the technical implementation staff and the compensation consultants into those separate facilities too? I would argue against it, but I would know it was likely to be a losing battle.

It seems so logical that it would be more efficient to have the techies talking to techies and the business talking to the business consultants. It'll make the project go twice as quickly, right? Logically, that's true, but in my experience we always end up with gaps in the requirements and design if the teams are siloed that way, and some of those gaps are schedule killers when they turn up later in the project.

And the reason goes back to some of what we talked about in the "**WHY IS ICM HARD**" section. Knowing the comp plans, I cannot tell you how the data is going to behave. And knowing the data, I cannot tell you how the plans are going to consume it or what interactions the operational staff will perform with it and on it (or because of it). The technical consultants need to hear the business requirements if they are to contribute to the system design, and the comp consultants need to know what gyrations the data is encountering in order to know if their plan logic will solve the problem or not.

Where the customer has organizational issues (remember the whole business-won't-talk-to-IT discussion?), this is only magnified. But sadly, those are the organizations where it is almost impossible to co-locate business and IT for the project. While I am not suggesting that everyone needs to be in every meeting, I do feel strongly that both sides need to be in enough of the same meetings to be knowledgeable about what the system really needs to do. It will become apparent early on which meetings can be strictly IT-to-IT or business-to-business, but I think it's safer to err on the side of inclusiveness.

When project work is being undertaken onsite, a fairly standard approach is for the customer to reserve a conference room (usually *not quite* big enough) for the duration of the project, and to plop down the implementation team there. This is their new home-away-from-home. This is not a bad thing, especially when there is adequate phone and network access piped to the room. Several thousand square feet of whiteboard space is also highly recommended – and let's get some fresh markers, while we're at it! It sometimes happens that the vendor staff will be given cubicles as well, but that is by no means the norm.

Now, this might be a little out of line for this book, but I'm going to make a plea for courtesy and understanding from the customers out there. Please recognize that the vendor and system integrator teams need the ability to have private conversations, even on great projects where a real partnership is being cemented between them and the customer's team. But just as the customer's staff would not want the vendors attending every internal meeting they need to have, vendor staff sometimes need privacy for their internal communications as well.

To that end – please don't camp out in the vendor's project room unless invited or attending meetings? There are conversations that need to occur that should be private. These are not for the purpose of being sneaky or pulling something over on the customer. There might be personnel management issues, strategizing, clarifications of requirements, design, or functionality that must be made, calls back to corporate HQ to clarify contractual or other issues, or any number of other reasonable things. When someone from the customer side is parked at the work table - "Oh, don't mind me, I'm just reading my email" – those conversations cannot happen. So the project team has to go wandering around looking for a discreet place to talk, but then they don't have access to the network and the whiteboards.

The customer usually has far greater access to offices and conference rooms than outsiders do, so if the customer team needs to have confidential conversations, they have an easier time making it happen. The vendor team often doesn't have that luxury. So if there is no separate office or conference room set aside for the implementation staff, it would be thoughtful to let them have the work room as a safe haven where they can talk openly with each other.

Okay, back to the conduct of the project.

PROJECT MECHANICS: SCHEDULING

In "The Mythical Man-Month",[33] Fred Brooks make the observation that, "Nine women can't make a baby in one month" in response to the idea of throwing staff at a late project. He's making several different points with that statement, but one of them is that some things take exactly how long they take, regardless of the resources you might be tempted to apply to them. I bring this up because customers sometimes require the vendor to certify that the system will be ready to go live by a certain date. The implementers' usual response is to throw more consultants on the fire to see if it will burn hotter. It doesn't.

The bottleneck here is that the customer staff, who provide the knowledge needed to specify and design the system, have day jobs.[34] Incentive comp doesn't stop while the project steams full-speed-ahead. The sales guys still expect their checks to go out. And the SMEs were already overworked before the project started – that's why the new system is going in, remember? The upshot is, the implementation team cannot expect, nor even ask for, 100% of the SMEs' time. We are lucky to get 50%, with 25% - 30% a more likely allocation, even if the vendor decides to throw 10 extra consultants at the project. And sometimes it's less, and it might be unavoidable if business must go on. So how do we make the best use of the staff who are already stretched too thin?

During the Planning Phase, it's important for the customer's and the implementation team's Project Managers to discuss the known crunch periods and to block those out on the schedule. If checks always go out the week of the

---

[33] Frederick P. Brooks, Jr. "The Mythical Man-Month". 1995 [1975]. Addison-Wesley.

[34] At least they do if they actually know anything about incentive compensation. If they are brought onto the project as SMEs – Subject Matter Experts – but haven't administered comp or the source systems for it for the company before, they are not likely to add much value to the process.

15th, then don't expect that week to be a good one for scheduling long meetings. If new plans are being rolled out the last week of January, again, plan on doing documentation or other work that doesn't require hand-holding from or for the customer's project team.

Then with the blocks of time available, a common practice is to schedule meetings for either all of the mornings, or all of the afternoons, for each week. Assuming morning meetings, the afternoons can be used for documentation or development, and quick and surgical phone calls, emails, or quick hallway conversations can take place to clarify a detail as needed. Flexibility is needed to adapt to the customer's rhythms, and travel time for the consultants must be born in mind as well. But this is a pretty workable project cadence and staff from both sides of the relationship can plan their work around it fairly easily.

PROJECT MECHANICS: THE SINGLE POINT OF CONTACT

Ah, the **SPOC** – the **Single Point of Contact**. It seems so logical to put one in place so the project team won't be interfering in the lives of the Comp Team as they do their day-to-day jobs. Establish some well-defined communications channels, we're talking real efficiency now.

Except, we aren't. Have I mentioned the problems of applying human language to the comp domain yet? Both parties in the conversation have to know and agree on what the words mean. And Tammy, the person who knows, is never the SPOC. It's usually someone bright and hardworking from the corporate Program Management Office, but not someone who has ever administered compensation.

So the usual routine is for the project team to ask a question. The SPOC applies more or less interpretation to it, then asks the SME, who gives an answer to the filtered question. The SPOC applies more or less interpretation to the answer, and brings it back to the project team. It's like the old children's game of Telephone – the project team might not know how deeply the question and answer were impacted by the interpretations put on them by the SPOC. I have nothing against the SPOCs I have worked with, many of whom were really smart and wanted to do a great job, but I have never seen them actually improve the communications process.

When I hear that there will be a SPOC in place on a project, I immediately spring into action. I ask a really challenging technical question that implies a lot of background knowledge. The SPOC comes back in a day or so with an answer – it doesn't matter what it is, because I'm barely listening. I then ask a highly granular and picky clarifying question about the answer. A day or so later when the SPOC brings me the answer, so I ask another clarifying question that's the opposite of what the SPOC just told me. It usually takes a couple of cycles, but at that point the SPOC will put me in touch with the SME directly. Then the floodgates for real knowledge transfer open. Crushing the SPOC's spirit is the value-add I bring to a project.

Meanwhile, the rest of the team has been "accidentally" running into the SMEs in the hallway and getting fast and accurate answers to their questions all along.

PROJECT MECHANICS: WORKING TO A DATE

In the US, it is just a given that projects all but grind to a halt between the second half of November and the first week of January. Some companies shut down completely the week between Christmas and New Year's, but even if they don't, critical people take vacations and the HR department won't let us tell them they can't. In parts of Europe, August is a complete washout. So it's important to be realistic about a schedule that has important milestones occurring during times when we can't even count on anyone showing up to the meetings.

Another more horrifying scenario is the IT lockdown. It doesn't happen everywhere, but it happens. The project is rocking along, everyone's behaving, work is being done, and the IT Enterprise Architect drops by the War Room one day and casually lets it drop that, "Oh, by the way – if your system isn't completed by October 1, you won't be allowed to integrate it with any critical IT systems until January. Corporate end-of-year lockdown, y'know. Have a nice day!" This is something even the customer staff generally were not aware of, and the sound of careers going up in flames can be deafening in the silence following the Architect's departure.

I bring this up because during the sales cycle, one question that's often asked is, "If we sign the deal with your company, when will the project start and how long will it take?" So we put together a tentative schedule, and assume that if the project starts in early-March, we should be able to go live by, say, November. Then the contract negotiations hit snags. Legal won't approve this wording, Procurement insists on certifications that no one has ever asked for before, both sides pound on the table, both sides threaten to walk away from the deal, and eventually, the contract is signed in late-April. A team is assembled – that usually takes a couple of weeks – and work begins in May.

But the project sponsor has already promised that the new system will be online in November. This is awkward. It was a risky assertion anyway, because the project wasn't scheduled from any real knowledge, just assumptions, and honestly, IT projects do sometimes, occasionally, run long once in a while anyway, even with good teams on both sides. So at that point people start scrambling to see if there's some way to bring it all in faster than promised, or whether scope can be cut to deliver something before the end of the year. Huge holes get torn in the schedule, and at the end of the day, the project ends up taking even longer than originally promised anyway.

I attended an ICM Round Table discussion at a vendor's User Conference a couple of years ago. Representatives from four companies that had successful ICM implementations sat around discussing their projects and answering questions from the audience. Someone asked what mistakes they felt they had made. And all four customers pointed to working towards a completion date, rather than working towards a quality deliverable, as something they wish they had not done. There are always unforeseen circumstances that impact a schedule, and in the rush to get the job done, compromises must always be made.

No one would sign up to an open-ended project completion – a business cannot run that way. But a realistic assessment of risks, and a little flexibility in addressing stumbles, can mean the difference between crash landing on a particular date (plus or minus), as opposed to a smooth landing when the project is genuinely done.

PROJECT MECHANICS: THE SIXTY-HOUR WEEK

Related to working to a completion date is the 60-hour project work week. When deadlines approach, especially if the project is late, then overtime is expected and reasonable – it's part of being a professional. But I have seen projects **begin** with the schedule in panic mode, and I have never seen the work proceed any faster because of it. When the project manager demands outrageous efforts before the project has even had a chance to hit any snags, the project staff nearly universally drag their feet and start doing second-rate work.

The exception to this is the world of the large Systems Integrators. They behave like law firms with associate lawyers. They hire consultants straight out of school and throw them at projects. The consultants are there to prove themselves, and they will self-select out of the company if they aren't willing to work like maniacs in their new hire days. And heck, they're young, they have stamina, they're not old and broken like me, so sure, they can handle it.

But seasoned professionals know that if a project manager is scheduling nights, weekends, and holidays before the project starts, then either the project schedule is already known to be doomed to fail, or else the PM is just being a control freak for the fun of it. Neither scenario is conducive to solid effort and good deliverables.

It is completely fair to demand accountability and solid work from the staff. If they screw up, then they should work extra hours to fix it. But if everything is an emergency, then nothing is an emergency. And it's a fact of life that if people put in too much time and don't get time to rest and clear their heads, then the work they do will eventually become sub-standard even if they want to do better. And this works on both sides of the project relationship – customer and implementer.

CHAPTER SIX – THE PROJECT COMMENCES

Okay – the papers are signed, the project teams on both sides have been assembled, looks like we're a 'go'. So what happens now?

Requirements Phase

It is impossible to stress too highly how critical the **Requirements Phase** is to the success of an ICM project. A well-run Requirements Phase provides the foundation for everything that happens afterwards. The Requirements Phase is one I will never willingly cut to save budget, even if the customer says the documentation of their comp requirements is complete before it starts.

DELIVERABLES

The Requirements Specification Document

The primary deliverable from the Requirements Phase is something that for the purpose of this book we will call the **Requirements Specification Document**, or **RSD**. Every vendor calls it something different – I've never actually seen anyone call it an RSD – so this name is as good as any.

Sez me (and therefore, sez every project methodology I have left behind at each of my various employers along the way), the RSD is an *application-agnostic view of all in-scope compensation functionality and system and operational requirements that will be delivered as a result of the ICM implementation*. The RSD should reflect any in-scope deliverables from the Statement of Work or the contract, plus any others mutually agreed to during the Requirements Phase.

Typically vendors expect a signature from the customer confirming that the RSD exactly describes their requirements and that the system will be accepted if it supports what is in the document. This is how the vendors can protect themselves, but it also protects the customers. When we get to the end of the project, the customer can't say, "Yeah, but your system *doesn't do THIS!*" If "*THIS*" has not been described in the RSD, then it is not a requirement that prevents acceptance of the system. The vendor may decide to do it, or there might be a Change Request generated for it, but shy of those two outcomes, it is not in scope for the project. Conversely, if the solution doesn't handle something that is in the RSD, the customer has a stick to use on the vendor. Do it, or we don't accept the system.[35]

Application-Agnostic

"**Application-agnostic**" is the operative term in the description of the RSD above. It means, simply, that the problem cannot be written in terms of the solution. It is written in human language, not application language. It should tell a story that is clear even to someone who has never used ICM software, and especially not the vendor's ICM software.

If I write a requirement stating, "System will use 'McGillicutty Algorithm' functionality to do sales crediting", how can the customer know that I have understood the requirement without having taken a class in the internal workings of the ICM system I am implementing? Even if I explain it to them – or even if they take the class – we haven't described the business requirement, we have just said what we will put into the system, so we have no

---

[35] And more importantly, we don't pay the invoices.

way of showing that it will meet the business need. Nothing in that description suggests test cases to use to validate the results. And if I discover an even better way to accomplish exactly the same thing, or get backed into having to use a different system function because of some source data anomaly I discover later, I have made it a requirement that I will use specific functionality, and I have a customer signature on the RSD, so now I'm stuck with it.

Therefore, that requirement should be written in the form of something along the lines of: "System will provide direct credit to payees using a combination of X, Y, and Z transaction attributes that will be defined for each payee and maintained outside of the system but fed into the system nightly", or words to that effect. With that description, it doesn't matter what functionality we use to do it, so long as we do it.

What You Are Not Allowed to Do

One common but unacceptable practice is to copy and paste the customer's requirements documentation into the RSD – sometimes even pasting in their 15-page comp plans. And what could be more efficient? The customer has to sign off on the doc because we're promising to do exactly, to the letter, what they have asked for, no?

No. Just as putting the requirements into system language means that the customer cannot make an informed decision about whether we have understood what they need, leaving the requirements in the customer's language means that we cannot prove that we have understood them. Remember how I mentioned that no two comp consultants agree on what a "commission" is? The customer and we won't agree either. We must, without fail, translate what we hear in the Requirements Workshops into neutral, human language. It takes longer, it's annoying, it's extra work, I get it. But not as long or annoying as finding out during Testing that we fundamentally mistook the meaning of a word, or worse, discovering that someone used an "or" instead of an "and" in the source documentation.

There should absolutely be a glossary attached to the RSD to define terms like "credit", "commission", "bonus", "territory" and the like. But those terms should not imply the specific functionality that will be used to solve the problem. The solution comes later in the Design Phase. It should theoretically be possible to get an RSD from one vendor and give it to another vendor to implement in their software. This would not be a recommended practice, but it is the goal of a good requirements document.

REQUIREMENTS WORKSHOPS

Caveat

Every implementation vendor (whether the software vendor or an SI) has its own methodology for performing projects. Each has its own deliverables – sometimes dozens or hundreds! Each has its own variations on what the conduct of the project and the workshops will be. So who am I to lay down the law and say how it's going to be for you?

Oh, just some guy who wants your project to succeed. For any project of medium (or greater) size or complexity, I think that the method I'm laying out here provides a solid foundation, and I think doing any less introduces serious risk to the successful outcome. As I tell the teams I work with, "Use your own tools, so long as they are at least as complete as the ones I am proposing. You can do more, you can do it differently, but you cannot do less than this."

So to that end, I will display my breathtaking ego by defining the minimum recommended requirements for requirements gathering as though they are a natural law that will allow no argument. Now, I know that any team you hire to implement software will use their own methods and tools for the project, and just because they don't do exactly what I propose in this book doesn't mean that they are wrong. They might do more, they might do it differently. But if they do any less, be wary that there may be gaps.

The Workshops

So what do we put in this RSD we're going to be delivering to the customer? Can we just grab the comp plans, the customer's enterprise data dictionary, and some reports and paste them in, call it a day? Erm, no, actually, that doesn't work. That is not to say I haven't seen requirements documents done just that way, but not on successful projects. The Requirements Phase is a lot of work, so let's get to it.

Incidentally, you do need to get hold of the comp plans, the data dictionary, the reports, and any other supporting documentation you can – these are critical source documents and they can help with the inventory of functionality needed for the system and provide additional perspectives on the words we hear. But they provide only one view into what you will be delivering, and it's not necessarily the most helpful view. The real way forward is to gather the customer SMEs together in workshops and hash out, in a systematic way and in excruciating detail, what the system needs to do to support the customer's compensation operations today and in the future.

What kinds of workshops? A representative list might include:

- End-to-End Processing
- Compensation Plans
- Payee Data
- Transaction Data
- Other Reference Data
- Downstream Feeds
- Reporting & Analytics
- Modeling Requirements (if applicable)
- Administration & Maintenance
- Workflow Requirements (if applicable)
- Testing Strategy
- Non-Functional Requirements

Of course, there can be others as well. The list depends on what the customer wants from the system, what was sold to them, and any unique challenges they bring to the problem.

So great – a dozen meetings or so and we're done, right? Sadly, no. Each workshop could represent a week's worth of four-hour meetings, or even more, depending on the size and complexity of the topic with respect to the customer. This is just a logical way to break up the requirements gathering to make it easier to get the right people in place.

I know no one wants to commit too many resources to too many meetings, especially when those resources have real work they are also responsible for that won't get done if they aren't there to do it. But as bad as it sounds, having representatives from the business side and the IT side attend each of the workshops is generally a more effective approach than keeping them siloed. In ICM, everything affects everything, so knowing what a business requirements means from a technical perspective – and vice versa – is very valuable to understanding what to build into a new system. It is up to the customer and implementer Project Managers to find ways to respect everyone's time commitments to the project and to their day jobs, but too much time spent during the Requirements Phase can prevent *way too much* time being wasted during the Test Phase.[36]

Now let's discuss the workshops in more detail.

---

[36] And the Redesign Phase, and the Rebuild Phase, and the Retest Phase…

End-to-End Processing

This is the workshop that should always be held first, and this one above all should have representatives from the business and IT. It sets the stage for everything that happens afterward.

In this workshop, we discuss a week, month, quarter, even year in the life of the Comp Team and the relevant IT systems folks. It includes everything from data availability to specific maintenance tasks to preliminary calculations to final calculations to report generation to dispute management to feeds downstream to whatever else Tammy and her crew do month in and month out. This workshop shouldn't get into the weeds of specific plans or file formats – try to keep it at 10,000 feet or so. We want to learn enough to be able to confidently point to where in the process everything we learn in the rest of the workshops goes, but not enough to try to code a comp plan or a feed.

I like to use timelines on a white board or a projected spreadsheet, or really, any other way of making it brutally obvious to everyone what we're talking about. Meeting attendees sometimes need to go to the board and point to a specific day and say, "You mean, *THIS* moment?", and get approving or disapproving nods to show that this is indeed what we are talking about.

Then, to make it even more complicated, I like to include at least three months in the process, but to visualize them next to each other, not in a long line. There are reasons other than my twisted sensibilities for this. One is, comp work typically happens in arrears – often a month or two after the business that is being compensated. And in incentive comp, we often go back in time, and sometimes that's not an exception, but a full-fledged process that must be scheduled for.

By doing three months side by side, I can see that *on this one particular day* Tammy's team might be preparing new quotas for the current month's business that will be paid next month, finalizing reports for the previous month's business that will be paid in the next payroll run, and recalculating the commissions for the month before and preparing the file of delta payments for Payroll. Time is part of the ICM challenge, remember? We need to build a system that recognizes the role of time in ICM operations, and the best way to do that is to lay January, February, and March on top of each other. Or better yet, October, November, and December, since you might have some scheduled planning or analytics requirements that come about at year-end.[37]

It's important to make the distinction between the fifth calendar day of the month, the fifth business day of the month, or the first Tuesday of the month, when describing a given process, by the way. In other words, if you plant a task on a given day, is it because that day is the *ninth calendar day* of the month, the *seventh business day*, or the *second Monday* of that month? Depending on the month, it could be all three, but the odds are, that process is dependent on it being a particular one of them.

This makes for a very confusing looking multidimensional spreadsheet by the time you're done, especially when you put months side by side. I've developed templates to document this, but I've noticed that people clutch their temples, laugh nervously, and back slowly out of the room when I demonstrate them. But hey, no one ever said this would be easy.

---

[37] In this book we will assume that the fiscal year is the same as the calendar year – January 1 to December 31 – unless otherwise stated. If your company uses a non-standard calendar, and many do, I hope you will bear with me and do the conversion as you read this. **Note:** I also will refer to the month as the smallest meaningful unit, but I recognize that for some customers it's the week, while others have the quarter as the most granular financial period that matters to them.

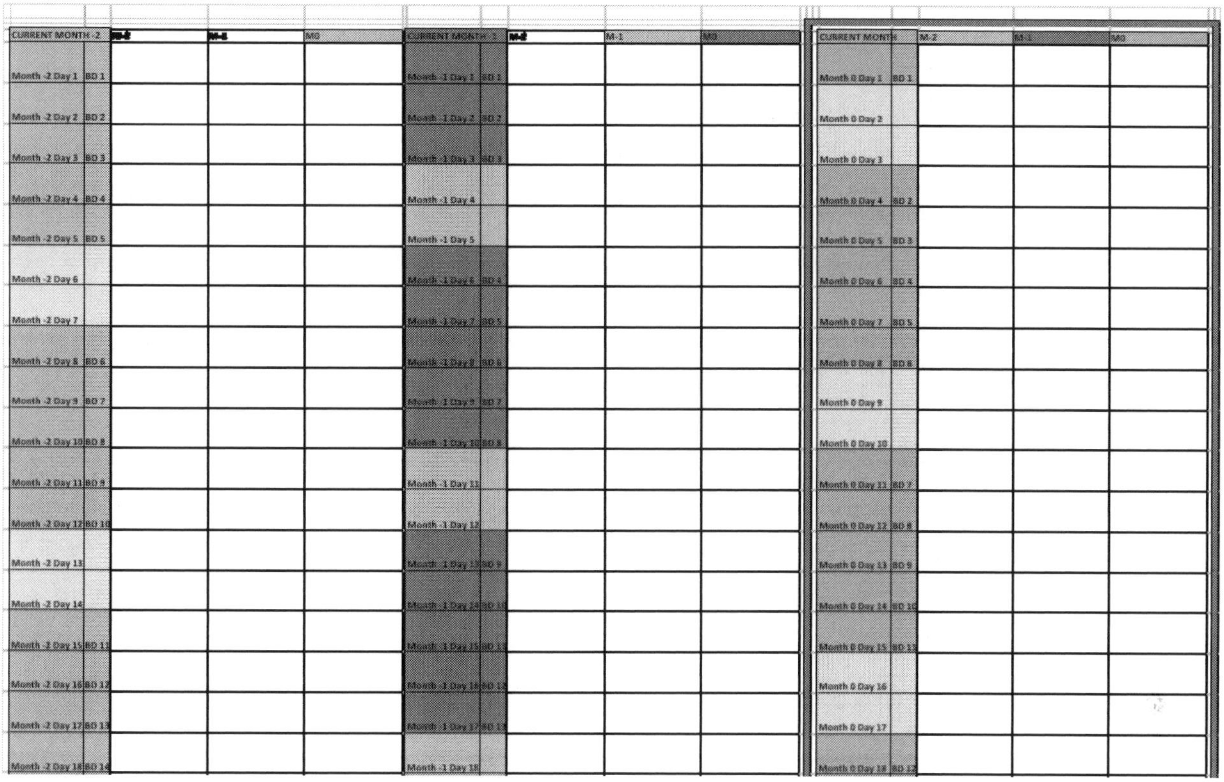

Figure 28 - End-to-End Process Workshop Template Fragment

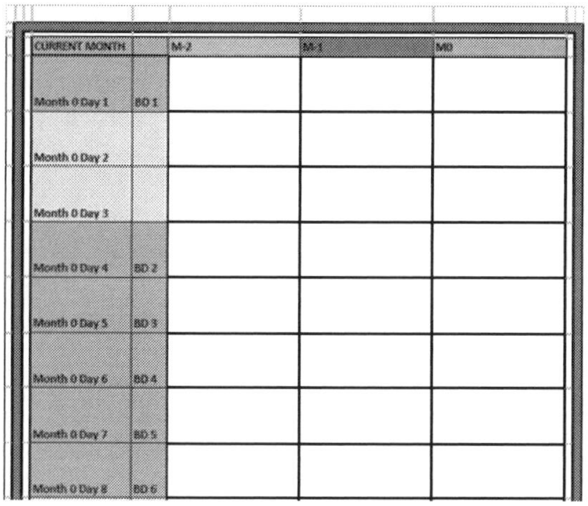

Figure 29 - Calendar Day vs. Business Day times Three Months

The implementers can prepare for the meeting by knowing what they need to learn, and by presenting an agenda that goes over the kinds of information expected. They might also want to draw a simple picture of what the outcome of the meeting will be.

The customer SMEs can prepare by having a pretty clear vision of what they do on a regular and semi-regular basic in the fronts of their minds. Often customers will want to document the complete process and bring that to the workshop. I'm happy to see that level of commitment, but I'd almost rather they didn't. I will read anything put in front of me, but that won't stop me from going through the process anyway. I may know more and go faster than I would without the documentation, but the documentation is not a replacement for the meeting. I know that can be frustrating, and I apologize, but what customers document and what I need to learn do not always line up neatly.

Remember, we don't always agree on what words mean, so if I try to read what you wrote, I won't necessarily understand what you meant. So prepare, bring some notes, but don't write the Great American Novel about your business operations and expect it to take the place of the workshop.

Compensation Plans

I like this workshop to follow the End-to-End workshop, but if that's not possible, I will deal with it whenever it can be scheduled. Comp requirements tie all the rest together, so even if I don't completely grasp what metric you are measuring or what the data looks like to support it, I will at least know what you are talking about when we get to the workshops where they are presented.

In the Comp Plan workshop we should go over all active plans needed for the system, and to describe them systematically. I use this structure when I'm conducting a workshop:

- Plan name
    - o Population on the plan (i.e., who is assigned to the plan)?
    - o How are they assigned?
    - o How many payees are currently on it (more or less – exact numbers don't matter here)?
- Plan Components
    - o A plan might have multiple metrics or multiple logical flows through it. I want to break down the description to the individual component level. But first, I want a list of them.
- Metric description (per component)
    - o The "business" name for it.
    - o The unit type.
    - o Any calculations that go into the metric ((("Transaction.Revenue * Payee.ShoeSize"), for instance).
- Plan conditions
    - o Any special requirements that are outside the component "math" (e.g., Payee.Status must equal "Active")?
    - o Anything else that must be checked?
- Transaction crediting (per component)
    - o The payee name on the transaction (ICM implementers love this)?
    - o Territories? If so, what elements make up the territories?
    - o Rollup/rolldown/roll sideways?
    - o Some other mechanism?
    - o The minimum set of data objects needed for crediting or eligibility.
- Incentive calculations
    - o What is the math?
      This should be in the form of a step-by-step "cookbook" of the logic needed to calculate the right answer, and it should be presented in business language, not system language. Essentially, we need to get to:
      Formula 1 = X * Y
      Formula 2 = Formula 1 + Z
      Formula 3 = Formula 2 / J etc.
      Every value referenced should be something we can figure out the source for, whether it is a data object, a derived metric value, a lookup value, or anything else the system needs to find to do the math. If we cannot figure out the source for a value in this cookbook, then that's a red flag that indicates we need to dig deeper.
      Always include calculation examples for the common states (both payment and recovery of

commissions if the order cancels, for example).

And here's a huge hint, in the form of **Ol' Unka DK's First Law of Example Calculation Documentation**:

You may never, ever, use the numbers 1%, 10%, 1, 10, 100, or 1,000 in your calculation examples. Ever."

You start throwing those numbers around to document a complex calculation, and I don't know whether that "10" is a result of dividing (100/1000) or multiplying (1% * 1000) or what. At the very least, use numbers with 3s and 5s, since they don't divide neatly into something that equals 3 or 5. And better, use examples that look like the real numbers you would expect to see in the system. Yeah, I know it's a pain because you can't do the math in your head when you're writing the doc, but tough. We live in a hard world and only the strong implement ICM.

- o What intermediate calculations are needed?
  For example, we might not know the commission rate directly, so we may need to calculate: Commission Rate = ((Payee.TargetEarnings * Plan.Component.Weight) / Payee.Component.Quota). Again, use business – "human" – language, not system language, to describe the math.
- o Are there any separate conditions pertaining to performance before (or after) the incentive can be calculated (e.g., "Component 4 >= 100%")?
- o The minimum set of data objects needed for incentive calculations.

- Common adjustments and exceptions
  - o What values might be overridden that we need to provide "knobs and levers" to manipulate? In other words, (2 + 3 = 5). If the Comp Team sometimes needs to make (2 + 3 = 7), we need a way to take the results of the calculation and allow them to be modified. Many ICM systems won't let you override the value of a formula (quite rightly, by the way). So if we know that 2 + 3 must be made to = 7, we might need to make the formula into (2 + 3 + **Offset** = 7), with the offset value something that can be maintained by the Comp Team, but whose default value is zero unless adjusted.

- Values for reporting
  - o Do we just need to report on the total incentive for the component for the month?
  - o Do we need to roll that up for the quarter and year as well?
  - o Do we need any of the intermediate values too?
  - o The minimum set of data objects needed for reporting

This is a lot of information per component, and there are often lots of components per plan. Sometimes components are dependent on other components. In that case, it's perfectly acceptable to just say, "Component Three equals the greater of Component One or Component Two". And obviously, if the same component is used on multiple plans, you can be smart about how you document those other plans.

Sometimes it is possible to overthink these things. On a recent project, we spent a lot of cycles trying to decide whether we wanted to make a grid of "This component is on these plans", or whether it made more sense to do "This plan has these components" (**hint**: it doesn't matter, just do *something*). The important thing is, describe the plans in human language in such a way as to make it impossible to misinterpret the requirements. And always err on the side of too much documentation, rather than too little.

You might notice that I have "**The minimum set of data objects**…" called out several times in the list above. The customer might want to feed Payee.IQ to the ICM system, but if I don't see that attribute as one of the minimum set I need to credit, calculate, or report, I need to know why we would want to bring that one in. I tend to be a jerk – erm, I tend to be fairly rigid – about bringing more data into the system than is needed. So every object that is called out in the workshop should go onto a master list of objects and attributes, and that Data Master should most definitely be referenced throughout the Design, Build, and Test Phases of the project.

The implementation team can prepare for this workshop (likely over the course of several long meetings) by providing this logical structure to the customer SMEs. The implementers should read all the plan documentation available to have a list of plans and potential components to discuss. And they should be prepared to guide the SMEs through this process – we really do want it to be very systematic and not get too far off the subject. After about the fourth component, the meeting will run itself. Be prepared to follow interesting paths if something unexpected arises – like, the IT representative blurts out, "That field on the transaction doesn't mean what you just said it means!" – but try to keep on task as much as possible.

And of course, the customer SMEs can prepare by knowing the plans and components and by being ready to discuss them in this structure. Bring sample calculations any time something unusual is called for. Maybe have payee reports available to show exactly how values are used. Again, don't bother writing up a huge amount of documentation for this beyond what you already have, but do be ready to discuss the plan logic in depth and systematically – step-by-step.

Payee Data

A workshop to describe the payees who will be in the ICM system – both who they are, and how we know about them – is a good foundation for later workshops. It sometimes happens that the payees come from multiple business units, have multiple roles, and the data about them is sourced from multiple HR or other systems. This is the workshop where we lay all of that out.

For each business unit ("Direct Sales" or "Independent Dealers", for example), we should know something about who the payees are from a business perspective, and then we want to learn about how they will be represented in the system. The kinds of questions we are interested in include:

- What system provides the data? What is it called?
- What types of payees are included in the system?
  What are their roles in the selling process?
- What format is the feed?
  - Direct database connection?
  - Staging table?
  - Flat file?
  - Other?
- How many records are in the feed?
  - On average?
  - Maximum volume during rush periods?
- How often and when do we get the feed(s)?
- Does the system feed a full snapshot of data, or just new/changed records?
- Is the data filtered to just eligible payees, or are there non-payees in the feed as well?
  What is the attribute that tells us which ones we are interested in?
- How accurate is the data?
  How timely is the data?
  How complete is the data?
- Do feeds ever need to be deleted and re-fed?
  How often, and why?
- What value or values uniquely identify a payee in the system?
  (This is a critical question for tying different payee records together in the event of a change or modification to an existing record.)
- What attributes are fed? Of those, which are needed?

Note: for this and all other data feed workshops, I like to use a matrix for each object and attribute identified. There are column with checkmarks filled in as appropriate for:

> Needed for Compensation
> Needed for Reporting
> Needed for Operations
> (e.g., research, queries, etc.)

If there is no checkmark for a given attribute in any of these columns, I will try not to bring in that object or attribute.

- May we see a sample feed from the system?
- What payee conditions or attribute values are meaningful in the ICM process?
  - Employment Status?
  - Others (e.g., Shoe Size)?
- Which dates are significant?
  - Hire date?
  - Termination Date?
  - Others?
  - Are there any special date conditions that must be born in mind (e.g., if the Payee is hired in the first 15 days of the month, then the Payee is eligible to be on plan and paid, but if not, then plan assignment starts the next month)?
  - Are there training periods or special assignment periods during which payees come off of plan?
- Leave of Absence (LOA)[38]
  - Do payees go on leave?
  - Are there different types of leave?
  - How does LOA affect the compensation process?

Implementers need to ask at least these questions, even if the answer for some of them is "not applicable". And further, they should not feel limited to these questions. Where an answer opens up a line of inquiry, follow it for at least a few moments to see if it will impact the system design. I never cease to be annoyed when I see a consultant just reading off the laundry list of questions and jotting down a yes or a no or a number without following up or thinking about what they are being told. Requirements gathering is an active process on both sides of the table.

Customers should have answers to these questions near at hand, but also think about why the questions might be important to see if that triggers other information that might need to be conveyed that isn't already covered in these questions, or in whatever questions the implementers have prepped you with. Maybe it would have come up during another workshop, but maybe it wouldn't. It is far better to bring it up early than not have it brought to the surface at all.

Transaction Data

In ICM, transactions are the business events used as the raw materials in the calculation of commissions and bonuses. These typically represent sales orders, but could also be artifacts of other activities as well, whether Call Center metrics, customer satisfaction scores, or anything else that is used in measuring performance for which a

---

[38] For whatever reason, many ICM systems have trouble with leaves of absence. Switching payees on and off for compensation calculations is just something that many of them do not do neatly or elegantly. It's important to be really clear about LOA requirements early on in the Requirements Phase to be sure that any gaps in system functionality can be mitigated in the system design later.

payee will be compensated.

Companies often have many different sources of transactions. There are the transactions they control directly themselves, which might come from one or several Sales Order Management systems. If they work though agents or third-parties, those third-parties might have their own sales tracking systems that get reported to the company for use in ICM. Some companies use reports from their enterprise data warehouses as sources of transactions too.

One thing that might make transactions different from other kinds of data is that, depending on a company's products and business model, transactions can represent stages in the life cycle of an order. In many industries, orders can be created, changed, cancelled, rebooked, billed, shipped, paid, or resold. Various payees might be compensated (or have compensation "**clawed back**") depending on the latest event in the order life cycle. So for a given sale of a Widget to a customer, any number of different transactions might be generated. Depending on the source systems, it will be more or less easy (or more of less impossible) to reconcile those events to the same sale. (See **FIGURE 8 - ONE EVENT, MANY SYSTEMATIC REPRESENTATIONS**)

Similar to some of the questions from the Payee Data workshop description, the kinds of questions we are interested in for each feed include:

- What system provides the data? What is it called?
- What types of transactions are included in the system?
  What types of event does the feed include?
  - o Booking? Debooking? Rebooking?
  - o Invoice? Payment? Shipment?
  - o Resale?
  - o Contract signing? Cancellation?
- What format is the feed?
  - o Direct database connection?
  - o Staging table?
  - o Flat file?
  - o Other?
- How many records are in the feed?
  - o On average?
  - o Maximum volume during rush periods?
- How often and when do we get the feed(s)?
- How accurate is the data?
  How timely is the data?
  How complete is the data?
- Do feeds ever need to be deleted and re-fed?
  How often, and why?
- What value or values uniquely identify a given transaction in the system?
  (This is a critical question for tying different transactions together in the life cycle of the event.)
- What attributes are fed? Of those, which are needed?
- May we see a sample feed from the system?

Note: and again, for this and all other data feed workshops, I like to use a matrix for each object and attribute identified. There are column with checkmarks filled in as appropriate for:

Needed for Compensation
Needed for Reporting
Needed for Operations

(e.g., research, queries, etc.)

If there is no checkmark for a given attribute in any of these columns, I will try not to bring in that object or attribute.

Other Reference Data

The Other Reference Data Workshop is, not surprisingly, where the feeds from the systems that provide data to the ICM system are described. We've had a separate workshop for payee data and transaction data. This workshop is to identify and describe any other feeds into the system that have been identified as necessary. However, there are other kinds of data that might not be administered in other systems, or that are used once during setup and then only revisited occasionally.

Where the data comes from ongoing and systematic feeds from other systems, the usual questions apply –

- What system provides the data? What is it called?
- What types of data are included in the system?
  What types of event does the feed include?
- What format is the feed?
  - o Direct database connection?
  - o Staging table?
  - o Flat file?
  - o Other?
- How many records are in the feed?
  - o On average?
  - o Maximum volume during rush periods?
- How often and when do we get the feed(s)?
- How accurate is the data?
  How timely is the data?
  How complete is the data?
- Do feeds ever need to be deleted and re-fed?
  How often, and why?
- What value or values uniquely identify a given objects in the system?
  (This is a critical question for tying different records together in the life cycle of the object.)
- What attributes are fed? Of those, which are needed?
- May we see a sample feed from the system?

Some reference data, often including plan variables, doesn't come from source systems. It might be maintained by the Comp Team in spreadsheets, or it could come from a report they get from Finance. IT might not even be aware of them. The implementation team must provide a way to get it into the system, but it might not be in the form of a scheduled job involving technological handshakes between monstrous, bullet-proof systems. It might even be a matter of typing them into the UI.

Sometimes – always – the customer has something we can call **foundational data** that we need to gather requirements on. An example of this might be **G/L codes** – **General Ledger**, or accounting codes – that get applied to payment files on their way to the Payroll or Accounts Payable system. How many do you have? Oh, 18, I think. How often do they change? We added two new ones in 2008. Do you have them now? Yeah, let me just email you the list. That can be a short conversation. Make sure there's nothing tricky about them, but then move onto the next thing. It doesn't need to have a feed defined, it just needs to be included in the system setup, with a provision for adding or modifying the codes provided to the users if anything changes down the road. Document that the data exists, but don't go crazy about it. Still, I guess it's better to be slightly too fixated than not fixated enough.

Downstream Feeds

ICM not only has data coming in, but it also has data going out. The systems we will send data to have their own requirements, and this workshop is where we describe them. An obvious example – the most common one – is the Payroll system for employee payees, or A/P – the Accounts Payable system – for external agents who are compensated for bringing the company's products to the marketplace. But other systems need feeds as well, including finance systems, data warehouses, compliance systems, and various others. It's hard to know in advance what systems will be affected by a change to the ICM system, but research is clearly called for before, during and after this meeting. It's embarrassing to flip over to the new ICM system and have the CFO come crashing into the room two hours later demanding to find out where that critical report went.

To define system requirements, then, we need an inventory of downstream systems that depend on ICM for data. These are the kinds of questions we must ask for each:

- What system consumes the data? What is it called?
- What type of data is included in the feed?
  What format is the feed?
    - Direct database connection?
    - Staging table?
    - Flat file?
    - Other?
- How many records are in the feed?
    - On average?
    - Maximum volume during rush periods?
- Are there deadlines for sending the feed?
  A given day or time?
- Do feeds ever need to be deleted and re-fed?
  How often, and why?
- What objects and attributes are fed?
- May we see a sample file from the legacy system?

In this case, I am less likely to fight over including attributes. If the downstream system is expecting them, I usually figure I have no choice but to include them. Unless they're really **goofy** (another technical term) – then I might want to ask the downstream system owner if they are really necessary.

Reporting & Analytics

As discussed previously, I like to break out reporting and analytics into broad categories when documenting them:

- Canned reports
- Canned analytics
- Operational reporting
- Research and ad hoc reporting

To reiterate my definition of reporting and analytics, I see reports on an ICM system as the well-defined presentation of data. There might be some math in the reports, say to aggregate results at the quarter or year level, but not a lot of logic. I see analytics as a deeper dive into the data to uncover trends, patterns, provide visualizations and dashboards, and to bring more intelligence to the display of data. Operational reporting is the display of data about the ICM system itself and about the processes that make up the ICM or SPM function. And finally, I also see the need to provide the Comp Team and other administrative users the ability to learn more about some object or set of objects on an irregular, ad hoc basis by way of queries as a meaningful distinction. If we know that certain kinds of questions will be asked of the team and the system, we can design the system configuration to provide easy access to the right answers.

For **canned reports**, the kinds of questions we need to answer include:

- What is the name of the report?
- What is the format for the report?
  Web based?
  Spreadsheet or CSV?
  Other?
- Who is the audience for the report?
  Payees? Sales Management? Admins? Finance?
  How many are there in the audience?
- How will they use the report?
- How is the report generated?
  On demand?
  On a schedule? If so, when?
- What objects and attributes are on the report?
  Do we know the source for each?
- Are there data visualization requirements?
  Charts?
  Graphs?
  Dashboards?
- What report navigation requirements are there?
  Will the users drill down from summary to detail, or aggregate up?
- How will report access be managed?
  By way of a portal?
  Is there a single-sign-on (SSO) mechanism?
- What data restriction requirements are there?
  Can certain people only see certain data?
- Are there requirements to make the report downloadable?
  In what formats?
- May we see samples from the legacy reporting system?
  Or mockups of new reports (they don't have to be beautiful!)

For **canned analytics**, most of the same questions pertain, but we also want to dig into the kinds of analysis being performed. Analytics are often performed for period-over-period comparisons (e.g., year-over-year, or quarter-over-quarter). Getting a sense of how the users will use the reports might work best in a conversation, rather than a question-and-answer oriented workshop. In this case, mockups or existing reports are a must.

Operational reporting gives the people supporting the team the ability to see into the workings of the process and systems. Essentially the same questions as above are used to drill into the requirements, but the focus tends to be on system operations, performance against SLAs (Service Level Agreements), workflow tasks, and the like. Mostly access and navigation are less of an issue than with the more public-facing reports above, but instead you might want to discuss warning and notification mechanisms for problems or potential problems.

For **ad hoc reporting** and **queries**, the questions revolve around the kinds of questions the Comp Team are called upon to answer when the phone rings and there's an irate payee or Finance person on the line. If the system UI allows simple queries on the data (and most do), providing training on the query mechanism can save a lot of report requirements by showing the Comp Team that they can use self-service to get to the information they need. If patterns of queries are apparent, it is often possible to save queries as templates for use by individuals or the team on an ongoing basis just changing the variables in the search box. Again, it is important to be sure that the system configuration be designed with these types of queries in mind. It is sometimes too easy to bury relevant data.

Modeling Requirements (if applicable)

The promise of modeling in SPM has sold a lot of ICM software. CFOs go crazy with (completely professional) desire when they hear about the possibility of playing what-if with the revenue and the plans to help predict compensation expenses. Unfortunately, that promise has gone largely unfulfilled.

It's not that modeling cannot happen in ICM. Most of the off-the-shelf applications have a provision for it. It's just that the system needs to be implemented with modeling in mind in order for it to work, and generally, that becomes the first thing cut when the calendar and the budget are taken into account. We'll get the system up, then think about modeling sometime later. And 'sometime later' sometimes never comes.

There are a variety of reasons for this. First, modeling can be very resource intensive. Despite what the vendors tell you, it is generally not a good idea to put modeling into your production system. Remember, this is a mission critical financial application, and putting extraneous data or plans into it has an impact on day-to-day compensation operations. The strong recommendation is always to create a sandbox environment for modeling. Some companies have adequate resources to take a copy of the production instance for modeling purposes, but many don't.

Another reason is that ICM systems are the very definition of "micro". They are all about the detail level application of rules and plans against real transactions for individual payees. In order to do macro-level modeling – modeling about large-scale data, results, and trends – you don't want to have to go in and mess with individual plans, quotas, and territories for all 5000 of your reps. You (generally) want to turn a crank and raise quotas in the west, lower target earnings in the east, increase the Widget revenue in APAC by 8% and lower the Rugalator revenue in EMEA by 4% to see what comes out. Making that work in a micro-level environment is very time and labor intensive. Again, if the data and the plans are not implemented to allow interesting manipulations for the purposes of modeling, the models you can run are limited.

If modeling is a primary reason why the system is being implemented, this needs to be kept in mind all the way through the Requirements and Design Phases. Someone from Finance needs to be there at the table making sure the modeling requirements are clearly stated – which dimensions are most likely to be modeled, how will they change, how often does it happen? It's an ongoing conversation, rather than a set of template discovery questions.

Having said that, I must offer something in the way of hope. A particular class of modeling relating to commission expense forecasting is called "**accruals**". Accruals are a flavor of modeling that can generally be performed in ICM, under the right circumstances. Accruals tell a company how much to set aside for future expenses.

Essentially, accruals are written into the comp plans in the form of incentives that are based on well-defined growth, but which are never submitted for payment. The plans calculate where we are as of this point in the quarter or year, and then forecast where we will end up at the end of the period if we continue to perform at this rate, or possibly, at a ramped rate based on analytics of prior performance. The non-linear growth rate is sometimes called "**seasonality**". If we know that no one sells in Q1, 50% of the business comes in Q4 (and 90% of that comes in December), then we build that growth into the accrual rules and formulas. Since many comp plans are non-linear – there are accelerators and bonuses based on performance – the ICM system, with the plans already in place to pay the reps or agents, is the perfect place to perform this level of modeling. Generate a report for the accrual incentives, ship it off to Finance, and we can pat ourselves on the back because we have improved the process.

Administration & Maintenance

If every piece of data going in or coming out of the ICM system will be completely automated, and there are never any exceptions to be managed or queries from payees to answer, then this will be a short workshop. But since, here on Planet Earth, that has never happened, this workshop is where we get to the nuts and bolts of how the Comp Team and their IT support will interact with the new system.

A good place to prepare for this meeting is with the notes coming out of the End-to-End Processing workshop, and with the "common exceptions" that came out of the Comp Plan workshop. These should provide a good foundation on the ways the Comp Team administer and maintain data and processes today. Clearly, some of those interactions will change with the new system, but some of them are there because of issues surrounding ICM as much as from the system itself. So this workshop should be a conversation about problem solving as much as it is about, "Which kinds of data do you have to modify and adjust today? How often?" Those are good questions, but the answers are not the requirements you need to document. You need to understand what the underlying problem is that causes administration tasks, and try to address that.

There are some processes that are just part of the bread and butter of the Comp Team's lives, and of course you need to document them and design a system to support them. But there will also be some processes that seem ornery, and those are the fun ones to dig into. If you can find a system design that eliminates one or two that weren't expected to go away, then you have made the comp world a better place. Bravo, Sir or Madam!

Conversely, if you start down a rat hole about some process that seems convoluted and incomprehensible, that might be a time to step back and ask questions like these:

- How often does it happen?
  Once a year? 1,000 times per month?
  (Hint: once a year is the perfect candidate for finding a manual workaround. 1,000 times per month is a strong candidate for automation. Anything in between? Use your best judgment.)
- Is it preventable?
  Would one extra piece of data eliminate the problem in the first place?
  Or one extra validation of data on the way in?
- Can we make it go away?
  If it's based on a bad process that has somehow become a company standard, can we change the process (assuming it doesn't add anything positive to the bottom line, of course)? Tammy will likely not be in a position to say 'yes' to the proposal to change the process (if she had that authority, she already would have), but can we escalate to Tammy's boss or the Exec Sponsor?

Then do the best you can and build the system to make it as easy as possible.

Workflows (if applicable)

By workflows, we are talking about the systematic initiation, routing, resolution, and reporting of business processes. It is becoming increasingly common for enterprise software to have workflow mechanisms built in to apply a level of control on important processes. ICM is no exception, and where workflows are to be implemented, they must be defined.

The most common ICM workflows are for submitting the payroll (or A/P) file, and for managing payee inquiries and disputes. Others might be in place for plan and quota approval. Some of these workflows might be supported by the software out-of-the-box, while others might need customization.

The flowchart is your buddy when defining workflow requirements. Those starting points, boxes, arrows, decision points, inputs, outputs, and end points force you to really look at a process from end-to-end to see what you do, especially if you're honest with yourself when filling it in. The temptation is to put in what ought to happen, rather than what really happens. But that's valuable too – if you can build a new process that matches the "ought-to-happen", you might end up with greater efficiency and rigor.

In addition to changes of state for a workflow, put in timings, deadlines, and alternative actors, and you have got the workflow section of your RSD 90% complete.

Which processes need workflows? Sometimes making the flowchart can give you a good look into that decision. If the current process comes down to, "We send the VP an email, he replies, 'Go ahead', and we do", does that justify spending the time and trouble defining, building, and testing the workflow? Remember, it's not free to create them – someone is getting paid by the hour to build each one. So if money changes hands based on the VP's email reply, or if that VP "OK" enables you to pass your Sarbanes-Oxley audit, then yes, absolutely build that workflow. Or if the VP tells you to, then do it. But otherwise, weigh the cost and the benefit. Not everything needs to have technology attached to it.

Another line of questioning for this workshop that is well worth pursuing is to explore the root causes of payee inquiries and disputes:

- How many inquiries and disputes come in per month?
- What is the most common kind of inquiry or dispute?
  How many do you get per month?
  What is the most likely reason for inquiries of this type?
  Is there something systematic we could do to prevent them in the first place?
- Okay, now what's the second most common type?
- And the third?

This can lead to a process change, a data integration change, an operations change, or no change at all. But the conversation is a valuable one even if there is nothing to be done in the short term to fix things.

Testing Strategy

Testing is so critical on ICM projects, yet is often so neglected. It needs to be pretty close to the forefront of the project team's minds (both customer side and implementer side) from the very beginning of the project, and every requirement stated and documented should also generate any number of test cases. But way too often, the Test Phase creeps up and the team is caught flat-footed and unprepared. Therefore, I believe it is important to call out the test strategy during the Requirements Phase.

This is one set of requirements that is most dependent on the customer team, by the way. There is testing the implementation team must perform if only to keep from embarrassing themselves when they hand the system over to the customer. But the customer has the responsibility to assure that the system does exactly what they need it to do. So this isn't something to gloss over.

For purposes of the RSD, the testing strategy lays out the ground rules that will be used during the Test Phase. It answers fundamental questions about how testing will be conducted. For example:

- Will there be a parallel system test, where transactions will be run both in the legacy system and the new ICM system, or will the test be against generated test data and cases?
- If parallel, how long will it be?
  One month? Three months?
- If parallel, will all results for all payees be compared, or just select test cases?
- If parallel, what constitutes a passing score?

All results for all cases match 100%?

Plus/minus 5%, as long as the deltas are explicable?

- If against generated test data, where will the data come from?
- Who will assure that it the test data matches the data from the source systems for the new ICM system? (This is important: if the data doesn't exactly match the format of data from source systems, when the new ICM system goes live, there can be disconnects when it receives real data.)
- What will be the mechanism for raising issues and test case defects?
- What will be the mechanism for managing versions of the application configuration?

Will there be a formal promotion process for code, or will changes just be entered and the system tested again?

There are people who specialize in testing, and they earn their pay by thinking through questions like these and many more. But it's important to note that application configuration testing is different from software testing. We are not too concerned about asking if the system got "5" when we added "2+3". With luck, the vendor tested that, and if they haven't, it will become apparent very soon. But we do want to know if combinations of rules and formulas on complex comp plans generated the expected and desired "7" when we fed it a "2" and a "3". We need to test the complex scenario, not the bits and bytes making up the engine. The test cases need to reflect the interactions inside the comp plan.

Non-Functional Requirements

Non-functional requirements are the "system-y" requirements, not the compensation requirements, per se'. Non-Functional Requirements workshop questions include, but are not limited to:

- User roles and permissions
    - Who can do what in the system?
    - Are different users restricted in what they may see?

        By objects? (E.g., Payees, but not Plans or Results)

        By attributes? (E.g., Payee.ID, but not Payee.Salary)

        By row? (E.g., Payees in the West, but not the East)
- Auditing requirements
    - Must the system track who made changes?
    - How will that be managed? Reported?
- System uptimes and maintenance
    - When will the system be online for users and payees to log in?
    - When may it be offline?
    - Who will perform which kinds of maintenance?
- Processing performance requirements
    - If run in batch, when will the system receive data?
    - When must it be finished processing?
    - When must reports be available?
    - How much growth in data must the system accommodate?
- Archiving requirements
    - How much data must be maintained online?
    - Offline?
    - Is this different for different types of data?

Historical Data Seeding Requirements

As we will discuss more thoroughly in the "DEPLOYMENT PHASE" section, determining the requirements and strategy for populating the new ICM system with the right amount of the right production quality data is an important factor in allowing the system to go live. It cannot be left for the final week of the project. Thought must go into it from the beginning because of the challenges that go with it. A set of historical data seeding requirements and a design to meet them must be factored into the project timeline, since almost any choices you make will have an impact on the schedule.

THE MOST IMPORTANT REQUIREMENTS PHASE QUESTION

"What question are you waiting for me to ask you?"

When I think the meeting or workshop is about ready to start winding down, I ask this question, especially for customers who are just starting out in the early days of their project. I have been nailed on too many projects where the customer PM corners me after the workshop to say that the SMEs are very upset and worried because I haven't asked them about the "217 Report", or the special "Birthday Bonus" the payees get. Um, I didn't ask because I didn't know it existed and I've never seen it anywhere else.

The SMEs know their company's Weirdness better than any outsider can ever know it. If the subject doesn't come up during the relevant workshop, the SMEs need to feel comfortable bringing it up proactively. But until I know they do, I ask the question. I usually get a laugh with it, but sometimes I get "You forgot the 'Double-Top-Secret Eligibility Status' requirement!" Oh yeah, silly me – I sure did! So why don't we just talk about that now?

Incidentally, does the order of workshops matter? In general, no. It's the implementers' responsibility to keep the intellectual balls in the air and be able to slot every new bit of knowledge into the right mental compartment. Sometimes the order of workshops is dependent on the availability of the SMEs, and that is something that has to be respected.

That said, I really do like to have the End-to-End Processing workshop come first, and then follow that with the Comp Plan and the Payee Data workshop sometime soon after. I believe that they provide the best context to make sense of all the others – we know better what the words mean after End-to-End and after the comp requirements. But I will take any workshop in any order that makes the most sense for the customer.

A METHOD AND MINDSET FOR REQUIREMENTS GATHERING:
THE STATE MACHINE

Requirements gathering is not a passive task. It requires active engagement on the part of the implementation team to pull out all the hidden parts of any stated or written requirement. And it takes a mindset that allows you to turn every statement of requirements over to see what might be underneath.

I was fortunate enough to attend a brown bag presentation more than two decades ago in which a database consultant presented the concept of the **State Machine**. I was totally knocked out by what he showed us, and have been using it more or less formally in requirements discovery, design, and testing ever since. It works for me; maybe it will work for you too.

A State Machine, simply, is an organized list of every relevant condition (or "**state**") a system can find itself in, and all of the relevant desired outcomes based on each state. In some respects it is like a decision tree or a flowchart, but I find it more useful in terms of allowing me to fully define a business problem, find an efficient solution for it, and give me scenarios to test the solution. The use of a State Machine can prevent you from missing edge cases that could have an impact on the system you are building.

The State Machine will often have multiple intersections or states with the same expected results. Finding and recognizing these patterns can make your solution more efficient if you can combine these different states into small rule sets with the common result as the action. And it can help prevent you from unintentionally leaving out a condition or set of conditions because you were too focused on the others.

And when it's time for unit and system testing, your State Machine provides you a list of every interesting condition or scenario that must be tested for, along with expected results.

The State Machine Mechanism

Building a State Machine is easy, at least in theory. Just take a scenario and consider every meaningful alternative for every dimension of the problem. Make a list of alternative conditions, and then create a matrix of the alternatives with different dimensions on the X & Y axes. Give yourself room to enter requirements or expected outcomes in each cell of the matrix. Use a spreadsheet or a word processor, use a white board, use whatever tools you have to hand, though soft copy allow you to keep the State Machine alive after housekeeping comes through and cleans up the room. Easy, right? So let's look at some examples and how to use them.

Let's start with an easy one. The business requirement is to pay a bonus when the payee is over quota. The bonus is paid with the end-of-year incentives – let's call it December to make it easy. What might that State Machine look like?

Revenue <= Quota	Revenue > Quota
No Bonus (Do Nothing)	Pay Bonus in December

Figure 30 - State Machine Example 1

See? Not so bad, right? So you need to write rules for two conditions and results – one for under quota, one for over quota.[39]

A problem like this one is too simple to really need a State Machine, of course, so let's expand it. Now my payees get a bonus if Widget Revenue is greater than Widget quota, and Rugalator Revenue is greater than Rugalator Quota. Here's that State Machine:

State Machine #2	Widget Revenue <= Widget Quota	Widget Revenue > Widget Quota
Rugalator Revenue <= Rugalator Quota	No Bonus	No Bonus
Rugalator Revenue > Rugalator Quota	No Bonus	Pay Bonus in December

Figure 31 - State Machine Example 2

One rule with the "Widget Revenue > Widget Quota AND Rugalator Revenue > Rugalator Quota" condition and you're good to go. Still not hard, and still not very interesting, honestly. But this is where the probing question comes in. This is really more a domain experience question than a State Machine driven question, but I'll include it here.

The scene: A gray conference room in a gray industrial park on the outskirts of a gray city:

- Fearless Comp Consultant (FCC): "So they only get the bonus if they're over both quotas, right?" If their

---

[39] In some ICM applications, not writing a condition is the same as saying that the opposite condition is false, so you might not need two sets of conditions or rules for this State Machine in practice. But it is still worth thinking about the negative or "false" condition when designing, so the State Machine still can provide value during Requirements.

total revenue is greater than the sum of the two quotas, but they are under one of the quotas, no bonus, right?"

- Customer SME (C-SME): "Right. Or, well, kind of. If Widget Revenue is greater than the sum of quotas, they DO get their bonuses. But that doesn't happen very often."
- Customer Comp Manager (C-CM): "Are you sure we do that? I never heard of it!"
- C-SME: "Yeah, remember when the VP of Sales called that time about the Cleveland rep...?"
- FCC: "Ahhhh... So what about if Rugalator Revenue is greater than the sum of quotas. Do they get a bonus then?"
- C-SME: "No, of course not! Only if Widget Revenue is."

The State Machine for that expanded requirement is illustrated here:

State Machine #3	Widget Revenue <= Widget Quota	Widget Revenue > Widget Quota AND Widget Revenue <= (Widget Quota + Rugalator Quota)	Widget Revenue > (Widget Quota + Rugalator Quota)
Rugalator Revenue <= Rugalator Quota	No Bonus	No Bonus	Pay Bonus in December
Rugalator Revenue > Rugalator Quota	No Bonus	Pay Bonus in December	Pay Bonus in December
Rugalator Revenue > (Widget Quota + Rugalator Quota)	No Bonus	Pay Bonus in December	Pay Bonus in December

Figure 32 - State Machine Example 3

In a case like this I would be tempted to leave out the "AND Widget Revenue <= (Widget Quota + Rugalator Quota)" in that cell, but when in doubt, or for more complicated scenarios, by all means err on the side of caution and put it in. And you could argue that the third row ("Rugalator Revenue > (Widget Quota + Rugalator Quota)") is unnecessary, but I'd usually put it in for the sake of completeness and to demonstrate that I have thought it through all the way.

A little analysis shows that your rule condition is marginally more complicated – "(Widget Revenue > Widget

Quota AND Rugalator Revenue > Rugalator Quota) OR (Widget Revenue > (Widget Quota + Rugalator Quota)".
But not brutally so. So let's make it worse.

- FCC: "Alrighty, so I think we have a handle on the bonus thing."
- C-SME: "Right. If they have at least a '4' on their MBOs, then they're eligible for the bonus we talked about."
- FCC: "Um, 'at least a '4' on their MBOs'?!?"
- C-SME: [tiny voice] "Did I forget to mention that…?" [/tiny voice]
- FCC: "Golly ha-ha yeah, you did neglect to mention that."
- C-SME: "I did? Right. No bonus unless they have at least a '4'".
- C-CM: "Unless the Widget Revenue is higher than both quotas, of course. Ho ho, wouldn't want to forget that!"
- FCC: [thin voice] "Ho ho. Right, right…" [/thin voice]

So here's that State Machine:

State Machine #4		Widget Revenue <= Widget Quota	Widget Revenue > Widget Quota AND Widget Revenue <= (Widget Quota + Rugalator Quota)	Widget Revenue > (Widget Quota + Rugalator Quota)
MBO Score < "4"	Rugalator Revenue <= Rugalator Quota	No Bonus	No Bonus	Pay Bonus in December
	Rugalator Revenue > Rugalator Quota	No Bonus	No Bonus	Pay Bonus in December
	Rugalator Revenue > (Widget Quota + Rugalator Quota)	No Bonus	No Bonus	Pay Bonus in December
MBO Score >= "4"	Rugalator Revenue <= Rugalator Quota	No Bonus	No Bonus	Pay Bonus in December
	Rugalator Revenue > Rugalator Quota	No Bonus	Pay Bonus in December	Pay Bonus in December
	Rugalator Revenue > (Widget Quota + Rugalator Quota)	No Bonus	Pay Bonus in December	Pay Bonus in December

Figure 33 - State Machine Example 4

Time: The Often Forgotten Dimension

On the surface, we have done a pretty solid job of describing the business requirements around this hypothetical bonus. But in compensation, there is always the issue of time to deal with as well. It's not enough to describe what happens when you run December in December. You must at least give some thought to what should happen if you run December in March of the following year. Out of the box the system will just recalculate and generate a positive or negative balance if something changes, but is that what the customer wants?

- FCC: "So, if there are prior period debookings, you recover the bonuses, right?"
- C-SME: "Of course we do!"
- FCC: "…?"
- C-SME: "Well, unless their Widget Revenue is over the combined quotas, of course…"
- FCC: "Right, right… Say – would you happen to have any aspirin?"

Here's the time dimension version of the State Machine, then:

State Machine #5 "December in December"		Widget Revenue <= Widget Quota	Widget Revenue > Widget Quota AND Widget Revenue <= (Widget Quota + Rugalator Quota)	Widget Revenue > (Widget Quota + Rugalator Quota)
MBO Score < "4"	Rugalator Revenue <= Rugalator Quota	No Bonus	No Bonus	Pay Bonus in December
	Rugalator Revenue > Rugalator Quota	No Bonus	No Bonus	Pay Bonus in December
	Rugalator Revenue > (Widget Quota + Rugalator Quota)	No Bonus	No Bonus	Pay Bonus in December
MBO Score >= "4"	Rugalator Revenue <= Rugalator Quota	No Bonus	No Bonus	Pay Bonus in December
	Rugalator Revenue > Rugalator Quota	No Bonus	Pay Bonus in December	Pay Bonus in December

		No Bonus	Pay Bonus in December	Pay Bonus in December
	Rugalator Revenue > (Widget Quota + Rugalator Quota)			
"December in the following March"		Widget Revenue <= Widget Quota	Widget Revenue > Widget Quota AND Widget Revenue <= (Widget Quota + Rugalator Quota)	Widget Revenue > (Widget Quota + Rugalator Quota)
MBO Score < "4"	Rugalator Revenue <= Rugalator Quota	Recover Bonus if Paid	Recover Bonus if Paid	Pay Bonus (Do not recover)
	Rugalator Revenue > Rugalator Quota	Recover Bonus if Paid	Recover Bonus if Paid	Pay Bonus (Do not recover)
	Rugalator Revenue > (Widget Quota + Rugalator Quota)	Recover Bonus if Paid	Recover Bonus if Paid	Pay Bonus (Do not recover)
MBO Score >= "4"	Rugalator Revenue <= Rugalator Quota	Recover Bonus if Paid	Recover Bonus if Paid	Pay Bonus (Do not recover)
	Rugalator Revenue > Rugalator Quota	Recover Bonus if Paid	Recover Bonus if Paid	Pay Bonus (Do not recover)
	Rugalator Revenue > (Widget Quota + Rugalator Quota)	Recover Bonus if Paid	Recover Bonus if Paid	Pay Bonus (Do not recover)

Figure 34 - State Machine Example 5

Some Other Considerations

Clearly, I believe in the value of the State Machine or I wouldn't have wasted umpteen pages writing about it. Having the principles of the State Machine in your head when you hear requirements automatically feeds you the question, "What if the opposite of that condition is true?" This is crucial when the SMEs are focused on a specific dimension of a problem to the exclusion of all the other dimensions. And here's a Pro Tip for you younger consultants just starting out on the road of life: you get a reputation for being insightful and asking the tough questions if you always have the opposite state in mind from the one being presented.

Deciding what your dimensions should be and what conditions you model in your State Machine is an art form based on some experience. Theoretically you'd probably need many more dimensions and cells than I'm showing, but you have to use domain knowledge and experience with the software to help you be most efficient without leaving anything critical out. But when it doubt, put it in.

The real pros at this kind of process modeling have the concept of **transformations** – what happened to change a condition. I haven't demonstrated many transformations in my examples. I tend to treat transformations as conditions – "Revenue is Positive for the Month" or "Revenue is Negative for the Month" would be conditions or states that represent "Add Revenue" or "Subtract Revenue" transformations.

And finally, here's a little bit of a carrot to use the State Machine during Requirements: depending on how you put your State Machine together, you might be able to copy and paste it into your Requirements Specification Document, either in the section next to the component, or as an appendix. And don't get me started on how many great test cases you can develop from using it.

REQUIREMENTS TRACING

How do you follow a requirement from the customer's operations to the implementer's RSD to the system design to the build to the final handoff? Beats me. How do you think you should do it? I'm open to ideas.

Okay, I do know the answer, but it's so time- and resource-consuming that I keep hoping the problem will go away when I say, "Just trust me – we'll get it right." But it doesn't.

You really need to build and maintain a matrix – often in a spreadsheet – that allows you to uniquely identify every business and system requirement generated on the customer side, every requirement from the RSD, every design element, and every test case. Then you cross -reference them. So Customer Requirement 1 maps to RSD Requirement 22, which maps to Design Element 333, which maps to Test Case 4,444. But understand that since the RSD is documenting scenarios, it might mean that one customer requirement is addressed by a dozen RSD sections, and one RSD section might address a dozen customer requirements. What should be clear is that it is nearly a full-time job keeping this matrix up-to-date. For a small project, this isn't nearly as complicated, but for a large one, it is very challenging, and the large projects are the ones where it is needed most.

The implementation team can contribute to this, especially during the Requirements and Design Phases, but ultimately, I believe it is the customer's responsibility to verify the tracing since it begins and ends with their input. And if there is a gap that somehow slips by, the customer is most negatively impacted.

And understand that maintaining the matrix can increase the time and expense of a project – this level of documentation is time consuming, and time does equal money on system projects. It's not cheap, but it is generally well worth it for the peace of mind that the system will do what you ask of it.

Business Consulting & Organizational Change Management

Now that we have talked about how requirements will be documented, let's take a step back and think about which requirements we want to document. It may seem that this section is in the wrong order, but I'm putting it here because I wanted the depth of the Requirements Phase to be understood before bringing it up.

I submit for your consideration that you are most likely only considering implementing an ICM system because things are broken. No one has ever done it for fun. There must be some pain, or else no one would consider spending the time and money to change things.

What's broken might be the legacy ICM system – that's always a possibility. But it might well be all that bad data, or all those bad processes, bad plans, or bad organizational interactions that make the ICM process seem broken. It might be that a lot of things are wrong. So the question is, do you want to swap out the ICM application and leave the rest of the ecosystem intact? Or would you rather fix things, then implement the new software?

That's supposed to be a rhetorical question, by the way. Jamming in a new ICM system while neglecting to address the underlying issues of what makes the old system inoperative is not a strong strategy.

Think of it this way: the legacy processes and systems in place likely grew together somewhat organically over years of business operations. A change was made here, so another system had to respond to that stimulus by changing there. Or the Comp Team needed something they couldn't get from System X, so they made an end-around raid on a report from System Y to get something that looked sort of right, then built a bunch of processes around it to cobble it all together. So the systems and processes that make up incentive comp in a company resemble jigsaw puzzle pieces. Pull the ICM system puzzle piece out and drop a vendor's off-the-shelf software in, will it fit? Most likely not, or at least, not without shaving off corners and taping some new chunks on.

Figure 35 - I Think I Can Make it Fit

I'm not putting it this way to defend vendor's products from charges that they don't work. Most ICM applications have normal or best practices built into them, plus a few not-so-best practices put in to satisfy a particularly valuable customer or two. But too much Weirdness will always fall outside the lines. If your ICM process is broken, it might still be broken in new software – software that, paradoxically, fits less well than the old, organically grown one.

So this, then, is a plea to at least consider the possibility of bringing in business consultants and/or ICM experts to take a look at what you are doing today with an eye towards eliminating as much of the Weirdness as possible *before the ICM implementation project begins.*

Why before? Why not during Requirements whenever we stumble across examples of Weirdness? The pragmatic and cynical and completely correct answer to that is because the project team has a deadline to hit. Rearchitecting business processes is a schedule killer. And because the only people with the authority to make changes to eliminate Weirdness don't come to the Requirements meetings very often. They leave those meetings to Tammy, who we already know does not have the authority to make the changes – if she could, she would have done so already. These two reasons together make meaningful process change impossible once the project starts.

That leaves doing it before the project, or after. And after doesn't happen. If we just spent a fortune implementing based on what's in place now, we don't want to have to reimplement to match the new processes later. So looking at processes is something you have to do before the project starts.

In nearly every project kickoff meeting I have ever attended, the Finance VP or the CIO looks the team squarely in their collective eye and growls, "We want to do this smarter. Don't implement what we do today; implement where we should be tomorrow." Then the project team never sees that person again. So we implement what the company does today, since those are the only requirements we have.

I worked on a huge ICM project once that was spiraling down into the black hole of what-we-do-today, and both sides were extremely frustrated by the slow pace of the project and the byzantine nature of what we were designing and configuring. And in the course of it, I ran into the customer's executive honchos at the vendor's Users Group meeting. They were really angry and they asked me, *"What the %#&@ are you guys building down there?!?"*[40]

I told them we were building what Tammy asked us to build. If they wanted anything different, perhaps they could actually come and attend the workshops and make that fact known, because otherwise, no one had the authority to do anything differently. We were all very polite to each other, but it was clearly a very quiet shouting match.

In a more ideal world, they would have had that conversation before anyone from the implementation side ever showed up on site. At the very least, someone at a honcho level should have been part of the Requirements workshops to say, "That may be how we did it before, but that's not what we'll do moving forward." It's often a revelation to the execs just how wacky some ICM practices are at their own companies, and when they find out, they sometimes step in to make changes.

So what does a **Business Consulting** – **BC** – or **Organizational Change Management** – **OCM** – engagement look like? Very much like a set of requirements workshops, except without the level of detail needed for the implementation workshops. They're kind of like a visit to the doctor. A poke here, a poke there – ooh! You just winced! Let's talk about how that made you feel!

If nothing makes you wince, and it seems like everything is more or less under control, then there won't be a lot of recommendations. On the other hand, if Tammy gets her IT counterpart into a headlock and begins administering an Atomic Noogie to him during a meeting, and the CFO downs half a bottle of Scotch when the subject of Sarbanes-Oxley comes up, then there most likely will be some recommendations for ways to mitigate the problems and risks.

And if you do happen to get a lot of recommendations for system or process improvement? You might want to consider implementing some of them *before you bring the ICM implementation team on site*. We know that if the problem is the HR system or the Order Management system, you probably don't have the budget to rebuild them in addition to dropping in a new ICM system. But if there are process changes, comp plans full of unintended consequences, exceptions that break the intent of the comp plans, or other human or departmental factors, this

---

[40] "Down there", because the project war room was in the basement of their office building.

would be a most excellent time to address them.

Incidentally, I have had consultants and consulting managers – typically new to the business – tell me in all seriousness that I should tell the customers that the process or logic they want us to implement is bad. They should change the requirement, and here's what we will do instead.

Um, yes, it is bad, and yes it should be changed, but that's not our decision to make – it's the customer's decision. Maybe there are contractual reasons why it can't be changed, or data issues that drive it, or it's an industry standard practice. So while I do believe in being consultative, and in telling customers the high cost of continuing down a bad path, the blithe assumption that the requirement will change just because I say it should has just never panned out in real life. I am arrogant, but I'm not *that* arrogant.

Design Phase

REQUIREMENTS VS. DESIGN

I've made a point of discussing the Requirements Phase as being application-agnostic – that is, we are not allowed to document the problem in terms of the solution. This is not always a popular stance to take with consultants, who usually come back with, "What if the customer wants something we (or more properly, the system) can't do?" Consultants always ask questions with parentheses in them.

And I reply, *"You can't help but do the design while you are hearing requirements*. You'll do it whether I give you permission to or not. That's just what technologists do!" And it's true – we listen to requirements through a systematic filter – we can't help it. It's how consultants are wired. So if we hear something impossible, we know it's impossible the moment we hear it in 98% of the cases. Granted, the *hidden impossibilities* sometimes sneak by, but I am not sure those would be caught if we documented them in system terms anyway.

What are hidden impossibilities? Those are the scenarios in which:

- A is possible if B is true;
- B is possible if C is true;
- C is possible if D is true;
- D is possible only if B is false.

They don't come up very often, and it's impossible to describe a real life example since it would be dependent on a perfect storm of data and comp plan Weirdness that would only make sense to the Comp Team of the company where it takes place. But I promise, situations like this do exist, and they are not always discovered during the Requirements Phase. The realization usually creeps up on you during Design if you're lucky or good, the Build Phase if you're not. Or during the Test Phase if you are cursed.

But the normal kinds of impossibility are not usually so well hidden, and we generally know what we are up against while we are documenting requirements. If something won't fit into the system (or calendar, or budget), we try to raise the question about how to resolve the problems early.

Another reason I don't like to do the formal design for the system configuration during the Requirements Phase is because we all tend to fall in love with the fruits of our labor. I am as guilty of that as anyone, as you can probably tell from some of the ideas and word choices I have left in this book that a real author would have taken out. If I thought of it, it must be brilliant and elegant and virtuous, right? Don't change anything!

So on an ICM project, once we have an idea for a cute way to configure the system, we start twisting what we hear into a shape that fits inside that idea. We start restating requirements back to the customer in a form that works for our idea, and if they don't actually come out and say, *"WRONG!"*, we take it for agreement. If we can't completely fit a requirement into the cute idea, we start glomming extra bits onto the idea to accommodate it. Eventually the idea becomes too misshapen from all the Weird things we have tried to shove inside it, and if we're smart, we start over. But in the meantime, we have made the requirements we have heard mean something a little more ambiguous than the customer intended them to be.

Like it or not, then, the time to do the formal design is during the Design Phase. I guess that's why they named it that.

WHY DO WE EVEN HAVE A DESIGN PHASE?

Isn't this ICM system I'm buying supposed to be a packaged application? Why do I have to figure out how to make it work? Run the installer, connect some pipes, isn't it good to go?

This kind of question does get asked, and it's not unreasonable for the CIO to wonder what actually got bought with that huge check the company just wrote. Many applications are like that. Install a G/L system, okay, you tell it what your fiscal year looks like and you feed in your chart of accounts, it's ready to go, right? Set up that HR system, make a couple of choices about the attributes you want to track, load in the employees you already have, and boom – fire it up.[41]

ICM systems are much more flexible than most other systems because they have to be. The incentive comp process in every industry is different, and it's different in every company in every industry. To build a packaged application that works for all companies in all industries calls for the creation of an environment in which incentive comp can be performed, rather than a more highly constrained kind of system. There are laws and regulations in finance or HR that provide guard rails around what the system can do. The only laws in ICM are… Well actually, there are no laws.[42]

The Design Phase is all about making the comp plans work in the ICM system, given the constraints of data and processes. The comp plans might have a lot of logic built into them, and that logic is dependent on source data – reference data and transactions – behaving a certain way. During the ICM implementation, data must be brought into the system in a way that conforms to the expectations of the comp plans, results must be generated, and data must be made available for downstream systems and reporting.

So the Design Phase is about finding the balance between several somewhat conflicting but generally desirable qualities. These, then, are **Ol' Unka DK's Sometimes Contradictory System Virtues**:

- **Accuracy**[43]
  We have got to get the right answer.
- **Performance**
  We usually have to get the right answer in a screaming hurry.
- **Thoroughness**
  We want to create lots of usable data for reporting and analytics, but it takes longer to process lots of results than it does to process just enough results to pay on.
- **Flexibility**
  The system must work for what we do today, but also for what we might do in the future.

---

[41] Yeah, yeah, I know. Neither one is that easy. But they do have their usage built into the product, in the way the UI works and in the sorts of things you can do with them. ICM is much less well defined, both as a process and as a system.

[42] Yeah, yeah, I know. There are laws in insurance and other financial services with respect to how the producers get paid. But work with me here. Even in insurance, there are many different ways to write the producers' contracts, and many different system configuration implications associated with them.

[43] Yeah, yeah, I know. Nothing conflicts with accuracy. Without that, nothing else we do matters in ICM.

- **Robustness**

    The system can't be fussy. It should be like a train – it just goes. Let's just wire it up to do what it's supposed to do. But that conflicts with the flexibility we also want.

- **Automation**

    The system should do the job, and the whole job. Don't make the admins do all the work.

- **Maintainability**

    If the system is too complicated, it becomes a bear to maintain, now and in the future. So make the system do the right things that neatly fit inside its core functionality, and leave the rest for the admins. But we are now conflicting with the full automation we were hoping for.

Hang out in the project war room during the Design Phase and you will hear passionate disagreement about almost any design decision because of the conflicts between these qualities. "If we do that, the customer will lose flexibility!" "If we *don't* do that, it won't perform!" In the abstract, we want all of these qualities, but sometimes we can sacrifice one or more of them because we have no choice.

THE TOOLS

The ICM implementation team has a few basic tools they can bring to bear on solving the customer's incentive comp challenges. These include:

- System Functionality
- Data Integration
- Reporting
- The User Interface
- Process Change
- Customization

These are the places where work can be done to effect the solution to the entire compensation process. We will discuss each of them.

System Functionality

That nice shiny ICM system is where we would like to do as much of the heavy lifting as possible. ICM systems are designed to handle logic, conditions, math, and data grinding. It's what they do. The better your team knows the specific functionality of the ICM system they are implementing, the more cute tricks they'll be able to pull out of it. And they'll also be better able to avoid the pitfalls and missing functionality that might be part of the system as well.

Every system is different. I won't even try to address what you can do in any off-the-shelf ICM application because it's a huge subject, and because whatever I tell you will be wrong by the time you read this book. Suffice it to say, each system has strengths and some bizarre tricks it can pull off. But each also has weaknesses and some frankly silly functionality gaps built in. So if you have a complicated problem, there will likely be some surprises about what will be done by the core ICM application, and also some about what won't be.

The things that can't be handled in the core ICM application are really what we are interested in for this section.

Data Integration

Moving data from source systems is the first thing we look to when we have a problem that can't be handled neatly using the ICM application's built-in functionality. **ETL – Extraction, Transformation, and Load** – hides a multitude of sins. No one would argue that we shouldn't be smart about taking data from one system and putting into another, but how much smartness should we bring to the problem?

In the simplest of solutions, all we want to do is move data from system to system, with maybe some simple formatting to be sure it's consistent. This is the minimum level of data integration we ever do. In a case like this, we have essentially told the customer to bring exactly the data they need to the ICM system, and make it look *just like this*. It sometimes happens.

Nah, who am I kidding? It never happens.

A step up from there is to apply validations to the data. For example, this field must be numeric, that field cannot be empty. Or possibly the ProductID on the Transaction must be a product in the ICM system's Product table – otherwise, don't bring the record in. We check to be sure that those things are cool before we bring the data into the system. It's a simple validation and it prevents processing errors. Nearly a no-brainer.

We might also want to filter out records that we know are not applicable. But even there, we shouldn't hide that filter in a black box. Some of the records we filter out now might be needed in next year's comp plans, and we don't want to limit the customer's ability to have the system respond to changes in the business. Most customers and consultants would still call this a fairly simple data integration solution. We're just saving the system from stumbling over dumb, mechanical errors in the data, or from having to sort through a lot of known extraneous data.

Beyond that, we start looking at a concept we call **preprocessing**. Maybe we need to look at a value in a field on the source data – say, CustomerID on the Transaction and from there, go to the Customer table in the CRM system to find the postal code on that Customer record, which we then add to the data we're bringing in so the ICM system can use the postal code in its processing. This is a simple preprocessor, and it or something like it has been built for dozens, or hundreds, of ICM projects. Yes, it's doing work that the ICM system might be able to do itself, but ICM might not have access to that data, and either way, SQL database queries perform faster than application processing.

Transactions from Sales Order Management...

OrderID	Date	Qty	Product	Price	Customer
123	8/14/14	2	X19 Widgets	$525,000.00	RedCorp
124	8/15/14	4	B9 Rugalators	$125,000	GreenCo

...joined to Customer Data from CRM...

Customer	Address1	Address 2	City	State	Country	PostCode
RedCorp	543 2nd Ave	Suite 1000	Bay City	CA	USA	91234
GreenCo	345 1st St	9th Floor	Suburb City	NY	USA	12321

...to create Transactions for import into ICM

OrderID	Date	Qty	Product	Price	Customer	PostCode
123	8/14/14	2	X19 Widgets	$525,000.00	RedCorp	91234
124	8/15/14	4	B9 Rugalators	$125,000	GreenCo	12321

Figure 36 - Simple Data Enrichment Preprocessor Example

And then there is the full-fledged *preprocessor-that-looks-like-an-application*, the kind with heavy-duty processing logic built into it. If this field is X, then bring in this piece of data over here and multiply these two values, but if it is Y, then subtract Payee.ShoeSize from Payee.IQ and put that value here on the record. At this point, we have started to embed plan logic into the preprocessor. That's generally regarded as A Very Bad Thing, but sometimes it's A Very Unavoidable Thing.

One kind of mini-application we end up with quite often is the territory crediting preprocessor. Territory definitions are stored in some system or table that is external to the ICM system. The preprocessor has crediting rules, and it slaps the PayeeID onto the transaction based on those rules and the territory definitions. Then the ICM system creates the direct credit for the transaction based on the work that the preprocessor did upstream. The SQL queries that perform this magic are pretty huge.

Who would be so dastardly and despicable as to build a preprocessor-that-looks-like-an-application? Well, any ICM consultant who has been in the field for more than a year has probably seen at least one, and worse, probably helped design it. We don't do it for fun or because we think it would be cool to play with high-powered technology. [44] We do it because there is sometimes no other choice to meet the customer's requirements using the data and systems available to us. A big pre-processor might be the *least-bad* answer.

The biggest problem with super smart preprocessors is that they take control away from the Comp Team. Most ICM systems provide access to the compensation logic to the business users – Tammy's Comp Team. With a monstrous preprocessor, though, if the crediting rules change, or the logic of the data enrichment changes, there is no way for business users to go in and modify the system to make it work for the new plans. Either IT must step in to rebuild the logic, or the implementer gets a call for a consulting gig to fix it for next year's plans.

And further, if the preprocessor breaks for whatever reason, it is usually not covered by the vendor's Tech Support agreement. It was built by the consultants, not the vendor's engineers, so Tech Support doesn't have any way – or obligation – to fix it (depending on the contract you have signed, of course).

With luck we will see fewer and fewer of the crediting preprocessors over the next few years because there are companies building off-the-shelf territory applications to do this kind of work. But I think it's a safe bet that none of them will handle every kind of crediting Weirdness that we run into, at least in the near-term.

Figure 37 - Preprocessor that looks like an Application

Incidentally, if there is such a thing as a pre-processor, is there such a thing as a **post-processor**? Yup. They are not as common as pre-processors, but they are out there. It sometimes happens that there are so many moving pieces and parts to the plans and data integration that a result can't be known until all the rest of the processes have run and the dust has settled. Then you create logic in the database to compare two of a payee's results to take the larger of them, or do math on them, or perform whatever other follow-on processing you need. Put whatever answer you come up with on whatever object makes the most sense. Often that object is a new transaction, which is then fed back into the ICM system for further processing.

Ranking is a common requirement for post-processing, because ranking is something ICM systems have some

---

[44] Maybe not entirely true. Technologists like to solve problems, and they like to use technology. If the easiest best way (in their minds) to solve this problem is a big preprocessing machine, well, so be it.

challenges with. Many will do a flavor or two of payee ranking, but in the **Pharma** and **Life Sciences** world, complex ranking is a must and the rules for it are beyond most ICM systems. So the usual routine in the ICM implementation world is to run the regular transactions, do a post-process to figure out the various rankings of the various payees, then put the rankings on new transactions that are then fed back into the system. After the system processes the ranked transactions, there might be another round of ranking, with more transactions carrying the ranks into the system. Lather, rinse and repeat until all the necessary ranking is done. Throw in the usual problem we have in ICM of needing to rerun prior paid periods, and this turns into a lot of processing every night.

Reporting

Using reports to generate comp results is similar to post-processing. When the dust has settled in comp plan processing, there might still be some value or values that haven't been brought to the surface. So the query that populates data on a report can be extended to do the rest of the heavy lifting that the core ICM system couldn't quite pull off.

Just like preprocessing, I am generally opposed to putting logic into the reporting layer beyond adding up the monthly results to get quarterly and yearly values. From my perspective, reports are all about displaying information: I don't want them to create the data they display. But that's maybe just me being dogmatic.

The User Interface

Not everything needs to be automated. If you are scrambling to work an exception into the comp plan logic and the data layer and the reports, and nothing much is working, don't forget that, if the problem is small enough, Tammy's team can enter the answer in the UI of the ICM system. But that has to be for a small problem, not a 1000s per month kind of problem, and you have to remember to give a mechanism to handle it.

Process Change

If none of the other tools we've mentioned so far can handle the problem, have we considered asking if the problem can be eliminated by doing something differently? Maybe not a wholesale plan change, but do we really need to do this Pair-of-Jacks-or-Better-to-Open validation for which we cannot find data or logic? How about we make that go away by doing something different upstream or in the daily processing or what have you? Hey – it's worth a shot.

Suggest it, show the problems we are running into trying to put it in the system, maybe do some analysis about the cost to implement it, and offer the customer the option to make a decision on it. If the decision is to keep doing it, okay, at least we tried to find a cheaper way.

Customization

This is a dirty word for most customers and for most ICM vendors. If you have to get into the application code to make changes to the way it works, that's a big, serious undertaking. Many vendors won't even offer the option of doing it, while others have a more open architecture into which you can at least drop plug-ins to try to create additional functionality. Before going down the customization route, investigate what this will do to your warrantee. And then consider a pre- or postprocessor anyway.

HOW DO WE DESIGN: THE STATE MACHINE

How we conduct design is clearly very dependent on both the problem to be solved and the system and tools available to us. Each project is different, and each customer's best balance of the system qualities – performance, flexibility, completeness, etc. – to be optimized is unique to them as well. So you're mostly on your own here. But the STATE MACHINE we talked about earlier is another tool to use in solving the more complex and multidimensional comp requirements that come up. Designing solutions for groups of cells in the State Machine that have similar outcomes, or conversely, if your system design handles every state and every outcome, then you can have confidence that your solution is complete. And don't forget to use all of the tools we identified: sometimes the solution to handle a cell can be "manual adjustment".

And sometimes you might have a cell that represents a condition that is enough of an edge case that you and the customer both agree that it won't be handled at all. In this case, be absolutely certain to document that decision. It's sometimes okay to decide not to deal with a scenario, but it must be with your eyes open.

A State Machine isn't a universal cure, but it is a valuable tool to have in your tool chest to deal with complex situations and requirements.

So now I'd like to propose some rules to live a healthy ICM life by.

OL' UNKA DK'S FIRST LAW OF ICM SYSTEM DESIGN

- *Sometimes there is no good answer.*
  Sometimes there is only the least bad answer.

Believe it or not, I do try to be hopeful and optimistic and to bring the light of reason and clarity to ICM projects and to build systems that will delight the users every day. I do. But sometimes, the Weirdness is pretty intense, and we have to make tough choices about how we will build the system for the customer. Sometimes an essential quality is tossed aside because of an overriding data or processing issue or comp requirement that prevents us from optimizing for it. It is important to be transparent with the customer about the choices we have to make to help them weigh the cost of optimizing one quality over another.

OL' UNKA DK'S SECOND LAW OF ICM SYSTEM DESIGN

- *The work has to happen somewhere.*
  Moving it doesn't make it go away.

ICM vendors often fall into this mental trap, and having worked for ICM vendors for many years, I have fallen into it myself on numerous occasions. The system is taking too long to finish – it's taking 12 hours to run every night. We just know it's because we're doing work in the ICM system that should have been done upstream – we're fixing a customer data problem, darn it! So we kick and scream and finally the customer's IT group moves the work into a preprocessor before they feed us the data. Great – now the ICM system in running in six hours and we're all heroes! Yay us!

Except… Except that the new preprocessor takes five hours to complete and one hour to feed the results to the ICM system. Net savings: 0 hours. So all right, we've shown that the ICM product can run fast, but we haven't solved the underlying problem – it still takes 12 hours to run end-to-end.

Doing the work with the right tools will speed it up, and it's important to always consider performance in every design decision. So to that end, I give you…

OL' UNKA DK'S THIRD LAW OF ICM SYSTEM DESIGN

- *Render unto SQL the things that are SQL's, and render unto application logic the things that are logical*
  - *Keep logic out of the preprocessor (whenever possible)*
  - *Keep data lookups out of the comp calculation engine (wherever possible)*
  - *Keep calculation out of the reports (whenever possible)*

Okay, maybe it's more a set of guidelines than an actual law, but you have to try your best to follow it anyway. Unless you can't. I understand.

OL' UNKA DK'S FOURTH LAW OF ICM SYSTEM DESIGN

- *If implementing it in the system will make the system more onerous to manage than handling it as a manual exception would, then handle it as a manual exception*

The ICM system vendor put a nice shiny user interface on their product just for times like this. But creating a way that a tough exception can be handled manually is not always as easy as it sounds; sometimes some heavy duty design creativity is necessary. Don't get complacent just because you pulled the "**manual-exception-get-out-of-jail-free**" card.

DELIVERABLES

Every vendor or SI has its own documentation, but two things I really want to see out of the Design Phase are a **logical design** and a **physical design**. These might be in the same document, they might be buried in other deliverables, and for some systems the implementation is almost exactly the same number of keystrokes as the physical design doc, so there's no real point in doing the document. But however this shakes out, there are reasons for having both documents.

The Logical Design Document

The **Logical Design Document (LDD)** is where we tell the story of how the system is going to solve for the customer's full set of requirements. Not every methodology has this deliverable, but I will try to show you why I think we need it.

For each major requirement, we write *human-being-type paragraphs* describing:

- The requirement from the RSD
- Constraints and challenges, if any
- The end-to-end story of how we will configure the system to manage it
    - From data integration, including preprocessing, if any;
    - To high-level comp logic, but now expressed in terms of system functionality;
    - To reporting logic;
    - To human processes needed, if any;
    - To downstream feeds;
    - With pseudo-code where helpful.

There are several reasons this story is important. One is because this is where the customer will be introduced to the system, and the Comp Team needs to start thinking in ICM system terms and concepts. This is a valuable first step, and it's not just valuable for the customer. The implementers need the customer to understand the system if the project is ever going to be completed, so starting them down the path during the Design Phase is a good strategy.

More important, however, is the fact that no one could look at a comp plan in an ICM system and know what problem it thinks it's solving, any more than you could look at a complex formula on a spreadsheet and know what problem it is trying to solve. All you can know is what was built. You might see that it is syntactically *correct*, but that doesn't tell you that it's *right*. ICM solutions involve data, logic, math, and reporting, so just seeing one piece of that puzzle doesn't tell me that the piece is doing its part of the heavy lifting.

The Logical Design Doc helps the implementers know they are supporting the solution when they document and build the physical design. Does this piece I'm building support the story we told? I can apply my own sanity checks to it, and if I have doubts, I can raise them instead of just blindly doing what I have been told to do in the Physical Design Document.

And finally, it makes a great foundation for the **Operations Guide** we will need to leave behind when the system goes live.

The Physical Design Document

The **Physical Design Document** (PDD) is where you get down to the specifics of how the LDD will be coded or configured. It has sections for Data Integration, Compensation Plans, Reporting, and sometimes Processes. This is an incredibly detailed document, because it provides the implementers with the exact recipe they need to follow to build out the customer requirements. The PDD should exactly align with every design element in the LDD (see above).

For each feed in the **Data Integration** section of the PDD, the design calls out specific:

- Systems, tables, keys, and columns; or
  File formats; plus
- Validations
- Transformation pseudo-code
- Job scheduling
- Error handling

In short, everything that must be coded to make the system function.

In the **Compensation Plan** section, the logic for every plan, component, and rule or formula is specified, including:

- Conditions to be checked in processing
- Objects to be created – by name
- Variables used
- Exception handling logic
- Any other plan configuration required by the ICM system

For the **Reporting** section, we want to see:

- Report mockups with every value identified by name and source
- Report navigation
- Query pseudo-code
- Security mechanisms identified, including single-sign-on protocols and report access
- Other requirements, such as download or mobile access defined

Where customer requirements will be addressed using process change, there will be a **Process** section that will describe how users will interact with the system and data to manage the requirement.

Customer Approval of the Design

This is a delicate one so I will dance around it a little. In general, I don't believe we or the customer should plan to have a formal "sign-off" on the design docs. There are reasons for this, and not just because I'm lazy and don't want to take responsibility for my work. First, and this is not meant to be a slam on the customer, but they (presumably) do not yet know the internals of the system they are implementing. So their ability to be certain of the correctness – or incorrectness – of a system design might be based on knowledge of other complex software plus good strong common sense, but it's not the certainty that comes with knowing *this specific application*. Of course, if this is a reimplementation project, then I withdraw this particular concern, but even then, they might not know why this design is better (or worse) than it looks.

The second reason is because, in building a complex system with lots of moving parts, we might find a different, better way to accomplish something than we came up with originally. As we start slotting the pieces together, we might realize that there are aspects of the design that can be improved. But if we have a formally signed off document that says we will build this way and no other, our hands are tied when we want to improve the build. We would need to get Change Requests for the design docs, and that would be a time-sink in the Build Phase.

I do believe the implementation team need to present the design documents to the customer team for review, sanity checks, and milestone approval. But unless the customer comes up with significant concerns that cannot be explained away about the design – "Wait a minute – you're planning to hire 100 high-school kids to come in every month after school, calculate our comp, *then type the results into your system for payment?!?*" – I don't think the signature should be considered "binding" on the implementation team. But others disagree on this point, so I'm prepared to be convinced otherwise on a case-by-case basis. Mr. Open-Minded, that's me.

TRACEABILITY

This document should provide the implementation and the customer teams the ability to tie each requirement documented in the RSD to an implementation method in the product. And each implementation method or element should then be tied to specific test cases in the Testing Phase.

What if there are gaps? What if there is a customer requirement called out in the RSD, on which the customer and the implementation teams have signed off, that haven't been addressed in Design? Sometimes it happens where it turns out that we don't have a good answer for a requirement in the system design. That's where the Project Managers go to work to determine what the options are.

Those options might include:

- Remove the requirement with a Change Request to the RSD
- Go back and find a way to make it happen in the system
- Handle it as a manual exception or a process change

Stalemate between the vendor pushing to remove the requirement and the customer demanding a systematic resolution can happen, which sometimes leads to escalations to the Steering Committee. This is where the SteerCo is critical, and a fast and reasoned decision is necessary to keep the project on track. And in return for that, both sides have to raise issues proactively. Just because it's embarrassing to tell the SteerCo that the application is missing some key functionality, or that a process you have been using for years is actually counterproductive, is no excuse not to raise it earlier rather than later.

ADDITIONAL REQUIREMENTS IN THE DESIGN PHASE

Earlier in this section we discussed the separation between the Requirements and Design Phases and the importance of keeping them separated. But just as I pointed out that design happens during the Requirements Phase just from the nature of the way implementers think, I also need to point out that new requirements will often continue to pop up in the Design Phase after the Requirements Phase is complete and the RSD is signed off.

Remember all that talk about how ICM is hard and how no one can agree on what the words mean and how data and processes and plans all interact with each other in a stew of Weirdness? Those things are still true. And that means that a requirement you explained and that the consultants read back to you might suddenly turn out to mean something totally different to each of you, despite each of you using the same words. Or the consultants might not have known to ask a question about a requirement that would have opened the door to a universe of functionality that no one thought about. There's no bad guy here; this stuff is just really complicated.

Even without the failure of human language, it is quite common that ICM projects take quite a while, so the requirements gathered early in the project change when the project crosses plan years. We take, design, and build for requirements for this year's plans knowing that next year's plans will be different, even if we don't know what the difference will be. We have to write that risk into the RSD and note the possibility that things will change when it's time to implement. And then Finance hands down the new plans and there is a scramble to see how the project requirements and the work done so far will be impacted.

However it happens that additional requirements pop up, and however much we wish it wouldn't, we have to at least keep it in the backs of our minds that they might. So what do we do? We document the new requirements or the new understanding of the old requirement, and then go through the same processes above. It might be a Change Request to the RSD, it might be something we put on hold, or it might turn into an escalation to the SteerCo. But this is one reason why ICM system vendors and implementers try not to sign up to fixed price contracts.

Build Phase

Once the design is complete and everyone agrees it's time to build, then it's time to build. And hey, just as design creeps into the Requirements Phase, it is not the least bit unusual for implementers to start building the bits they are pretty certain of even before the Design Phase milestones are hit and signed off. It's a way to be sure the design is really going to work, for one thing, and it helps the project timeline to have some work done early. That's the sort of thing that buys the Project Manager a little stress relief later on.

THE TURN-KEY BUILD PARADIGM

There are a couple of common paradigms used in large IT projects that apply to ICM implementations. The most common is for the implementer team to build a **turn-key** system. What this means is that the implementers go off to the top-secret labs in their secret subterranean lairs (or maybe the project work room down the hall) and configure the system exactly as documented in the RSD and the PDD. Sometime later they come out and say, "She's ready – go ahead and turn the key and start 'er up!"

This is the first time the customer's Comp Team really sees and gets their hands dirty in the new system. They run their User Acceptance Tests, pronounce themselves satisfied, and everyone is happy. Or just possibly, they run their tests and say the system has failed some percentage of them, and let's get those fixed now, okay?

Now, very few customers will let the vendor or SI run off for weeks unsupervised, so there are often build reviews scheduled throughout the life of the Build Phase. But however that shakes out, the vendor is responsible for the entire build, and the deliverable is the system itself. There are one or two other deliverables as well, but the working system is the main one.

THE COLLABORATIVE BUILD PARADIGM

But turn-key is not the only way the Build Phase can be performed. There is another paradigm that's sometimes called **collaborative build**, and it holds many intriguing advantages. In collaborative build, the mantra is, "The implementers build one with the customer watching, the customer builds one with the implementers supervising, and the implementers and customer teams split up the rest." "One" and "the rest" refer to any reasonably similar system elements, whether data integration routines, comp plans and components, reports, or anything else on which the implementers can train the customer team. If there are five similar comp plans with only minor variations between them, the vendor builds one as a template, then the customer staff follow that template to build some of the others.

I am a big fan of collaborative build whenever practical. I think it is absolutely the best known way to have the customer "own" the system when the project is done. I continually go back to the fact that *incentive comp is hard* blah de blah *ICM systems are complex* yadda yadda and **WHY DO WE EVEN HAVE A DESIGN PHASE ANYWAY?** As we discussed in that section, we have to balance the several desirable but sometimes conflicting qualities of an

ICM system in our design and configuration to come up with the best,[45] most balanced configuration overall. This means we might choose to optimize for one quality – say, processing performance – by giving up another quality – maybe flexibility or automation. After all, when implementation consultants yell at each other in a meeting over design decisions, it strongly indicates that there are at least somewhat credible alternatives to any design we finalize on.

When we build a large and complex turn-key system to support difficult operational processes, we end up presenting the results of our compromises with respect to desirable system qualities to the customer at the end of the Build Phase. We tell them to do their UAT on the system we give them. But they probably do not know why we made the decisions we made and what we gave up for what else in return. It will not be obvious that this bit of manual work *here* bought us a ton of automation *there*.

On the other hand, if the customer team has been building the system alongside the implementers, the choices – and the reasons for the choices – will be much clearer to them. The customer's operational team will know the system and understand how to test it better, and they will have had opportunities to propose alternative design approaches that might perhaps better support their business processes. If those approaches wouldn't work, the implementers can explain why not, but if they would, there might still be time to make changes that will make the system work better for the customer operations teams.

When we are designing, we consultants think we know what's important, but we aren't the ones doing the day-to-day work of paying commissions. An activity that the implementers might think is trivial might actually cause significant pain point for the Comp Team. If the Comp Team is there getting their hands dirty in the system during the Build Phase, they can raise the issue. This value of this in terms of customer satisfaction is not to be underestimated.

While I like collaborative build quite a lot, there are disadvantages to it as well. One is, the customer Comp Team has day jobs that are already getting squeezed by their responsibilities to the project. Now put them to work in the comp plan factory with deliverables that impact the project schedule, and you have piled a lot of pressure on them.

Another is on-the-job-training. Sure, you plan to send the customer's build team off to the vendor's product training before they start their tasks, but they will still need a deeper understanding of the system than they can get from the canned training classes. They need the knowledge that comes with implementing and using the system for more than just a single project. Just as implementation consultants need time to ramp up on an application, even though thinking as system implementers is their job and modus operandi, the customers will be less than 100% effective when they first start to configure the system.

So collaborative build generally does not decrease the time it takes to do the project, and in some cases, might even extend it. The customers are amateurs in the system, so they don't work as efficiently as the implementation "experts". And the implementation team has to spend a fair amount of time hand-holding and keeping the customer team inside the lines of what they are working on, which costs them some productivity. Collaborative build is expensive on both sides of the relationship. We have made the implementation team larger, but we have also imposed extra tasks on them.

If it didn't generally make the customers better users of their system from Day One of Go-Live, I would say collaborative build might not be worth the extra effort. But in my experience, customers who contribute to building their own system are happier than they might be if they were just handed the keys later.

---

[45] Or least-worse.

DELIVERABLES

Well, there's the working system. That right there is a pretty significant deliverable. Transactions go in, they generate answers, and reports pop up, so let's give ourselves a big hand. But there's more we need to leave behind at the end of this phase.

One is **updated Logical and Physical Design Docs**. Why new versions of the Design Phase deliverables? Because as we build, we realize that we can do *this function* more efficiently *this way*, or by doing that different thing, we can eliminate a couple of comp plans. Because of the complexity of even a medium-complexity project, and because of the compromises and balancing of system qualities we have made, we often do find different ways to accomplish our ends. But just because we can do it better than the original, documented design, doesn't mean we can ignore the design docs. In a utopian world, the implementation team is keeping the LDD and PDD up to date as they work through the project. Here on Planet Earth, however… well, I'm sure it's actually happened somewhere sometime. I mean, it stands to reason, right?

Another is **Unit Test** and **Assembly Test** documentation. You might think of these as Test Phase deliverables, but I would say no, they are actually part of Build. As an implementer builds a piece of the puzzle to satisfy a requirements and conform to the PDD, there is also the requirement to run tests against what she or he built. It's just a good practice, but it also helps prevent preventable humiliation later when the customer fires up the piece for the first time and it bursts into flames. A quick test while no one is looking can help save red faces later. We call that "Unit Testing". The test cases run by the implementer should be documented, as well as the results of the tests.[46]

"Assembly Testing" is when the individual pieces of the puzzle are fitted together and tested to be sure that what I built doesn't break what you built, which can easily happen in complex systems. If I write a plan that creates a value called "Widget Revenue", but you write a report query that's looking for "Hardware Revenue", your report won't be able to find the result I generated. Both of our puzzle pieces might be elegant and beautiful individually, but the system won't work unless one of us changes what we did. Assembly testing allows us to throw the system over the wall to the customer test teams knowing that at least the easy stupid mistakes have been caught. The harder stupid mistakes are now the customer's responsibility to catch.

ADDITIONAL REQUIREMENTS IN THE BUILD PHASE

Sigh… Yes, it sometimes happens.[47] Too often, actually.[48] As you build and as you run things by the customer, questions come up that lead to unpleasant surprises. The same remedies apply – either document the new requirement as a Change Request to the RSD and then figure out how to design and build around it, or make it go away until a later project phase. When is the next SteerCo meeting? Maybe we'd better call an emergency meeting.[49]

Test Phase

The Test Phase is where the customer steps into the limelight. This is where they determine to their own satisfaction whether the system will do for them what they expect. The vendors must support the phase, but the

---

[46] Unit Test results had better be "pass", or else there's no excuse for putting the configuration piece out where the customer can see it.
[47] [*COUGH*]*It always happens.*[*COUGH*]
[48] [*COUGH*]*It always happens.*[*COUGH*]
[49] Okay, it doesn't always happen. But it happens a lot.

customers drive.

Which means it's really unfortunate how hard testing can be, especially for large, complex, bad-data-and-exception-driven systems. Again, not a slam on customers; it's just that this kind of testing is not generally part of their expertise (with some exceptions, of course). Unless Tammy and her team have implemented an ICM system before – whether the same vendor's solution or a different vendor's solution – the testing that must be done on an ICM implementation is pretty unnatural. Throw in their responsibilities to their day jobs and it only gets harder.

Even their IT departments don't always have this kind of skillset. They are all about keeping things going and making them work, but not necessarily about rigorous, systematic testing of complex business requirements in unfamiliar systems. There are exceptions; some are good at it, but many are not.

Some customers have PMO roles that handle testing, but again, how often do they have the experience and insight to test business scenarios where the answer can be determined absolutely, but for which the questions are so difficult to verbalize?

All of which explains a request I've heard many times working on projects for ICM system vendors: "Can you take over the testing for us?" Well, yes, we could, but what exactly is our incentive to uncover problems in the configuration? I always joke that if you put me in charge of testing the work my team and I did, I can pretty well assure you that we will pass.[50] That doesn't stop us from owning the Test Phase if the customer insists, but it is a built-in conflict of interest. And when we are done, where is the confidence that the system will do what the customer needs?

So having raised the flag of surrender and broken everyone's spirit, is there no hope at all? Well, yes, there are things you can do to improve the testing process. So let's talk about them. Various methodologies have various names for the various parts of system testing, and I'm too lazy to try to reconcile them all. But there are a few broad categories that must be tested, regardless of how the implementation theoretician breaks them down. I would say these categories fall out something like this:

- Integration Testing
- Functional Testing
- User Acceptance Testing (UAT)
- Performance Testing

Every delivery team will have its own version of this (and every testing methodology is *the only correct one*), so whatever I say about them will be subject to argument. But that said, let's examine what each might be about and how best to get through it in one piece.

But first, let's discuss the mechanics of testing.

TESTING LOGISTICS

There are several practical considerations that must be planned for in testing. These include:

- Defect Reporting & Resolution
- Environments
- Code Promotion
- Test Data vs. Production Data

These are the kinds of things that Test Leads and Project Managers will lose sleep over in the weeks leading up to the Test Phase, and which will keep them on their toes during it.

---

[50] [*COUGH*]*It's not a joke.*[*COUGH*]

Defect Reporting & Resolution

Testers are going to test, and no matter how good or how careful the implementation team is, the testers will find defects – bugs, flaws, mistakes, errors, crises, what have you. These defects need to be tracked and given to the implementation team to fix.

There is a lot of software out there for tracking this kind of thing, but you could use a spreadsheet or yellow stickies if that's how your company wants to do it. The important thing is to include enough information to know what went wrong. Commonly that includes:

- Tester's name
- Date
- Version or build of the system configuration (if applicable)
- Test case number and/or description
- Severity
- Priority
- Description of the defect
- Steps to reproduce the defect
- Assigned to which implementer (if known)
- State (it starts with "entered" and ends with "resolved", with luck)
- Resolution type
- Comments where appropriate

Severity and **priority** are the two most interesting fields here. Severity indicates how big a problem it is. Is it merely cosmetic – "We specified 'teal' for the report background, but this is more 'aquamarine', don't you think?" – or does it cause the servers to catch fire and the city to go dark? This tends to be a four or five point scale, depending on the tracking software and the methodology. But an "S1" bug defect means that we cannot move forward with the testing because of this problem. The system is down.

Priority is about how important it is to fix the defect. This is where arguments start. Again, there might be a four or five point scale for this, from "low priority, fix it if you have nothing better to do" up to "drop everything and *fix it NOW!*" Stereotypically, customers mark everything as "S1P1" – high severity, high priority. Or at least, that's what most consultants *think* the customers do, whether it's true or not. There's no question that if the system crashes, or if it calculates entirely wrong results on the comp plan that 10,000 reps are being paid on, that is a high severity and high priority defect. But much less than that, there is room for discussion. That's why tempers run high during the daily bug review meeting.

Resolution type is another interesting one, and there can be a dozen different versions of that. We hope it will end up "resolved – fixed", meaning that the configuration was changed to handle the defect, and the defect can be closed and set aside.

But then there's "resolved – will not fix". Sometimes we will decide not to fix one, for whatever reason. Maybe it is a low priority defect, or maybe it is for an unusual edge condition that we agree won't come up very often. "Cannot reproduce" is another resolution that makes people unhappy. The tester found a problem, but no one else can find it. The tester is sure the issue is lurking out there, and is just waiting to say "I told you so!" when it rears its ugly head later, usually the day before the customer is supposed to sign off on the system.

The unhappiest resolution of all is "rejected" or "working as designed". You found a bad behavior in the system. I agree you found it, but the behavior you wanted was never agreed to as a requirement and is not documented in the RSD. Can you live with the system doing what it's doing? Then we need to move on, or possibly agree to change it later, depending on how big a fix it turns out to be. If not, then see the "**ADDITIONAL REQUIREMENTS IN THE TEST PHASE**" section. Sigh. Both sides really hate this situation. But this is why the Requirements Phase is so critical – for *both* sides of the project relationship.

Once a defect is raised, it is discussed in the daily bug meeting. Assuming that both sides agree it's a bug and needs to be fixed, the person who coded or configured that part of the system will be sent off to fix it. It might be something small and bone-headed, or it might be a major rewrite of a chunk of the system. You hope for the one, but sometimes it's the other.

When the fix is made, the test case is performed again, and with luck, we can mark it "resolved - fixed" and move onto the next thing.

There is usually an agreed-upon metric for the number of defects that can be in the system at the end of the Test Phase. It might be zero S1 or P1 defects, and no more than X (3? 5? 10?) S2 or P2 defects, with a defect resolution time for the remaining bugs defined as well. So tracking this stuff matters. A quick, "Hey – the 'Widget Commission' component is calculating ten times too high on the 'Sales Rep Plan' – can you take care of that?" at the coffee machine is probably not a rigorous enough testing methodology.

Testing Environments

For a lot of customers and a lot of ICM vendors, a three-environment setup is pretty common on a project. These consist of **DEV**, **QA**, and **PROD** – the development box, the test box, and the production box.[51] DEV tends to be pretty minimal, since heavy duty processing and large data loads aren't normally needed while the implementation team is building and configuring the system.

QA often mirrors the configuration of PROD, and PROD is the big one. PROD has to be able to manage all the data and all the processing for all the payees, plans, and transactions once the system goes live. Since we'll be conducting performance tests on the system in QA, the hardware needs to match. There are usually different rules about how the different systems can be administered – DEV can be abused by anyone, QA might actually have more controls built around it – but PROD is something IT owns and guards jealously to prevent badness and vendors from happening to it.

Some customers have a four-environment setup, and I think I've run across five box setups as well. Whatever you have the need and the resources to procure, I'm not too fussy.[52]

Code Promotion

During the Build Phase, the implementers configure the system and write code for data integration and reports to comply with the customer's requirements. They're doing this in DEV, generally. Okay, the Build Phase ends today and the Test Phase starts tomorrow, so we need to get that configuration and all that code into the QA box for the customer to start beating up.

What does that entail? Depending on how the ICM software is built, it could be as easy as taking a dump of the database on the DEV box and importing that into the database schema on the QA box. Barring that, or in addition to that, there might be components of the system that must be copied across, and the tools to **migrate** – essentially, copy – those pieces will be more or less easy to use. The most frightening case would be having to

---

[51] "Box" sounds singular, but often refers to a bunch of hardware – a database server, an application server, the calculation engine, networking gear, the report server and perhaps others. But we devil-may-care consultants will often just say "the DEV box", and by that, mean as much or as little of the system as we mean it to mean. Know what I mean?

[52] I've written this section based on the software living on-premise in which the customer manages the hardware, but the same considerations apply for hosted or SaaS software packages. There will still generally be at least a three-box setup since the vendor won't want you developing and testing in their production instance. It just might appear to be more seamless to the customer.

completely rewrite everything that's been built in DEV into the QA environment, but I don't think there are too many modern software packages out there that require it.

So the configuration – let's call it the "code" – has been recreated in the QA environment and the testing team goes to work trying to break it. And they find some defects. So the implementers go back to work, fix the defects in DEV, and then migrate the changed code across to QA. Every configuration instance that is promoted from DEV to QA should be uniquely identified with a build number or a date so the testers and implementers can be sure they are finding and fixing the same bugs.

This process proceeds through many iterations until everyone's satisfied. That's the basic theory, but of course it's never quite that easy.

The Gold Copy

This goes by various names, depending on who's doing the talking. Whatever it's called, sometimes on some projects there is the notion of a **Gold Copy** of the configuration code. It consists of pieces of the configuration that have been completed and tested and found to be satisfactory. The Gold Copy acts as a checkpoint – everything up to this point is okay, and we don't need to test it thoroughly anymore.

The Gold Copy can be used in a variety of ways, depending on the application architecture and whether it allows additional pieces of configuration code to be migrated into it. You might want to just add newly passed code to it, "smoke test"[53] it to be sure you haven't broken anything, then create a new Gold Copy that includes the added configuration code. If the system doesn't allow the addition of code to a Gold Copy, then you must create an instance of the configuration that includes everything that is known to be good, and create an entire dump of that system to promote it from DEV to QA to PROD (when the time comes).

The Gold Copy is set aside and is not to be messed with by anyone. Development and acceptance testing is performed against a working instance of the configuration, not on the Gold Copy itself. There's usually someone whose job is **configuration management** – keeping track of the builds – who is responsible for managing the Gold Copy and the daily builds as well.

INTEGRATION TESTING

Does the system play and share well in the customer's IT ecosystem? Remember, development most likely took place on DEV – the development box, at least for larger companies that get nervous about putting untested code out there where the rest of the systems can see it. We test on QA, and then we promote it to PROD – the production box. So while everyone else is testing on QA to be sure they have the functionality they want, IT is putting a version up on PROD to see how it works in the real world.

Can the report server see the database server? Can the calculation server? Can the integration routines talk to the appropriate upstream and downstream systems? Can the report server talk to the company's reporting portal? A "yes" to all of these is a happy outcome. And as stated, a big chunk of this goes away if you are using a hosted or SaaS solution.

The new system is tested for a variety of good systematic qualities, including (but not limited to):

- Compliance with the company's supported platforms
- Adherence to security policies
- Connectivity to other systems
- Anything else that indicates that this hardware and software will become good corporate citizens,

---

[53] A "smoke test" is a focused test suite of known scenarios and data that is run against the Gold Copy. Results can be quickly compared, and if they are the same, nothing new has been added that broke the Gold Copy.

regardless of actual functionality.

This is something IT departments can do with their eyes closed so we won't spend a lot of time on this one.

FUNCTIONAL TESTING

If I feed in a 3 and a 2, do I get 5 (if it's adding) (or 6 if it's multiplying) (or 1 if it's subtracting)? In other words, has the system been configured properly to get the right answers as defined in the RSD? This is the core functionality of how the system will support business operations moving forward, and this is a spot for some seriously good testing to be performed. We want to know:

- Do the data feeds grab the right data and import it in the form we want?
- If there's a preprocessor, is it preprocessing properly?
- Are the right payees on the right plans?
- Do they get credit for the transactions they should get credit for?
  Are the rollups and overlays credited properly?
  Do they NOT get credit when they shouldn't?
- Are the performance numbers adding up properly?
- Are the correct commissions and bonuses being calculated?
- Are payments in the right format and for the right amounts?
- Are repayments (or recovery of payments) of paid periods only picking up the deltas?
- Does it work not just for one month of data, but for several?
- Are there places where identified exceptions can be managed?
  And if an exception does get managed, does the system take it into account when calculating and reporting?
- Do the reports report the right amounts?
- Do the reports honor the reporting security hierarchy we want to use?
- Are the right users in the right roles with the right permissions?
- Do the workflows route properly when approvals or rejections are entered?

In other words, remember all those things we wrote down in the RSD back in the Requirements Phase? We want to be sure the system does them all, and the way we hoped it would.

Easy peasy, right? Run some transactions, compare the results to the RSD, we're good to go, right? Uh, no. Not right. It's actually a little bit more involved than that. You need a strategy, some test data, and some expected results. Let's address them in the opposite order, since the story flows better that way.

Expected Results

When you are testing, you have to have some idea of what a "pass" or a "fail" might look like. The only way to do that is to know what answer the system should come up with. You could be completely passive in your gathering of expected results – run the system, see what comes out, and then work backwards to figure out if you think the answer is right. A better approach is to be a little more active about it, however. Look at your data before you process it, choose whatever number of test cases makes the most sense (and it could be all cases if that's how your methodology works), "process" that data manually according to the rules you have defined, come up with the answers, and only then run the system and compare the pre-calculated results to your system test cases.

The most active strategy of all is to proactively look for data that pushes the boundaries of the system (remember the STATE MACHINE?), pre-calculate the results from than, then run the system and compare the interesting test case results to the system generated results. This is likely to be the most valuable form of testing just because you aren't spending time working on the "easy" cases – you can concentrate on the edge cases that are where the system is more likely to miss the target.

However you choose to do it, be really careful in your pre-calculation of the expected results. It's embarrassing for the test team to flag an error in calculation only to discover that the new system got it right and that your expected results are flawed. Any consultant who has worked on more than two ICM implementations has stories to tell about how the new system pointed out an error in the way the legacy system had been calculating incentives for the last umpty-ump years. We take our gratification wherever we can find it.

Test Data

So what data do you test against? The sort-of-easy answer is to grab a few months' worth of real transactions and run them against the plans in the new ICM system. Check what the system calculates, pays, and reports against your expected results, and there you are.

Since I made it sound easy, you know there's going to be a "but". And the "but" is, you are implementing against next year's plans, but maybe you're using this year's data and plans to generate expected results. This comes up most often when the system is supposed to go live on the first of the year. There's no point in putting in this year's plans when the system needs to go live against next year's plans. So your data and expected results won't necessarily align with the system configuration.

But even if you are going live with plans and quotas and rates and territories that are exactly the same as the ones you are paying against now, there is still room for challenges in testing this way. It is very common for the Comp Team to have to step in and make adjustments to data and to process exceptions in the course of their day-to-day jobs – I think I might have mentioned something about bad data and processes, right? If you are going to test in parallel between the systems, every modification to the data in the legacy system must also be made to the data in the new system. This means doing maintenance twice. It's not impossible, but it's something to think about when you are coming up with your testing strategy.

The other choice is to generate data that does what you want it to for testing. This data might have no connection at all with anything coming out of production systems, other than a strong resemblance in terms of format. It's a lot of work, but it enables you to test results in the most surgical way possible; you know there's a test for this edge condition because you wrote data to test this edge condition. Without actively creating that data, there might be no test for a particular brand of Weirdness coming out of the source systems that month, or if there is, it might not be easy to find it.

Testing Strategy

As discussed, I believe creating a testing strategy begins around the time of the project kickoff, but is an important parallel effort during Requirements and Design. It can't wait until the implementation team throws the software over the transom on Day One of the Test Phase. I am a big fan of someone on the customer's project team owning testing from the beginning, and that person should be creating test cases, more or less formally, with every requirement discussed in the workshops. "We do this, unless it's Tuesday, then we do that." Okay, there's another test case – make a note of it. This is a time-intensive job, and it cannot be performed as an afterthought. It might be that person's full-time project responsibility. This provides fodder for the test data and expected results to fit whatever strategy you choose to use.

Remember the **STATE MACHINE** discussion in the **REQUIREMENTS PHASE** section? That can be a fertile source of test cases. Every cell in a State Machine should spotlight at least one test case for unit and system test. If you have a separate group doing testing, it is very important that they test these conditions, not the individual rules themselves. This is sometimes a difficult concept to get across to a testing manager who does not understand compensation or ICM software, but it's an important one. Try to make sure they test plan components, and that they test for all the possible conditions. Once they get the concept, they will probably be grateful to you for providing them with a State Machine.

So what is your strategy? The strategy might involve choosing between **black box testing** or **white box testing**, or both, first of all. Black box testing is when the testers don't know anything about how the system works; they only look at the results, and usually the final ones at that. They compare the expected results to the reports or feeds from the new ICM system, and if there's a discrepancy, they flag it and move onto the next test. It is up to someone else – often the implementer – to figure out where the error is.

White box testing is a more in-depth variety. White box testers see a discrepancy and begin working backwards from the result, or forwards from the source data, to find where the error occurred, which they then flag and report. Implementers prefer white box testing, of course, but it really depends on how deeply involved and knowledgeable the testers have been with the system.

What population are you testing? Every single payee? A random 10% of them? A targeted 5% of them? It really depends on testing resources and the size of the implementation. If you are paying 50,000 payees, it is darn difficult to test each and every one of them. If you have 100 payees, sure, go ahead, check all of them. If you are using generated data for targeted payees, well then, that's your answer. You check all the results for whatever data you brought into the system.

USER ACCEPTANCE TESTING (UAT)

User Acceptance Testing is where Tammy and her team work the system in a more or less real operational way to see if the system configuration works for their **Business As Usual (BAU)** tasks and responsibilities. If the system gets the right answer, but only after the comp admins calculate it manually and enter the number into the UI, we might regard that as a failure. Or if there is a common exception that must be managed, but the system design doesn't give her team the ability to override the regular result, again, that system doesn't support the business, even if it does calculate accurately.

A common approach is to have the users run the system in parallel with the legacy system for some period of time as though it were in production. This certainly gives the Comp Team the sense of what interacting with the new ICM system will be like, although it might be a bit random given the different kinds of work that happen at different times of the year. So it's probably best to have some specific scenarios planned for UAT, and perform them in addition to the parallel production-simulation model.

It's important to provide system training and the foundation of an operations guide to the UAT team because the system will be different from what they are used to, and you don't want them to be floundering while trying to learn the ins and outs of the new system. And it's equally important for the UAT team to understand that "different" does not necessarily equal "worse". No one likes anything that will slow them down in their job functions, but until the users learn the ropes of a new system, it will always feel like they can't work as efficiently as they could before. The question is, once the ropes have been learned, will the system be better than what they know now? If not, that's grounds for unhappiness and probably ought to be addressed.

Finally, the UAT score needs to look at the system as a whole, not just a particular facet of it. I attended a meeting during which the users just lambasted a certain piece of system functionality we had designed and built in. It was evil, it curdled milk left in the same room as the server, it was too many mouse-clicks and keystrokes, it was a huge step back from their legacy system, and we all know how bad *THAT* was! Finally someone – I wish it had been me – asked, "Well how about the rest of the system. Is it any good at all?" And the users talked for ten minutes about how great it was, how it streamlined their jobs, how they could get information they needed that they could never get before, and so on. But boy, this one piece of functionality was really awful. So can we call this a "win" overall? Well, sure, I guess…

PERFORMANCE TESTING

The system has to get the right answer. It has to be usable. It can't break the rest of the IT ecosystem. And it probably has to be big and fast and powerful as well. That last bit is judged in performance testing. The usual routine here is to put in all the real production data, plus a bulked out bunch of duplicated transactions and payees, and run the system to see if it will finish processing inside the window available.

It never does on the first try, by the way, but this is not necessarily cause for alarm. The implementation team will tune up their code, and the ICM vendor will likely toss out a few ideas about optimizations that can be performed. Sometimes it really is impossible to get the job done in the allotted time, but that probably won't come as a surprise – the implementers will probably have been putting out warnings and red flags about that from the early days of the project when they began to realize what they were up against. If that has not been a recurring theme during the project, then tuning both the application and the configuration to hit the processing window is just part of the normal give and take of the project.

I don't want to trivialize this; it is critical that the system perform, and perform well. But at the same time, you don't want to try to squeeze every drop of performance out of the system configuration until you know roughly how much more performance you're going to need to squeeze out. We always design and build for processing efficiency, but we don't really go nuts with it until we see whether we need to. If we take 14 hours to run when we have a two hour window, that's a source of concern and a lot of people will be sweating over it. But five hours for a two hour window? I bet we can add an index or two to the database schema and that'll take care of itself. If not, then we'll look hard at specific configurations. And actually, most ICM consultants have seen 14 hour runs drop to two hours with the addition of the right index. So I tend not to panic at the first couple of performance tests – unless the bits'n'bytes guys look like *they're* panicking.

Related to absolute processing performance, there is also the need to be sure the system will handle anticipated growth over the year / two years / five years. Not only will it receive its full load of monthly transactions, but depending on the system, it will also have to store 12 or 24 or however many months' worth of transactions along with them. There are database tricks that can be performed to enable these transactions not to clog up the works, but either way, IT is going to want to test the system to see if it can hit the window today and also in two years.

But let's be realistic about it, okay? I worked at a big European cell phone provider who gave us their anticipated growth requirements for performance testing. If you looked at them critically, you could see that the only way to achieve that level of growth would be to sell a phone and a contract to *every man, woman, and child in the country in the next three years*. Nice ambition, I like their self-confidence, but all the other cell phone providers in the country would probably question their ability to completely corner the market that way. So how seriously should we take that growth requirement?[54]

Another kind of performance testing that must be performed is load testing. The system is fast and accurate, but only 17 reps out of your 10,000-strong sales force can log in to read their reports at a time? That would not be good, not good at all. You probably ought to test for that. There are various applications and tricks out there to fool the system into thinking 1000 people are logging in. Consult your IT professional for the one you should test with.

ADDITIONAL REQUIREMENTS IN THE TEST PHASE

Sadly, the Test Phase is where we often see lots of new requirements as the customer starts running what we built through its paces and discovers that what they said and what we heard might well have been different. Or maybe it wasn't said at all, but someone should have asked. Or not. But this is where Project Managers start

---

[54] Hint: not very. But they still made us try to meet it.

developing ulcers.

I worked on a project where it turned out that the customer wanted the system to only pay positive deltas when a prior period was recalculated and a payee earned more than the original payment. If the payee should have earned less than the original payment when we recalculated, the system was required not try to recover the negative delta. This was discovered late in the Test Phase – like, right before the system was meant to go into production. The requirement was not documented anywhere because the subject had never come up during any requirements workshop or in any hallway conversation in the meantime. And here's a hint: that's something no off-the-shelf ICM system I have ever seen would want to do as part of its standard functionality. It takes real creativity to find a way to only pay positives but never recover negatives.

I will revisit this scenario later because it illuminates a variety of challenges. We cobbled together a solution for that new requirement, but it wasn't much comfort to find and deliver it late in the Test Phase, and honestly, the relationship between the customer and the implementers never recovered from it. We should have designed and built the system with that requirement in mind from the start, and we didn't. And it is now a question I always ask in the Requirements Phase.

So, how are we doing on project budget and schedule? Better call the SteerCo. Sigh…

DELIVERABLES

One deliverable is a thoroughly tested ICM system and set of processes that will completely support the customer's compensation operations for years to come. But there might also be a list of test cases and their pass/fail status, and a report from the defect tracking system showing cases raised, cases closed, and resolutions. If the totals fit inside the agreed upon milestone definition, we're good to go to put this baby into production!

Deployment Phase

So how do we take a test system and turn it into a production system? That's a slightly trickier proposition than it appears to be on the surface. The main issue is data – both reference data and transaction data.

TEST DATA VS. PRODUCTION DATA

While we are developing and testing the system, we are populating it with test data – data that looks the way we need it to look in order to generate results that we can check. While it's possible that we take ongoing feeds from source systems, both of transactions and reference data like payees, and plan data like Territories and Quotas, this is not a common approach since it creates a moving target with respect to validating results. In fact, while we talked about a Gold Copy of system configurations like plans and data feed logic, there might well be a Gold Copy of reference and plan data that is maintained as well. This data, with these configurations, will generate this set of known-good results when we run the smoke test.

But time marches on, and the reference data for the company is changing while we are testing. So we need to remove all the stale test data from the system and seed it with the right amount of accurate data for the day the system goes live. The easiest way to do that might well be do load the Gold Copy of system configurations into a brand new schema, as many systems won't allow the physical deletion of data – the test data will always remain if it can't be deleted. Maybe that's not the end of the world, but it's something to consider when making deployment choices.

SEEDING HISTORICAL DATA

This is a topic that has brought projects to their knees in the final moments before going live, yet even experienced consultants will sometimes only schedule a couple of weeks at the end of the project plan for it. It needs much more time and thought than that.

It's the idea that the system must have some minimal amount of transaction and reference data in it before the system can go into production. Sometimes results data is needed as well. How much? However far back the system will have to "look" to calculate correct results in production moving forward, generally.

If you have plans based on full years' worth of quota, and you go live in July (assuming a January through December fiscal calendar), then you very likely need at least the reference and transaction data for January through June. And hey, guess what – if there are effective-dated elements of the plans, then the date-effectivity of the source data must be honored. I can't just take the snapshot of HR data on June 30 and call it a day; I need to know what each payee looked like on any given day as well.

Do I need results data too? If I have plans that need to know how the payee has done year-to-date, then yes, absolutely. Some ICM systems won't actually allow you to import results – they have to be calculated by the application. If you are using a system like this, then you need to configure the system as if it were live in January and then run the calculation engine to populate results. Bad enough, but you also have to validate them. This is time-consuming, to say the least.

Okay, then how about we seed the payee's results with a single transaction per metric per month, quarter, or year-to-date to let the system "calculate" the historical results? Good idea, and a commonly used strategy. If you are lucky, you won't need to build plans that will be able to read the transaction and populate the results you need. If you're not lucky, based on plan complexity or calculation logic, you will need to create separate historical data seeding plans to populate results your "real" plans can pick up. And incidentally, if you have plans based on "rolling number of months" results, this becomes extra tricky. It's not insurmountable, but you need to think it through.

Will the prior periods ever be revisited due to Plan, Quota or Territory changes, or even due to late arriving data? If so, then the one-transaction-per-metric strategy might not work, or it might require some delicate surgery to make it work.

For these reasons, among others, it is often the simplest plan to go live on January 1 (for calendar-year oriented companies) to avoid the whole historical data problem. But that leads to an issue we alluded to before: you are running your legacy system on this year's plans, but configuring the new ICM system with your best guess at next year's plans. This makes parallel testing extremely challenging.

I think it's usually easiest to go live at the start of the second fiscal quarter. You are using the same plans on the old system that the new system will be configured with, but there are only three months' worth of results to populate. And in addition, that makes a great parallel test period.

The real point of this section is that historical data seeding cannot be left as an afterthought. It must be planned for from the Requirements Phase onward.

HISTORICAL DATA VS. ARCHIVING

Let us not confuse historical data seeding requirements and design with archiving requirements. A common requirement for financial data is that it must be stored for seven years. This does not mean that it all must be loaded into the new ICM system. I have had customers ask for it in the interests of being able to retire the legacy system and have an elegant repository for all comp data. But the considerations in the above section all still pertain. However you might want to do it, validating seven years' worth of synthetic results based on date-effective source data from systems that might not be able to provide it is at least a year-long project on its own.

DELIVERABLES

The major deliverable is a system configured with the plans, rules, data, and results (if applicable) representing the state of ICM processing and operations as of Day One – the day the system will go into production. Data feeds are hooked up and working, and report configurations are ready to feed the reporting mechanism.

Go-Live Phase

Technically, we're ready to go. We've tested everything, we know it works, or if it doesn't work, we know what to do about it. The data is clean and pristine. The systems folks are ready to support whatever comes up. So why are we so afraid to flip the switch and go live? Because it's a big change, and big change is always scary. But let's be brave and do it.

Data feeds flow in, we calculate results, we report them out to the payees, and we send feeds to downstream systems. It's probably not going to be a seamless cutover because there will always be new processes and ways of doing tasks that are different from the way we did them in the old system. And doing things in test systems is never quite 100% the same as doing them in the production system. And heck, I admit it – bugs that weren't caught during testing will arise. We hope they aren't big ones that involve logic changes.

For this reason, it is not uncommon to keep a skeleton crew of implementers nearby to make sure nothing gets dropped, any hiccups are addressed quickly, and otherwise perform a service that we highly-technical types call "hand-holding". It's just common sense to have them available for a period or two. What you do not want to do is keep them there for months or years afterward.

It's sneaky how that happens. It might not even be something the vendor wants, though if you hire a consulting company to do your project, they're generally pretty happy to keep billing for their consultants. But it might be the customer side making it happen. You plan a small Phase Two of the project to tie up loose ends. You bring another business unit on board. You make some plan changes you want the consultants to build for you. There are always new reports to write. And somehow, those guys just never seem to leave.

There is a concept called **Managed Services** that it taking off in the industry to provide this extended operations engagement. For a price, the vendor or the SI will provide a body or two to help keep things going by working side-by-side with Tammy and her team. ICM vendors who provide a hosted or SaaS delivery model provide a form of Managed Services by default: they keep the lights blinking on the machines in the background. They usually are willing to have a dedicated person or two support business operations as well. Managed Services should generally be a conscious choice, though. You don't want the realization to slowly dawn on you after a few months of being afraid to send the consultant home that this is actually an accidental Managed Services engagement.

Organizational Change Management Phase

The Organizational Change Management Phase really runs for almost the complete duration of the project. It's not a milestone on the timeline as much as it is an ongoing process. It includes training for the project team early in the project, payee training at the end of the project, and process change tasks that run all through it.

USER TRAINING

The users of the system – Tammy and the Comp Team primarily, plus IT support – must be trained early enough in the application to be useful to the project, but not so early as to forget everything they have learned when they finally get their hands on the system. Training usually begins with the vendor's "vanilla" training classes so the users can learn how the system thinks – how it's laid out – and what the words used by the system mean. A good time for this is during the Design Phase. At this point it would be impossible to offer customized training because the system hasn't been built yet.

As more users come on board during the Build Phase immediately prior to the Test Phase, customized training is an option for those vendors and SIs who offer the option. This kind of training is generally based on the standard training, but it sits on top of the customer's implementation and will often include specific tasks that the customer must perform. Custom training is a wonderful way to demonstrate exactly what the users will see when they log in, but it comes at a price, and not just a financial one. Developing this kind of training materials is time consuming and requires input from the implementation team to be as complete and accurate as possible.

PROCESS CHANGE MANAGEMENT

We talked about trying to make your systems and processes more rational in the **BUSINESS CONSULTING & ORGANIZATIONAL CHANGE MANAGEMENT** section a few dozen pages ago. That flavor of OCM was a more strategic concept. It was all about proactively changing the way you do business operations before the project starts, then making that the foundation of requirements moving forward. That idea is very valuable and ought not to be neglected. But even if you haven't made willful changes to the way you operate, the adoption of a new system to replace an old one (or an old non-system) will necessarily introduce some new ways of doing tasks, and introduce some new tasks as well.

Planning for this during the project is critical. Going live with a new system with no idea how to operate it is a recipe for unhappiness. As the system is designed and built, the **Operations Manual** for the new system must be developed as well. The Ops Manual is the instructions on the back of the box to help users navigate and get the best of the system. It is often in the format of step-by-step instructions for performing specific tasks.

I mentioned in the **DESIGN PHASE** section that the Logical Design Document – the LDD – could be a good foundation for the Ops Guide. It may not allow a cut-and-paste generation of the Ops Manual, but it should at least provide the outline of tasks and the logical approach for performing them. If customized user training has been created and delivered, it too can be leveraged in the creation of the Ops Manual.

PAYEE TRAINING & COMMUNICATION

At some point you are going to spring the new ICM system on the payees. As long as the checks are right, no problem, right? Well, not exactly. For one thing, they'll be using the new system's reporting functionality, most likely, and so they'll need to know where to look for it (which might be in their existing portal, or might not). You might be offering the payees the ability to raise disputes and queries from the system, rather than from phone calls to Tammy's team or by way of emails. They need to understand this mechanism as well.

And finally, there will almost certainly be minor variations from the legacy system in the way the new ICM system calculates, no matter how well we agree on and design for the comp plan processing requirements. It could be minor rounding "errors" depending on whether we multiply (A * B) and then divide that by C, or whether we divide (A / C) and then multiply by B, which might be something the system does better one way or another.[55]

Or it could be a situation where the new system actually calculates the plan rules accurately for the first time in years, and the overpayments the sales reps have come to expect stop. That's always embarrassing, but it is a great

---

[55] I've seen a VP of Sales call the Comp Team to complain about a $17 "rounding error" on a high-four-figure commission check when the new system went live. Sales guys care about accuracy. When it's in their favor, anyway. Which is why they always maintain their own spreadsheets and check every result out of the ICM system. Shadow accounting is rampant in the sales world.

ROI for the Finance folks. But this is another reason to keep the sales folks in the loop about the upcoming system and the ways they will interact with it.

To that end, some SIs, vendors, or customer PMOs have Communications Specialists who plan an information campaign to alert the payees to upcoming changes. They also provide end-user training for the payees about the logistics and their future interactions with the system. They will sometimes create contests to try to involve the payees in the system more. Sneaking verbiage into a comp report offering a $50 gift card to the first ten payees to call and say they've seen it is a trick companies have used to increase **adoption** of the new reports.

ADOPTION

It has taken me a long time to come around to the concept of adoption of the ICM system. It seems to me that once the payees have cashed their first checks, adoption is complete, *sir yes sir!* You might as well talk about adoption of a Payroll system. As long as the check clears, I'm fully bought in no matter what the system is.

But there is more to it than that, so I have grudgingly come to accept the idea that the company and its payees need to commit to the new system, and vendors need to be concerned with this and proactively address it in their customer relationship efforts. From the company perspective, this means bringing as many of their payees onto the new system as possible as soon as practical, rather than trying it out for a small group now, adding a few payees later, and maybe that country's Sales Ops after that. If the system works, it will probably bring with it economies of scale and reduced errors, and the sooner everyone is on board, the better.

For the payees, it means the conscious choice to use the system's reports, rather than continuing the practice of shadow accounting. This is especially critical where different systems provide different views of sales data with different filters and rules. Payees have been known to cherry-pick the reports from their favorite systems to make their numbers look as good as they can, then use their own calculations to beat up Tammy. Hey – it doesn't cost them anything to try, and if it works, then it's free money. So having the payees buy into the idea that the new ICM system is the source of truth about sales crediting and compensation data is a key factor in getting people focused on selling and not disputing commissions.

Vendors often will ask customers to shut off payee access to reports and systems that provide unreliable data, or data that will lead to disputes because it isn't in synch with the data the ICM system is using. The sales guys complain – "That report is the only place I can get the customer contact's wife's favorite color – *it's mission critical!*", but it really does increase the ROI of the new system to keep everyone looking at the same source data if it doesn't actually remove something the reps need.

A Note on Agility

Let me preface this section by saying that I am a fan of the **Agile** method of doing system development. I have friends who preach it, I have worked in organizations that practiced it, and I believe that it is a great tool – for certain kinds of problems. But (and you could probably sense that this was coming) I don't believe ICM projects are the kinds of problems for which Agile development can work effectively.

Here is a brief oversimplification of what the Agile methodology is in case it is something new to you. I described the standard ICM project methodology as a waterfall, one in which requirements lead to design which leads to the build which leads to testing, all in a well-defined sequence. Agile rejects the idea of monolithic "phases" of a project. Instead, it embraces the idea of constantly producing working code all through the project. The project is divided into two-to-four week long "sprints", during which the developers take a small piece of the problem and build a solution for it from soup to nuts – from requirements gathering to building to testing to documentation. At the end of each sprint, there is more working code. There is no Requirements or Design or Build or Test Phase: every sprint and every task includes all of those things.

What Agile is designed to do is to prevent a year-long project from reaching its conclusion with every piece almost, but not completely, complete. In Agile, at the end of a two-week sprint, there are a bunch of small but complete bits of functionality. Again, this is horrendously oversimplified, but it's beyond the scope of this book to present the methodology to you, and there are many online resources you can use to learn more.

Why don't I like Agile for ICM projects? Because it is *the mass of requirements that inform the design of the system*. Not having a full bore Requirements Phase means that the system requirements come in piecemeal – depending on how we break out the tasks, we might not know all the requirements for even a single bit of plan logic until several sprints have come and gone. And as I pointed out in the DESIGN PHASE section, an ICM system design for anything other than a small, simple system is based on balancing contradictory system qualities to come up with the one that is best, or at the very least, is the least worse. I can't make the determination of whether I have come up with a high-performing, flexible, robust, accurate system until I know *all the Weirdness*, not just a piece of it.

This is not a theoretical quibble, by the way. I've never done a fully Agile project, but I have done projects that were broken up into phases without taking the full set of requirements into account. And on one such project, a requirement we heard in Phase Three completely and irrevocably invalidated a fundamental design decision we made in Phase One a year before – one that could not be changed, and on which the entire system depended. Lawsuits ensued.

The reason I bring this up is because I have had the request to plan projects on Agile lines from various customers and even from vendor Sales and Services management. And I always have to push back to do it in a more traditional way. Again, Agile is a very cool tool, but you have to use the right tool for the job. I love my electric screwdriver a lot, but it's the wrong tool for driving a nail. And it's certainly the wrong tool to cut a 2x4 to length.

If you are absolutely determined to use Agile methods, I would strongly urge a hybrid approach: A full (traditional) Requirements Phase, followed by at least the Logical Design, if not the Physical Design as well. Then break the Build and Test Phases down into Agile sprints.

Yeah, yeah, I hear it a lot – I'm a dinosaur, I don't get modern technology and trends, I am over the hill. Fine. But do it my way anyway.[56]

---

[56] And *get off my lawn, ya little hooligans!*

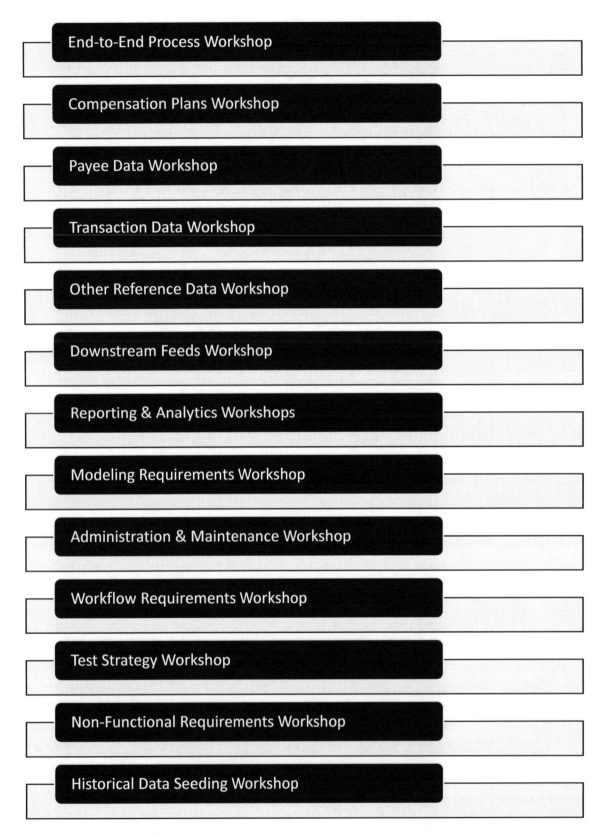

Figure 38 - Requirements Workshops

Requirements Phase

- Requirements Specification Document

Design Phase

- Logical Design Document
- Physical Design Document

Build Phase

- Working System
- Unit Test Status
- Assembly Test Status

Test Phase

- Integration Test Status
- Functional Test Status
- User Acceptance Test Status
- Performance Test Status

Deployment Phase

- Clean Day-One System
- Historical Data Seeded

Go-Live Phase

- Working System
- Post Go-Live Support

Organizational Change Management Phase

- User Training
- Payee Training
- Communications Plan

Figure 39 - Project Phases & Deliverables

CHAPTER SEVEN – ICM FUNCTIONAL CHALLENGES & ISSUES

This section will be a potpourri of some of the more challenging requirements that crop up on ICM implementation projects and in variable compensation in general. I'll try to illustrate them the best I can, but the problem with these things is that they make perfect sense to the company doing them and are completely incomprehensible to anyone else. But there are a few common themes, so maybe you'll recognize something you do and give some thought to why it might be making your variable comp life harder.

Every off-the-shelf ICM application has its unique strengths and weaknesses, so what might represent a challenge in one might be cake in another, and vice versa. I will be trying to call out challenges I think are fairly universal, but I will almost certainly miss something specific to whatever system you are implementing.

Transaction Processing

WHAT TRANSACTIONS DO WE BRING INTO THE ICM SYSTEM?

Every transaction on which someone might get credited and paid, of course. But what if the plans change next year? Maybe this year, we don't pay on Professional Services engagements for Rugalator installations, but next year's plan includes a 1% commission for all Pro Services revenue.

To make the system fast, we want to only process transactions that matter to us. Filtering out non-commissionable transactions is just good common sense in system design. But in ICM, it can be limiting.

It might be possible to make your ETL process for importing transaction data "**data-driven**" – maybe by providing a table that the users can manage to determine which products should be included on transactions that will be read by the query that pulls data from the Order Management System. Or you might just say, import everything and let the system churn through the mass of noise to find the good ones. You might want to do that anyway so you can have all of your revenue available for analytics, rather than just commissionable revenue. What you end up doing will be dependent on a lot of factors, so there's no cosmically "right" answer. But you do have to think about it before you can say your design is complete.

TRANSACTIONS AS AGGREGATED SNAPSHOTS

Many companies in the **Pharmaceuticals** and **Life Sciences** space don't actually track orders and shipments themselves. They use data from a centralized clearinghouse that provides a snapshot of the rolling 12-month period sales of specific products to specific locations – doctors, hospitals, and pharmacies. The products have a lifecycle that involves sales and returns over time, so the numbers for a given location can fluctuate over time.

Logically, the (oversimplified) feed might look like this for a particular product and location during the first week of August:

Product X Sales to Location 123		As of		07 August							
Month - 11	Month - 10	Month - 9	Month - 8	Month - 7	Month - 6	Month - 5	Month - 4	Month - 3	Month - 2	Month - 1	This Month
100	78	86	95	88	75	63	99	102	89	108	23

Figure 40 - Pharma Sales Data Feed Example 1

A week passes, and the feed for this product and location combination might look like this:

Product X Sales to Location 123		As of		14 August							
Month - 11	Month - 10	Month - 9	Month - 8	Month - 7	Month - 6	Month - 5	Month - 4	Month - 3	Month - 2	Month - 1	This Month
99	79	82	91	88	76	64	93	101	90	104	34

Figure 41 - Pharma Sales Data Feed Example 2

Most ICM systems expect to see sales data representing actual events – the plusses and minuses for each individual order taken and sold or returned. The view of the world we see in the Pharma space is an aggregation of business over time. What this means systematically is that we must artificially break the totals down into transactions. The way we do that is to build a preprocessor to compare today's snapshot of data with the last one we got, and do the subtraction to come up with the delta representing the change since the last snapshot.

It would be tempting to just take the total of all 12 months and do the subtraction, but life is seldom that easy. Pharma reps change sales territories like I change shirts, so we need to be sure that we credit (or debit) the correct rep based on when each owned the territory. This also indicates a fair amount of reprocessing prior periods. And some companies just give the current rep all the good and bad from prior periods on the assumption that it will usually come out okay in the wash.

This snapshot view of sales transactions is similar to the **Travel** industry, where cruise and resort reservations are in a constant state of flux. We don't see individual transactions for reservations made and cancelled; we see the current state of who is in which stateroom on which ship on which cruise, and which travel agent made that particular reservation. But there might have been three different customers in that room since the last snapshot.

Sales Crediting

ROLLUP & OVERLAY

The difficulty of managing and describing territories aside, most of the challenges we run into in sales crediting revolve around overlays: moving credits from the original credit receiver or receivers throughout the organization. We expect the direct rep's boss, and the boss's boss, to receive rollup credit. But when it needs to flow over *here*, then over *there*, but only sometimes up to that part of the organization *if it's a promotional product*, and then to this team *if it's a large deal*, the complexity of the implementation has increased significantly. And you have to wonder whether the company is getting a good return on investment of its compensation dollar by the time everyone gets paid for the sale.

The issue here is really more about best practices in sales comp, which we will discuss further in the next chapter, than it is about implementation. It comes down to how much each payee receiving credit actually did to influence the sale. If the answer is, "Not very much, but that's how we pay our people", then maybe it makes sense to rethink the comp plans. Incentive compensation is about directing the behavior of the payees. If the payees' behavior didn't make additional sales happen, then the incentives aren't incenting anything.

CREDIT SPLITS

There is one behavior that presents a special systematic challenge: the **credit split**. If everyone on a team gets X% of every credited transaction – in other words, a split based on rules – that's one thing, and ICM systems can do this kind of thing more or less well depending on the system and the circumstances. The credit split based on a percent that is determined per deal, though, that's something else. If there's no way to know that two (or more) reps split a deal based on information on the transaction or on their comp plans, and if there's no way to know what percentage of the deal each rep should get based on the data, then you are in the position of (potentially) having to look at every single transaction and compare it to your (non-systematically maintained) list of credit splits to know how to credit each transaction.

There are ways to handle this in the various ICM systems, but none that I've seen is particularly elegant. The credit split data may well be easily maintainable by the users, but the processing is inefficient because there's no way to know which transactions to ignore. Ideally, you don't want to perform a lookup or any logic on any object that doesn't need it, but there's no avoiding it when we don't know which transactions will have splits and which won't. If performance is not a concern, then this doesn't matter, but if you are trying to squeeze the system for speed, it is something to consider.

A workaround might be to let the system credit the direct rep in whose territory the transaction falls, then let the Comp Team manually split the credit after processing, rather than trying to find a way to force the crediting engine to do the job. Technically it's the same amount of manual intervention – we still need to tell the system that the credit for OrderID123 needs to go to Mary (50%), Sue (30%), and John (20%), but we just make that determination against the original credit rather than putting it into a table for the crediting engine to use. But every ICM system is different, so do what works best for your requirements.

BLUEBIRD DEALS

Many comp plans cap the deal size on which a payee can be compensated. If a sales person makes a cold call to just the right person who happens to have just the right requirement and a huge budget, a huge deal might result that really had nothing to do with the rep's skills or effort – it's called a **bluebird** in the sales world. Great for the company, sure, but the incentive you pay could well be ridiculously high.

While in general I'm not a big fan of capping payments in any way, I can see the point of this practice. I just think it has to be handled well. It should be communicated clearly in the comp plan terms and conditions, then the capped value must be set as fairly as possible. The capped value should be high enough to make the payee still want to keep selling for your company, but not so high that the rep can stop selling for the rest of the year.

Systematically, it's strictly a matter of creating or adjusting the credit value, regardless of the transaction value. And operationally, it's a matter of budgeting a couple of hours to listen to the rep whine about how unfair life is. Put up with it because the deal was valuable to the company.

Aggregation

In general, ICM systems don't have much trouble aggregating revenue or other performance metrics after sales crediting for a payee. Assuming the credits are defined well enough to be trusted to represent the payee's performance, then adding it all up isn't a challenge. Of course, if it is impossible to know for sure which performance events to measure for a payee, so you give credit for more than the payee has done in the hopes of filtering it out later, then the aggregation stage is where you would have to do the heavy lifting to not count unearned performance. But this is not a situation I have seen very often.

MULTIPLE POSITIONS IN PARALLEL

Where aggregation can be a challenge systematically is the situation in which payees hold multiple positions at the same time. If the application wants to process at the level of the payee, and most do, that means processing at the "Mary" level. So what do you do when Mary holds the Sales Rep – Minneapolis job from January 1, 2013, but is also holds the Sales Rep – St. Paul job from August 15, 2013 in parallel with the Minneapolis engagement? If each job should be measured independently, this is something that might prove challenging for some ICM systems.

You can't just throw all the revenue into the "Mary" revenue bucket. The clock for revenue going into the Mary – St. Paul bucket starts in August, and the totals have to be tracked separately. There are workarounds – create several instances of "Mary", for one – but it introduces inelegant usages of basic functionality of the system.

ACCOUNT-BASED METRICS

The one place where aggregation is almost always a challenge is for metrics based on sales to a specific customer or named account over different periods of time. This is common in **Financial Services** and for some **High-Tech** or **Manufacturing** companies. In the **Health Insurance** industry, for example, a common compensation plan component is a sliding scale commission based on the total premiums for the rolling 12 or 24 o 36 months *for the specific customer or policy*. So this $100 premium payment is not interesting as an event in itself: it is only interesting because it makes up a rolling 12 month total of, say, $400.

The rate table for that might look like this:[57]

12-Month Cumulative Revenue Low Range:	12-Month Cumulative Revenue High Range:	Commission Rate per Tier:
	$500	10%
$500	$1000	8%
$1000	$1500	6%
$1500	$2000	4%
$2000		2%

Figure 42 - Cumulative Revenue Rate Table

ICM systems generally calculate aggregations and incentives at the payee level. The customer, as an object below

---

[57] Note that the rate goes down. In the Insurance industry, acquiring a customer is sometimes perceived as more valuable than getting a lot of revenue from any given customer. Descending rates kind of freaked me out the first time I saw them.

the payee, is a much more granular level than the system will operate. There are all sorts of cute ideas that people come up with to try to solve this problem inside the ICM system ("How about if we create every customer as a payee and then roll them up to the agents?" "Um, yeah, there are 1,000,000 customers. So, no."), but at the end of the day, it's going to be a preprocessor unless the customer has a way of providing the rolled up data from the Policy Admin system. Which they don't.

The frustrating part of this is that it makes perfect sense to compensate this way – no one is being unreasonable. It's just the classic case where the data coming in is incomplete (from the ICM system's perspective). When you ask the customer how they do it today, they tell you they get the answer from the 30-year-old COBOL system that the new ICM system is replacing. This eventually becomes a really large and heavily logical preprocessor.

COMMISSIONS IN THE CREDIT PHASE

This is really a solution more than a problem. If the amount to pay for a sale can be known at the time of crediting – say, a flat rate per Widget, with no variable rates based on attainment – it is generally more efficient to create a credit for the amount of the commission during the crediting stage, rather than breaking it out later during the incentive calculations. This is especially true if there are many different products, each with its own flat rate. While you could bucketize each product, and then multiply the number of each by its unique rate, that would mean creating a lot of objects – a measurement per product.

Some ICM systems allow you to put all the credits into a single bucket, then "look through" them to find the specific product each represents, but that requires you to look at each credit individually a second time. A principle in performance tuning the application is to *process each object as few times as possible*. Knowing that Model X19 Widgets are paid at $2.00 each, but Model B32 Widgets are paid at $2.10, and knowing it during the credit stage, it's easiest and cheapest to create a "credit" (actually representing a commission) for $2.00 or $2.10 earlier rather than later.

Incentive Calculations

This section is rich with Weirdness, but some of it will be a little challenging to describe, so I hope you'll bear with me. The culprit behind most of our case studies here is **non-linear calculations**. Non-linear commission rates are a standard part of many comp plans. The rate table, with a base rate up to 100% of Quota, and an accelerated rate over quota, is a perfect and common example (See Figure 21 - **RATE TABLE EXAMPLE**). ICM systems handle that well, in general.

NON-LINEAR CALCULATIONS

The problems come when you try to "**unmake the omelet**". By that I mean, trying to determine the value of a particular small part of the non-linear calculation. Let's imagine that you have:

- Annual Quota = $1000
- Base Rate of 5% (for all revenue under quota)
- Accelerated Rate of 10% (for all revenue over quota)[58]
- One order each month for a HypoWidget for $100 each, for a total of 12 orders = $1200

Your total commissions for the year are as follows:

- $1000 * 5% = $50
- $200 * 10% = $20

---

[58] Having two rates based on performance against quota makes the calculation "non-linear".

- Total commissions = $70

So far, so good. No problems yet. Until you ask what the cost of sales for the September order was. Well, in September, you were under quota, so we paid $5 in commissions on the $100 order (the 5% Base Rate).

How about the cost of sales for the November order? Well, you were over quota in November, so we paid $10 in commissions for that $100 order (the 10% Accelerated Rate).

So was the November business worth less to the company than the September business? We paid a lot more in commissions for the same amount of business, right? So we should chase more of the kind of order we got in September than we should business like the November order?

No, and this is a critical idea in incentive compensation that is not as well understood as it should be. *There is fundamentally no difference in the two orders*. And this is the important fact:

- *Neither order contributed any more or any less to either the revenue or the commission expense. Their value per unit is exactly the same for either side of the ledger.*

Without the September order – maybe you took vacation that month and didn't close any deals – we would have paid you only 5% for the November order since you would have been under quota. So the September order (and all the other orders during the year, regardless of when they came in) influences the November order's "higher" or "lower" commission amount.

The lesson to be learned here is that where there is a non-linear calculation, with different rates for different levels of performance against quota, every unit of performance (like, say, "dollar") that falls inside the quota period (the year for annual quotas, the quarter for quarterly quotas, etc.) contributes equally and earns equally. By paying more frequently than the quota measurement period, we make it look like there is different contribution based on when the deal happens, but that's just an accident of history. *Mathematically, it's all exactly the same*.

Why am I making such a big deal about this? A variety of reasons. First of all, this was a simple example. We will explore a couple more that are less apparent. And secondly, trying to artificially apply a commission value to a particular order is something that ICM systems have trouble with. It's not too bad the first time you run a period (though this isn't always the case either), but if you rerun periods with new orders or including clawbacks for cancelled orders, all of a sudden the values you have assigned to the individual orders change. This leads to disputes from the payees.

In our example above, what if you had the 12 orders for $100 we talked about, but in December the October customer debooks – they cancel the order because they don't like blue Widgets and that's the only color the HypoWidget comes in. So we clawback the commission. Since you are over quota at this point, your total revenue would be $1100, not $1200. So we would take back $10, since that's the Accelerated Rate.

"But wait!", you cry. "I was only paid $5 for that order in October!" True, but you have only contributed $1100 to the company, yet you have collected commissions of $70 for revenue of $1200. Your higher commissions later in the year were predicated on that order continuing to exist. We need to get you down to $60, so that's $10 you owe us. Now we have changed the perceived values of some numbers we have gone to a lot of trouble to report on. Numbers that were, essentially, meaningless to begin with.

Systematically, this also contributes to the perception that the new commission system stinks. Where payees can make an argument that they are being cheated and Tammy is stealing the food off of their children's feet, the sales folks will do what they can to make the numbers work in their favor.

Let's look at another example, the slightly sneakier one we discussed earlier in **CHAPTER TWO**. We pay a flat $1000 per Widget sold, unless you happen to be over your Rugalator quota. Then we pay a flat rate of $2000 per Widget for Widgets sold *after you exceed your Rugalator quota*.

It's now October, and you can see that you're about to go over your Rugalator quota. But you also have some Widget orders in the pipeline. You can bring those Widget sales home whenever you want to. But you will almost certainly wait until that pesky Rugalator deal finally closes before you bring write up the Widget orders. Why? Because if you wait until the Rugalator deal closes, you make more money. In fact, this might even include orders from September that you have been sitting on – it's called "**sandbagging**" in the sales world – just because you are pretty sure you'll get the Rugalator deal closed in October.

COMP PLAN:
Pay $1000 per Widget until Payee exceeds Rugalator Quota.
Then pay $2000 per Widget for every Widget sold after that.

It's October 1st.
George has sold 98 Rugalators against a Rugalator Quota of 100.

It's October 10th.
Blue, Inc. agrees to buy 5 Widgets from George.
If George sends in that paperwork, he will receive $5000.
But George is negotiating a deal with LimeGreen LLC
for some Rugalators. It makes him forgetful.

It's October 29th.
LimeGreen LLC buys 3 Rugalators from George.
George sends in the paperwork.

It's October 31st.
George "remembers" he has the Blue Inc. Widget Order.
George sends in the paperwork and receives $10,000.
Same order, but by holding it, George pockets an extra $5000.
Bad George! B-A-A-D-D-D GEORGE!!!

Figure 43 – Illustration of the Impact of the Order of Transaction Processing

This is bad for two reasons. One is that the company has to wait until the sales line up to your satisfaction before you will get around to placing the orders. This is revenue they are waiting for, and this is business they could be closing, shipping, and invoicing.

The second reason is that many ICM systems won't allow you to process the orders in an arbitrary sequence. They process the way they process, and it's possible that the sandbagged Widget orders will process before the Rugalator order does. So the ICM system would want to pay the lower rate for the Widgets, while the rep wants and expects the higher rate. Therefore, the system is lousy and we all hate it.

Adoption aside, the other issue with this is how we have to deal with system testing. If the order of transaction processing matters, then any hiccups in the test scenarios will show up as wrong results. A lot of effort will go into tracking them down. It is not always obvious to comp consultants who are new to the domain that they need to ask the question of whether it matters if Transaction 1 comes in before Transaction 2 or after it, so this can turn into one of those **ADDITIONAL REQUIREMENTS IN THE TEST PHASE** issues. There may be heroic measures that can be taken to get the system to process in the arbitrary order we're looking for, but you want to build for this, not discover it during testing.

QUOTA CREDIT VS. COMMISSION CREDIT

Many have been driven to madness by this one. It too is a non-linear calculation problem, but it has its own twist. It's the idea that we need to calculate attainment against quota to determine the commission rate using one metric, but pay commissions using that derived commission rate against the second metric. Some customers will call the measurement that retires quota "Quota Credit", and the revenue basis for paying commissions the "Commission Credit". It seems reasonable – I have had many customers ask to do it. And the first time you see it, you think, "Sure, that makes sense. Let me just figure out how to put it into the ICM system." And you start doing formulas and figuring out rules and checking scenarios, and you get the dawning realization that the math will break when you try to implement it.

Let's take a look at the kind of situation that will break it. Imagine this payee has an Annual Quota of $1M, a Base Rate of 2% for revenue under quota, and an Accelerated Rate of 5% for revenue over quota.

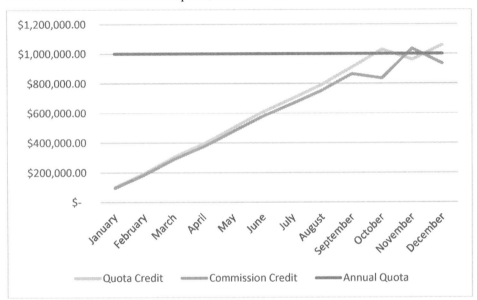

Figure 44 - Quota Credit vs. Commission Credit

From January through September, everything is fine. The Quota Credit measurement tells us the payee is under quota, so we would apply the Base Rate of 2% to the Commission Credit measurement value. The problem comes in October. Quota Credit goes up – it actually shows the payee exceeding quota. By the rules, I guess that means we pay the commissions at 5% (or at least, some portion of them). But the trouble is, the Commission Credit measurement went down for whatever reason – maybe a big order debooked. So do we pay something at 5%, recover something at 5%, or maybe recover the negative revenue at 2%. Or really, what?

Then the following month, the Commission Credit goes up over quota, but Quota Credit goes down, ending up under quota. Pay? Recover? And at what rate? And in December we have another situation where Quota Credit goes up and ends up over quota, while Commission Credit goes down. What is the system supposed to do here?

This is not a system or software problem. It is a problem with math. If the numbers can move independently of each other, then you could end up with a situation in which the expected result will be ambiguous. And the worst part is, if you do three months of parallel system testing before going live, you very likely won't catch this scenario since most payees won't be over quota in the first three months.

When customers insist on doing this, I show them these scenarios, plus one or two more, and I ask them to write the commission formula that I can just drag and copy under all of the scenarios that will do exactly what they want for each. I have never had a customer who was able to tell me exactly what rule or formula the system should always follow. If they pay this way today, it's usually using spreadsheets in which they can just decide of the amount to pay and type it in. But an enterprise system that wants to use rules and formulas can't turn on a dime like that. We need to know exactly how to handle it without human intervention. If the numbers can move independently, there are probably a half-dozen scenarios you could come up with that would put the outcome in doubt.[59]

GATES

This isn't so much a systematic challenge as a requirements definition challenge. "**Gates**" is a term used to describe the compensation plan requirement to not pay the Accelerated Rate (the "over-quota rate") for Product A unless revenue for Product B is also over quota. If the revenue for Product B is under quota, then you only pay the Base Rate for Product A. From a requirements perspective, that sounds pretty clear, but you have to ask all the right questions to be sure you really know everything that's needed. These include:

- If revenue for Product B is over, but revenue for Product A is under, do we pay Product B at the Accelerated Rate? In other words, does each product work as a gate for the other?
- If revenue for either product is over the sum of quotas for both products, does that get paid at the Accelerated Rate?
  If so, is it just Product A revenue being higher than the sum to earn the Accelerated Rate?
  Or just Product B revenue higher than the sum?
  Or both products?
- If we go over quota on Product A in August, but don't go over quota on Product B until October, do we make up the difference to the payee in October? (Hint: you have to hope the answer is 'yes'. The math gets Weird if the answer is 'no'.)
- Are there any timing factors?
  Reprocessing prior period factors?
  Common exceptions?

Any of the answers to these questions, with the possible exception of the last one, can be accommodated in most ICM systems more or less elegantly. But assuming the answer and building the system around it is very risky.

THE "50% ON BOOKING / 50% ON SHIPPING" COMMISSION PROBLEM

For a variety of reasons, many of them really good, it is sometimes desirable to recognize that selling has a lifecycle, and that the milestones in the selling process are good places to pay a portion of the sales reps' commissions. For example, you might want to pay half of the commission on booking – getting the order placed and some guarantee of payment by the customer – and half on shipping – sending the Widget to the customer, which might be delayed for weeks or months based on the way your business model works. Invoicing – writing an invoice to the customer, which usually means revenue is going to be recognized – is another milestone that might be part of the commission lifecycle. Returns or cancellations are other transaction lifecycle events.

This makes sense. If you have a sales cycle that can last months or years, the desire (from the company) would be to hold the commission until the customer's money is in the bank. But if the rep has to wait years for the commission, you would risk demotivation, possibly to the point of attrition. And the rep does need the money to

---

[59] In one case, the customer SME told me that the numbers never moved independently from each other anyway – Quota Credit always equaled Commission Credit in their company. So, uh, why are we going through this exercise, then? Choose one or the other and let's just get the attainment and the commission basis from the same measurement.

buy a new ski boat – a year or two is a long time to wait for that.

Of course the rep's desire would be to get paid for bringing in the order. This is good because it reinforces the good behavior – selling. The risk there is that the order could debook or change significantly over time. So now the rep has the commission money, and good luck getting it back if something bad happens. So splitting out payments serves a couple of purposes. It protects the company from the customer getting cold feet, and it keeps the rep actively interested in the order and in making sure it moves forward neatly.

There are a couple of challenges we face trying to make the milestone payments work in ICM systems:

- Reconciling events
- Determining the commission rate

Reconciling Events

For many companies (though not all), the milestone events come from different systems. Sales Order Management tells us the order was booked, while Fulfillment handles the shipment, Accounts Receivables handles the invoice, and who knows who handles any other events on which you might base payments. They don't always model the data the same way, with the same unique identifiers and with the same granularity of information. Sometimes they don't all agree on what the order is worth.

As we discussed in the **BAD DATA** section in **CHAPTER TWO**, Order123 from Sales Order Management tells us that $1M worth of Widgets were ordered. Funny, that order was forecasted for $1.3M in the CRM system – wonder what the disconnect was? Fulfillment tells us that $500K worth of Widgets were shipped to London on CustomerPO432, and $280K worth were shipped to Paris on the same PO. Where is the last $220K worth? We're out of stock on the SpaceWidgets. A/R tells us that $390K was invoiced on invoice number 847 (turns out that customer gets a 50% on shipping, 50% on approval deal).

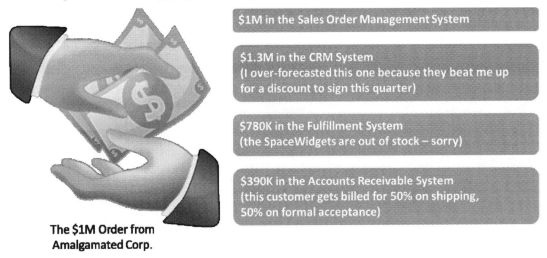

$1M in the Sales Order Management System

$1.3M in the CRM System
(I over-forecasted this one because they beat me up for a discount to sign this quarter)

$780K in the Fulfillment System
(the SpaceWidgets are out of stock – sorry)

$390K in the Accounts Receivable System
(this customer gets billed for 50% on shipping, 50% on formal acceptance)

The $1M Order from Amalgamated Corp.

Figure 45 - Reconciling Events in the Sales Lifecycle

Long story short – the first transaction that came in worked like a charm to get the rep 50% of the 5% commission on the $1M order, but from that point on, how do we even know that the later events are related to the first? Either the implementation team builds the preprocessor to manage it, or the customers already have one, but it's not a trivial task.

What Rate Do We Pay?

Assuming the existence of reconcilable transactions to tie business events in the sales lifecycle together, how do we know how much to pay for the second or third milestone? Remember all that stuff a page or two ago about non-linear rates being applied from one metric to another? If the rep happens to be over quota when this order is placed, but the rep's prior orders haven't been shipped yet, should we pay the under-quota rate, or the over-quota rate? Sez me, I think you should pay the under-quota rate because you haven't been able to recognize revenue on the earlier orders, but it's shocking – *shocking*, I tell you – how many sales reps and even comp administrators would disagree with me. Either way, unless every order ships for exactly how much the rep sold it for or every dollar can be recognized, there will be commission payments that might not be supported by the underlying revenue on which they're based.

My take on the mathematically acceptable way to do this, by the way, is to apply each dollar or unit for each event against the same quota value, then generate the commission times the milestone weighting. So if Sue books 110% of her quota, but only ships half, she gets her commission for the booking metric (times the weighting), and gets what she would earn for shipping (times the weighting) as a separate calculation that doesn't try to tie back to the original booking transactions.

SPIFs

SPIFs are tactical, surgical incentives to provide course correction mid-period, to act as sales contests, or to help get either hot new promotional items or obsolete merchandise off the shelves. SPIFs are usually tacked onto the comp plan, rather than being a defined part of it at the start of the plan period.

In its simplest form, a SPIF might consist of a flat payment amount per unit sold. If you go into a big box retail store and ask what the best DVD player is, the Knowledgeable and Honest Sales Person will tell you, "ZippyPhoton. Yeah, the ZippyPhoton (we call it 'ZP') is the best unit on the market. It gets great reviews. It's what I have myself!" So you buy the ol' ZP unit, and said Knowledgeable and Honest Sales Person collects a $45 SPIF for selling it to you. It turns out ZippyPhoton pays the store $50 per unit sold and the sales person gets some or all of it. Next week, when the ZippyPhoton SPIF has ended, MagiColor will be offering their own $60 SPIF for sales of their DVD players. Go in next week and ask the same question and see what answer you get.

A harder SPIF to manage is one where the first 50 units sold in the store earn the payee the SPIF amount. That is something most ICM systems won't do well right out of the box, though the right preprocessor can make anything happen – for a price.

Another flavor of SPIF is the extra bonus for hitting quota, or for hitting a special sales target during a period. That's easy or hard, depending on the rules and how the data is managed.

The point that should be becoming clear is that SPIFs are whatever Sales Management and Finance can agree on to goose the sales folk into making heroic efforts for a short burst of time. If your system has the data, it's probably not too hard to manage the SPIF. If you don't, or if it needs to be calculated at a different level than the ICM system wants to calculate (i.e., other than the payee), you might find it fiendishly difficult.

Companies that use SPIFs should provide the implementation team at least the most common varieties that have been used in the past and that are likely to be used again as supplemental functional requirements so the team can try to leave behind a system that can respond to any new SPIF[60] programs that come up.

---

[60] Oh, okay, I'll unpack the acronym, though I was hoping to avoid it. According to me, SPIF stands for "Special Product Incentive Fund". While I am happy to lay down the law on compensation term definitions, in this case, I have heard so many different definitions that even I don't have the arrogance to claim mine is the right one. In this case.

DRAWS VS. GUARANTEES

Fasten your seat belts. This section will arouse the ire of precisely 50% of the incentive comp practitioners because again, these are two words that no one agrees exactly what they mean. So we all fight like cats and dogs over our own interpretation. If only to bring the light of reason to the misguided people who use these words wrong, then, I will provide the Official Definitive Definitions as Handed Down by the Plenary Session of the Supreme Compensation Council.

Draw

A **draw** is a pre-determined *fixed payment advance* to a payee (e.g., $2000 per month). Regardless of how much the payee earns in calculated commissions, the draw is a separate payment. Sometimes when a payee is on draw, the company will not even track or calculate commissions separately.

It is usually only paid for a limited time (e.g., the first three or six months in a position. And it is either **recoverable** (the company collects it back from future earnings *after the draw period*), or **non-recoverable** (the payee gets to keep it.) Recoverable draws usually have a recovery schedule – it's not all recovered at once, but instead, might be recovered over several months.

Guarantee

A **guarantee** is a *variable payment advance* to a payee (e.g., $2000 per month). If the payee earns any money, the guarantee supplements it to bring it to the guarantee amount. If the payee earns more than the guarantee amount, no additional guarantee is paid that month.

It is usually paid for a limited time (e.g., the first three or six months in a position.) It is either **recoverable** (the company collects it back from future earnings *either during or after the guarantee period),* or **non-recoverable** (the payee gets to keep it). If the recovery is allowed to take place during the guarantee period, the recovery will generally not be allowed to take the payee below the guarantee amount.

Example: If Mary's guarantee amount is $2000 per month, and in Month One she earns $1400 in commissions, her Month One guarantee will be $600.

In Month Two, Mary earns $2400 in commissions. She owes $600 in guarantees from Month One. Her Month Two guarantee payment would be -$400. In other words, we would recover $400 from her, because that would still allow her to be paid $2000, her guarantee amount. If we recovered the full $600, it would take her below her guarantee amount to $1800. We would expect to recover the last $200 in the following month – assuming that didn't take her below $2000 in total payments. There might be a recovery schedule for guarantees as well – they might not be recovered in a single month.

Requirements Definition

Either way, the company wants to be sure the rep can afford gas for the car and a clean suit, so it is important to be sure some money is going out each month. The question is, do you just throw a lump sum at the rep now and maybe recover it later (the draw), or do you supplement the rep's earnings to bring it up to the minimum (the guarantee)?

Most ICM systems can be made to pay or recover draws or guarantees more or less neatly. The question is really, when the customer says, "We pay draws of $2000 per month", do you nod and smile and say you know what it means, or do you start digging deeper?

- Do they mean draw or guarantee? In other words, forget what I just told you – *what definition is the customer using for these two terms?*
- Is it recoverable or non-recoverable?

- If recoverable, what is the recovery schedule?

Some ICM products have "draws" and/or "guarantees" built into them as predefined domain functions. This seems like a good thing, and is, as long as the functionality matches the customer's requirements for it. Otherwise, the consultants will have to build it into the comp plans using standard calculation functions, rather than the spiffy domain-specific functions.

COMMISSIONS IN THE INSURANCE & FINANCIAL SERVICES INDUSTRIES

There's a book waiting to be written just about commissions and bonuses in the insurance world.[61] From an ICM perspective, they present some unique challenges. They can be solved, but they do require some creativity.

Insurance agents could be either **captive** or **independent**. Captive agents can only sell the products from a single carrier, whether as employees or as exclusive agents. Calculating their commissions is a little less complicated. Independent agents, on the other hand, can sell any carrier's products. So the carrier is not necessarily trying to get the independent agent to sell more of its products, per se'; they are really trying to get the agent to choose *not to sell its competitors' products*. So while it's kind of the same as selling more, it's also subtly but importantly different.

The Contract

The contract is the foundation of the relationship between producers and broker-dealers or carriers. It defines the products that can be sold, the hierarchies of agents to agencies to broker-dealers to the carrier, and it defines the commission rates to be paid based on a bewildering number of dimensions (product, state, age of policy, age of insured, the producer's role or level, plus no doubt a couple more) that must be populated in lookup tables.

For a given contract-product-state -age of insured combination for a new policy, the table might look something like this:

Level	Rate	Role
20	105%	Wholesaler
19	100%	Wholesaler
18	95%	Broker-Dealer
17	90%	Broker-Dealer
16	86%	Broker-Dealer
15	82%	Broker-Dealer
14	78%	Broker-Dealer
13	74%	Broker-Dealer
12	70%	Agency
11	66%	Agency
10	62%	Agency

---

[61] Actually, it's called the Requirements Specification Doc – the RSD – and it gets written on every project.

9	58%	Agency
8	54%	Agency
7	50%	Agency
6	46%	Agent
5	42%	Agent
4	38%	Agent
3	34%	Agent
2	30%	Agent
1	25%	Agent

Anyone else freaked out about how high the numbers are? Carriers might not make a penny – in fact, will most likely lose money – on first year policies. The rates go way down for years 2 – 10, and they drop even lower on years 11 onward, which should tell you that insurance companies take the long view on the value of their customers. And the other thing to understand, and this is very important in ICM terms, is that a given commission is the rate shown *minus the commissions paid for levels below the payee's level*.

So let's assume that Jill is a (level 3) agent selling through the Phil Agency (level 7), which sells through the Dill Broker-Dealer (level 13). If a policy premium is $1000, Jill gets $340. The Phil Agency gets $500 minus Jill's commission, or $160. The Broker-Dealer gets $740 minus the Agency commission, or $240. So the ICM system not only needs to know Phil's rate, it must also know how much Jill was paid.

That can be kind of a headache for ICM systems. When they are calculating Phil's commission, they don't necessarily know Jill's rate for that particular policy. And you can't just write Phil's plan to always subtract the level 3 rate because, if the policy was sold by Bill (level 1), the amount to subtract would be different. And don't forget – Phil can still sell directly himself, so there might not be a subtraction at all – he might collect the entire 50%, or $500.

A Grizzled Old Insurance Industry Veteran once tried to clarify this for me by telling me to look at the insurance industry as the original pyramid scheme – it's just a highly regulated multi-level marketing model. The negotiation agents and agencies do when they sign up with a broker-dealer or wholesaler is to get a contract rate table with higher numbers, or to come in at a higher level. These values – the rates and level numbers – will be used as long as they sell the carrier's products under that contract, which could be decades.

Annualization

For certain classes of products, some carriers will use **annualization** rules to pay commissions for sales of new policies or financial products. When the product is sold, the producer will be paid a commission on the total anticipated premiums or contributions for a year (or half-year or two years, or whatever the producer's contract specifies). So if Jill sells a product with monthly premiums of $100, she could be paid a commission upfront for the total of $1200 – the annualized value of the policy. Life is good for Jill, but meanwhile, the carrier wants to be sure that the premiums for the policy are actually collected. So the premiums are tracked, and in "**Month 13**", the total is trued-up to the annualized value for which Jill received her commission a year ago. If the total is less, she gets dinged out of future earnings, and if it's more, she gets another little something.

Now, I was being a little disingenuous when I said the premiums for the policy are tracked. That's more theoretical than actual – there aren't really a lot of systems that do it, and the new ICM system is replacing the ones that did it. So this requirement becomes a job for the preprocessor you were hoping not to need.

Payment

Payment is something else most ICM systems do well. Actually, it's kind of their job. Even rerunning and repaying prior periods – most ICM systems handle the task of only paying or recovering the difference in incentive calculations pretty well.

UNMAKING THE PAYMENT OMELET

This is very similar to unmaking the incentives omelet with respect to aggregated and non-linear calculations. If I have to determine your payment amount by combining various metrics and incentives, don't then ask me to break the payment out into different G/L codes based on products and geography – please! On the other hand, people do ask for this. If they can show me the math they want to use to break out the ledger accounts, then I'm happy to do it. But I won't make up the math myself. The exception to this rule is when we pay a flat rate per unit – then I won't be quite such a jerk about it.

PAYMENT CAPS

A **payment cap** is what it sounds like: it is the maximum a payee can be paid during a period. Companies will institute payment caps to cover themselves if they write their plans wrong. They don't want some rep to get a $17M payment because someone didn't think through an incentive component completely.

That's the (almost) reasonable reason for caps. In some cases, it is just executive ego: the VP doesn't want any reps to make more than he or she does. In 99.9997% of cases,[62] payment caps demotivate payees and cause them to stop selling. This is a Very Bad Thing. It often makes the best sales reps quit and take their skills to another company that doesn't cap payments.

Systematically, however, it isn't usually very hard to configure and administer. But if you are a comp consultant, tell your customer that, sadly, the new ICM system can't handle caps, darn the luck. You will be doing them a favor. Sure, *the sales guy said*, but no.

Data Integration

THE "TOO MANY ATTRIBUTES" PROBLEM

Okay, it's mainly a problem for me, but boy, is it a hot button issue where I'm concerned. I'll just lay it out for you straight:

- **Ol' Unka DK's Only Law of Data Exclusion:**
  The *only objects*, and the *only attributes*, that belong in the ICM system are those needed for *crediting*, *commissioning*, *reporting*, or *researching compensation*. The *ONLY* ones.

Every piece of data you import into the ICM system has a cost – maybe a minuscule one, but a cost. That cost is primarily about keeping it in synch with the system of record from which you got it. If the value of an attribute can change, you must be diligent about reconciling the source system with the ICM system to keep the ICM system up to date as the source system changes. If you don't, one system will have information that conflicts with the (allegedly) same information in the other system. You have now created a situation in which one system

---

[62] As determined in a very scholarly study, the name of which escapes me at the moment.

is not to be trusted. For me, the risk of introducing contradictory data into multiple systems, and therefore, the cost of keeping them reconciled, is far too high to justify bringing in data that isn't really needed in ICM.

I usually hear four flavors of data or attribute need. My default response varies according to the flavor:

- "We need it and we use it for XX and YY."
  Okay, you may have it. With my compliments.
- "We might need it sometime. We used it last year (or have plans for next year) to do…"
  Okay, I'll think about letting you have it.
- "We might need it sometime."
  For what? **Hint:** if you have to thrash around to come up with a scenario ("We need Payee.FavoriteStarWarsCharacter because, um, we might have a contest – yeah, a contest! And the award might be, um, an action figure! That could happen!"), then the answer is 'no'.
- "We don't really need it, but what the hey, the source system feeds it to us."
  No.

DATA INTEGRITY WITH UPSTREAM SYSTEMS

We touched on it a little bit in the section above, but where data comes from a system of record elsewhere in the enterprise, we must always be certain that the data is in synch in both systems unless there is a really compelling reason why they shouldn't be. But absent such a compelling reason, you never want information in two trusted systems to be in conflict.

Most ICM systems have user interfaces that allow the Comp Team to modify or adjust data in the system. So what happens if the HR system sends me a record for Gloria with Payee.IQ set to 128, but I have sound compensation reasons for going into the ICM system and adjusting it to 131 based on information received from a non-HR source? Maybe her bonus is dependent on it. But now I have ICM and HR disagreeing on what Gloria's IQ is.

The ideal solution is to communicate the new information to HR, have them update it there (they are the system of truth about the payees, after all), and then have them send a corrected record to ICM. Sometimes that's not practical, so the next best thing is to make sure that any data changes in ICM are communicated back to the appropriate source systems. The upstream might not be able to do anything about them, but you at least have to try. The worst case is no communication of changed data, and both systems storing different values.

Incidentally, there are operational reasons to worry about making changes to data in ICM. One is, the next time we see the feed from HR, it will have Gloria's IQ at 128. It will appear to be "wrong" in ICM (how can the feed know that we changed it intentionally?), so the feed will want to overwrite the ICM record to bring it in line to the "correct" HR data. Unless the data integration consultants plan for situations like these in their data acquisition routines, we will be in a constant state of the Comp Team changing values and the systematic feed overwriting them with the values in the source system. It can be worked around, but you need to have the possibility in mind when architecting a solution.

Reporting & Analytics

FAKING ANALYTICS

Before ICM vendors started including analytics packages as a standard offering, and when the only people who could figure out how to do business intelligence wandered around in cloaks and pointy hats with moons and stars on them, the next best thing (according to the customers, anyway) was to have the system calculate every permutation of every result across time and across products. The reports would pick up these non-compensation metrics and put them out where the Finance folks could get them to do their own trending and forecasting.

Great, sort of. Except that it destroyed the performance of the system to calculate tons of results that weren't needed to compensate the payees. This is less of an issue now that the ICM vendors have all seen the light that analytics is a huge part of the ROI of the ICM system implementation. But it still sometimes slips into operational reporting requirements that the customer would like us to do a quick pivot table of products by geography by commission amounts by revenue. You know, in our spare time. Without an analytics tool in the toolkit, that means doing the calculations during incentive processing. If all you have is a hammer, then everything looks like a nail.

It all comes down to using the right tool for the job. ICM wants to calculate commissions and bonuses and to report on the numbers that go into them. It can do more, but there is an operational cost to it. And honestly, the system won't be as flexible and powerful as an analytics tool would be. Use the right tool for the job whenever possible, and in this case, the ICM calculation engine probably isn't the right tool.

HEAVY LIFTING IN THE REPORTING STAGE

I fairly firmly believe that reporting should be a presentation of information created by the ICM system during its incentive processing. If you have a lot of math and logic in the report definitions, it probably means that you have a lot of complexity in the plans that didn't fit into the functionality of the application, or bad data that needed another phase of massaging, or both. If the report is the last and only place you can get to a result, then so be it – you gotta do what you gotta do. But ideally, the report should be about putting information in front of people, not about creating that information.

REGULATORY REPORTING IN THE INSURANCE & FINANCIAL SERVICES INDUSTRIES

As we've discussed, these industries are very highly regulated, and part of the regulation is about reporting. There are standard reports that must be generated on a regular basis for the producers (the payees), their customers, and the government. The problem is, the regulations aren't very clear about how some of these reports are supposed to be defined.

Take non-monetary rewards, for example. Insurance carriers and broker-dealers like to show the love to their best producers and agencies – lavish trips to warm places for selling a given amount of our product every year, or even just tickets to a Lakers game or a nice dinner. It's just a way to keep agents or agencies who could sell any carrier's products focused on selling ours, y'know?

Yeah, great, except that there are reports we've got to generate, including how much we have rewarded a given producer for each piece of business they have generated for our products. *So how do I account for the basketball tickets?*

This exact conversation has taken place, down to the specific words and inflections, dozens of times in ICM projects for insurance companies:

- Increasingly Desperate Customer (IDC): "So, your product can handle non-monetary rewards?"
- Wary & Wily Consultant (WWC): "Of course!"
- IDC: "And how does it do reporting for them?"
- WWC: "Any way you would like! You just tell us."
- IDC: "We'd just like the usual kind."
- WWC: "Oh, there are lots of usual kinds. How would you like it to be reported?"
- IDC: "Uh, maybe just the way your last customer did it."
- WWC: "Gee, that's customer-confidential, so why don't you just tell me your reporting requirement?"
- IDC: "Oh, just report on them the regular way."

- WWC: "Sure – we'll just do it the way you're doing it now. And how do you do it now?"
- IDC: "I don't *know*! *Please, just tell us how to do it! I beg of you!*"

The trip or the dinner or tickets could be just divided equally by the number of policy holders, or each policy, or pro-rated for total commissions earned per policy, or pro-rated for face value of the policies, or maybe in a half-dozen other ways. No one is really sure. [63]

Incidentally, tax reporting is the biggest regulatory report of all. And that gets challenging in the insurance space, where companies merge and consolidate over time, and where so many agents are independent. Back in the BAD DATA section we talked about the challenges of reconciling the identities of producers who are represented differently in all of the various legacy systems. Now imagine that you have one agent selling your products by way of contracts to multiple companies you have acquired – John H. Smith vs. J. H. Smith vs. J Henderson Smith vs. JS Associates, etc. The total commissions for each version of that producer might come to less than $600 per year, but combined, they might be well over that. And at $600 per year, the carrier is required to send a 1099 form. This isn't an ICM system problem. It's a source data problem, and the cost of solving it is huge.

Modeling & Forecasting

Modeling and forecasting in your ICM system will be as accurate and easy as the particular application you install. And they're all different – have I mentioned that? – so I don't want to go too far down the path of making prescriptions and pronouncements about what you'll need to do to make modeling work. I will raise a couple of philosophical points about the practice for your consideration. You can jettison them if they don't work for you.

ICM IS A PRODUCTION FINANCIAL APPLICATION

I like using the software for modeling and forecasting, but I don't like using the production system for it. First of all, the systems are generally under a processing time crunch – it's just a fact of life in our domain that we always need to make it go faster than it wants to go. So adding artificial data and processing to an already stressed system just opens the doors for conflicts where Finance needs an answer yesterday but so does Payroll. So on that practical foundation, I'd rather see modeling or forecasting happen in a **sandbox** environment (e.g., DEV or QA) whenever possible.

And also with regard to artificial data – this is the system of record for an important financial metric for the company. Putting forecast or plan modeling data into the system means you have introduced known falsehoods – your models – into your source of truth. The ICM system might well be architected to segregate the fake data from the real data – it's not terribly difficult to do that, if you do it thoughtfully – but it's still fake data and it's still living in your ICM system. This may just be one of my hot buttons and any right thinking person would know that I'm over-reacting. But it gives me heartburn, and therefore I always recommend performing this kind of activity in the sandbox.

MODELING HUMAN NATURE

ICM is all about changing payee behaviors to better align them to the company's strategies and goals by way of… well… bribes, really. But we call them incentives to make it seem more professional. So when you model a new comp plan component or different rates, the data you use to model doesn't exist in a vacuum. If you are using this year's sales to see the cost of a new bonus to the company, you might well be missing some important considerations.

---

[63] I hope these regulations have been clarified since the last projects I've done in Financial Services. But they hadn't been as of then and I haven't been able to find out for sure.

I had to parachute in to visit a customer who had called the vendor I worked for to say the comp plans weren't working. They sold service contracts, among other things, and had decided to bump up the rates for sales reps who brought in multi-year, prepaid contracts. So the sales guys did – on every deal. So was the system calculating wrong? No, it was getting the right answer. So what was the problem? The problem was, their model for the new incentive had shown a much lower commission expense – the plan was broken. They'd modeled using last year's data, and there weren't nearly as many multi-year, prepaid contracts last year.

So yeah, now see? From my perspective, the plan was working like a charm. They'd incented the reps to do something, and by golly, they sure did it! *Incentive comp worked!* They had just modeled badly.

I think there are three levels of comp plan modeling skills when evaluating a new component or different commission rates against current year sales trends:

- Level One: Using this year's data *as-is* to determine incentive expense;
- Level Two: Using this year's data, but *bumping up or bumping down a given metric to reflect the additional (or subtractive) value of the new component or rate*;
- Level Three: Using this year's data, bumping up or down the metrics to show the impact of the new component, *but also bumping up or down other metrics to show the different mix of behaviors that the new component will introduce.*

To illustrate, imagine that ConGlomCo pays a high commission rate for sales of Widgets, and a low rate for sales of Rugalators. The Rugalator business is pretty stagnant, so let's bump up the rate to see if we can increase sales. Great plan, but what will be our expense exposure?

The Level One Modeling Craftsman takes this year's data and commences modeling. "We will likely sell 100 Rugalators at $1M each this year. We pay 2% currently, so our expense this year will be $2M. We could bump the commission rate up to 3%, so using this year's data, our new expense would be $3M, or a $1M increase. That's reasonable."

The Modeling Artist sees that estimate and says, "No, you have to do Level Two modeling because, with the new incentive, the reps will sell many more Rugalators. Let's figure they'll sell 1.5x as many next year with the new incentive than they will this year, or a total of 150 Rugalators. Revenue will be $150M, at 3% commission, carry the nine, divide by the square root, our projected next year expense will be $4.5M, or an increase of $2.5M. Probably worth doing if we can corner the market."

But the Modeling Ninja looks at that estimate and asks, "Ahhh, but what will this do to our Widget business? If the reps are working at capacity and are only selling 100 Rugalators a year, if they do sell more Rugalators, how many fewer Widgets will they be able sell? The expense is not just the commissions, but the lost sales of Widgets as well!" He bumps down the Widgets number and runs that model.

And the Modeling Ninja has one more insight. "McDivot Labs is rumored to be developing a Boson Rugalator. That could be a game changer. It might not matter what commission rate we choose to pay on our GigaRugalator – next year might well be a bad year to be a Rugalator sales rep in the marketplace."

It's an art form. No one is always going to get it right, if for no other reason than that those pesky sales guys keep bringing their own agenda to the sales process. We sometimes think incentives are the perfect surgical tool to drive behaviors with pinpoint accuracy, but they're not. So a new incentive might have no impact at all, or it might have an impact far beyond what we anticipate. But I think the one thing we can hold true is that this year's sales, generated under one comp strategy in the current state of the marketplace, will likely not be representative of next year's sales generated under a different comp strategy in a changed marketplace.

Exception Processing

THE HIGH COST OF EXCEPTIONS

Aside from the questions they raise about how serious the company is about its comp policies, exceptions also have systematic implications that should be thought about before granting them. There are really two that come to mind:

Ol' Unka DK's Ninth & Tenth Laws of Exception Processing:

- Manual exceptions must be planned for
- Systematic exceptions have a cost

Let's examine both problems individually.

Manual Exceptions Must be Planned For

"We'll handle that as a manual exception" is the get-out-of-jail-free card for implementation consultants. If the requirement can't be kept straight in anyone's head, and if there's no data to support it anyway, you'll usually hear that as the favored solution. And sometimes, a manual exception is exactly the way to handle a problem. If the users know what they want the system to do, but it would cost $200,000 in consulting fees to get the scenario configured in the system, it's cheaper and easier to let the users just plug in the right answer.

But sometimes manual exceptions are not the right solution. Sometimes, depending on the architecture of the application you are installing or the data issues surrounding the comp plans, there is no object in the system in the right place in the comp calculation that can actually be adjusted by a user. If the value that needs to be overridden is in the middle of a long chain of formulas and rules, some systems won't allow you to just go in and change that "2 * 3 = 6" into "2 * 3 = 7". *There might be no object that can be changed manually.*

We might need to change that formula to "(2 * 3) + **Offset** = 7", where "Offset" is a variable we set up for each payee with a default value of 0. And the Offset variable can be adjusted by the user. It's not necessarily an elegant solution, but it works. Most importantly, it needs to be designed in. "We'll handle that as a manual exception" does not necessarily get the implementation team off the hook – there must still be some design thought given to the solution. You have to ask, "How?"

Systematic Exceptions Have a Cost

Every customer wants the system to handle every predictable situation, and who can blame them? I want to do that myself. But there are costs to automating every single exception, and those costs are processing time and difficulty of maintenance. I'm going to give a goofy example here to show how processing exceptions creates an explosion of conditions to be checked – possibly more than you think there might be.

Imagine this rule I ought to make for my life but most likely never will:

- Walk to work every day.

Pretty simple, the system that is my brain knows what to do. But wait, there are exceptions. A common one is bad weather, so I should include it in my rule definition:

- If it's not sunny, drive to work.

Okay, fair enough. But I haven't really built the system properly. To handle the rain scenario, it should look more like this:

- If it's sunny, walk to work.
- If it's not sunny, drive to work.

But what if I have a lot to carry? It's my turn to bring in donuts and bagels today. I can't carry them walking, so I have to drive anyway.

- If it's sunny, and if I don't have a lot to carry, walk to work.
- If it's not sunny, or if I have a lot to carry, drive to work.

But I'm very green-minded, so I'm seeing a problem here. On Spare-the-Air days, I should take the bus.

- If it's sunny, and if I don't have a lot to carry, walk to work.
- If it's not sunny, or if I have a lot to carry, and if it's not a Spare-the-Air day, drive to work.
- It it's a Spare-the-Air day, and if it's not sunny, or if I have lots to carry, then take the bus.

I could go on, but I hope you're seeing the problem. It's not enough to add a rule or condition to handle the exception. You must also *exclude the exception condition from the normal case*. Add enough exceptions to the problem and you end up with something that looks like the tax code – a multitude of very detailed conditions about what must be true in order for the system to do something.

Note: This example implies a rule evaluation model that isn't necessarily how your ICM system will work. Perhaps you have a system that has rule precedence – the ability to process rule conditions from the most detailed to the least, and then stop once one of the rules is fired. Or perhaps you don't. What I want to get across is the explosion of conditions that must be thought about, designed for, built and tested if you decide to include every exception to the common case in your ICM system.

This explosion of conditions necessarily creates a huge maintenance burden. If you decide to change any of these rules to add or delete an exception (where does riding my bike fit in?), now you have to wander through every single set of conditions and unpack them to handle the change to the system. People forget or miss things, and then you end up with either gaps in the conditions, or overlapping conditions.

I worked on a system for many years in which *the second rule to fire won* when there were overlaps in conditions. You couldn't know which rule would process first – even from one run to the next. So you would end up with results that would appear to change randomly. It drove the consultants and Tech Support nuts. But that only came about when the comp plans were so complex that it was impossible to keep all the nitpicky rule conditions straight to manage the exceptions we had to code for.

And operationally, every rule or formula evaluation for every payee or every transaction[64] has a processing cost. It might be measured in milliseconds, but it is there. The more transactions or payees you have, the more those costs add up. If your system is struggling to finish processing inside a time window, a few milliseconds, times lots of exceptions, times lots of data, can have a measurable impact on how long it takes to process and might possibly be the difference between finishing on time or not.

By all means, when it is a "common exception", automate it. But when it is an "exceptional exception", consider the cost of implementing it versus finding a simpler way to get the job done.

THE "VENEER OF LEGALITY" REQUIREMENT

The "**Veneer of Legality**" is what I call the desire to make an exception look like it isn't an exception. I see it less often than I used to, but it's still out there in scattered pockets of ICM administration. It's the idea that the plan says we have to pay *this way*, but we want to pay *that way* in this particular exception case. So can we cobble together enough transactions and variables to make the answer come out the way we want it to even though it

---

[64] The two most common indicators for the processing time for an ICM system are the number of payees and the number of transactions. There are other performance factors as well, including complexity as we are discussing now, but in most ICM system, calculations happen at either the payee or transaction level.

wouldn't if we followed our own rules?

Again, it's incomprehensible to anyone except the company doing it, but I once had to deal with a situation where the Comp Team needed the ability to throw some extra money at specific payees at random times. Okay, fine, we'll give you the ability to upload manual payments, job done. But no, because every payment has to be reported as a commission that ties back to an order. But this payment has nothing to do with an order, right? Right, but we have to have one. So how about uploading a dummy order and having the system calculate the amount you want to pay the guy based on his commission rate? No, because that isn't a real order – it has to be an order that's in our Sales Order Management system.

Lots of backing and forthing later, it finally became clear that the requirement was to take a random order from Sales Order Management – not even necessarily one that the payee got credit for – and attach a commission amount for the payee directly to the order. This turned out to be tricky because the ICM software we were implementing was not architected to allow that. You couldn't force results like that into the system – it had to calculate them itself.

The core problem was that they wanted to do something "illegal", but they had to pretend the system was doing it "legally". The easy answer of just giving the rep some money would look like they were breaking their own policies, so they made a requirement to, essentially, hide the payoff. They smeared a Veneer of Legality across the thing they wanted to do.

In one thoroughly fascinating case, we worked with a customer who would figure out how much they wanted to pay each rep. Then they would go into the plans and change the comp plan formulas to get the pre-calculated results they needed. That was fairly mind-boggling. Usually the desire is to just create fake data that leads to the payoff the customer is looking for according to the plan that's in there. Sometimes the fake data isn't even hidden – the dummy transaction might just have an OrderID of "DummyTransation1".

Please – if all you want to do is give a payee some money, just do it. Please don't put bad data or reverse-engineered plans into the ICM system and then pretend the system calculated the result all by itself. Please?

PLANNING FOR DISASTERS

On about every third project I find myself in a conversation about the system needing to automatically recalculate every result by automatically deleting every transaction and every result and automatically reimporting all new copies of the transactions when the users push the panic button. It's always based on that planetary alignment of disasters that happened that one time two years ago when the upstream systems all hiccupped and sent bad data at exactly the same moment that the plans were changed retroactively midyear and someone accidentally kicked the plug for the server out of the wall and everything went black.

I totally get that that was a terrible time in the life of the Comp Team – they still bear the scars. But I can't design a system to automagically fix every problem that ever might happen. The next perfect storm of evil won't look like the last one, so whatever safeguards we build into the system won't respond to the new disaster properly anyway. Just take system backups regularly and restore as needed.

THE TWO MOST IMPORTANT QUESTIONS TO ASK ABOUT EXCEPTIONS

When I am presented with requirements for an exception or any processing logic that makes my head spin and that I know will bring the system to its knees if I put it into the plans, there are two questions I always ask:

- *How often does it happen?*
- *How do you handle it today?*

How often does it happen?

If it last happened two – no, three – years ago, and it happened once, and the situation that made it necessary to put it into the system no longer pertains, I usually try to avoid it, and I certainly will try not to have to find a way to automate it. If it happens 1000 times per month, and twice as often every month during the fourth quarter? It's probably unavoidable, and it probably needs to be automated if the system is to provide value to the users. Something in between those extremes? I have to lay out the cost of designing, building, and testing the system to meet the scenario, and then try to guide the customer to the right answer (sez me).

How do you handle it today?

This is a big one. I sometimes get requirements that wrap not only me, but also the SMEs giving them to me, completely around the axle. So I ask how they do it today. And I sometimes get back, "Well, we don't. We were hoping you could find a way to do it for us." Maybe the reason they don't handle it today is because it can't be handled – maybe the data doesn't exist, or the maybe outcome isn't well defined for every possible state of the scenario.

I'm willing to try to make the system better for the users – actually, I kind of like it when I can. But sometimes a bad situation is a bad situation, and the new system doesn't have functionality to guess what is supposed to happen. It's always worth a try to ask, but if you can't see a way to do it now, then maybe one doesn't exist.

CHAPTER EIGHT – BEST PRACTICES IN INCENTIVE COMPENSATION

This isn't about how plans are put into systems; this is about what comp plans should do, and what they shouldn't. Interestingly, plans that follow best practices also happen to work best systematically, but I'm not writing this chapter to make my professional life easier. I'm doing it because bad plans make the ROI for your entire ICM program shrink, and not just the software part.

Every company, every industry, every division or business unit, yeah, they're all different. But there are a few ideas that seem to work, despite all of those differences. I'll put them here for you to pick from if you see ways to make them work for you. I can't and won't give you a recipe for the perfect comp plan. All I can do is point you toward practices that increase plan effectiveness, and away from the practices that decrease it.

The Comp Plan Virtues

When designing compensation plans, here are a few goals to keep in mind. Think of these as **Ol' Unka DK's Comp Plan Virtues**:

- Comp plan metrics must be *aligned with company goals*
- Comp plan metrics must be *focused*
- Comp plan metrics must be *within the control of the payee*
- Comp plans must be *motivating*
- Comp plans must *not conflict*
- Comp plans *must not be used in place of management supervision*
- Comp plans must be *measurable*
- Comp plan goals, targets or quotas must be *achievable*
- Comp plans *must never demotivate payees from selling*
- Comp plans must *NEVER motivate payees to kill business*
- Comp plans should *pay as soon after the sale as practical*
- Comp plans must always be written to *recover incentives in the event that the business debooks*
- Comp plans must always be *clear and unambiguous*

Some of these are pretty self-evident. That is, they are until you try to write a comp plan, then you realize how easy it is to fall into the traps hidden in trying to motivate people to do things that might be in your best interest, but might not appear to be in theirs.

COMP PLAN METRICS MUST BE ALIGNED WITH COMPANY GOALS

The reason we pay variable compensation is to align the behaviors of the payees with the direction the company needs to go. This is fundamental to the domain. Rewards for achieving high performance should necessarily fall in line with the goals of the company.

If a company is selling a brand new product, possibly in a brand new industry, market share is most likely the most important thing for that company. Many companies would give away their product or services to collect new customers to add to the logo page in their corporate presentation. So that company should not even mention high revenue goals or profitability in its comp plans. Whereas a consulting company might well look at profitability as the most important metric. Every company has different desired outcomes, but the plans must reflect the ones that will most directly affect the financial future of the company.

COMP PLAN METRICS MUST BE FOCUSED

We have all seen comp plans with a half-dozen metrics tied together. The plan might include everything from revenue, to new customers, to margin, to compliance with sales procedures and timely updates to the CRM system. As a sales rep, what should you consider the priority? The answer always comes back, "All of them!", but humans don't work that way. You will make a decision based on what's easiest to maximize balanced with what pays the most, and you will disregard the rest.

One metric on a plan is great. Two metrics? Maybe... Three? I'm doubtful. More than three? The plan is probably too unfocused to be useful for driving behaviors.

COMP PLAN METRICS MUST BE WITHIN THE CONTROL OF THE PAYEE

As a payee, I must feel that I have some control over my financial future. If my commissions or bonuses are tied to something that is outside my sphere of influence, then my plan isn't about my behavior, it's also got a big "luck" component built in.

The classic villain here is the **corporate profitability** clause. I only get my bonus if the company achieves its profitability goal. So this year I leapt tall buildings in a single bound, was more powerful than a locomotive, flew faster than a speeding bullet, cured cancer, and was good to my mother, but the meatheads on Exec Staff decided they needed gold plated taps in the washrooms of the new corporate jet? And I didn't get my bonus because we missed profitability? Excuse me, but I have to start sending my resume out to companies that appreciate the work I do.

I was asked to give feedback to a company that did high-level consulting on their proposed comp plan for an Inside Sales Rep – an ISR. And all the metrics on the proposed plan had to do with revenue. I pointed out that this person's job was to find and qualify leads and hand them off for the sales people to close. Once the ISR got the appointment for the rep with the prospective buyer, everything after that was out of his control. The lead could be perfect, the customer prospect aching to spend a million dollars, but the sales person could screw it up. Revenue had no place on that plan because it was out of the ISR's control. Qualified leads were the only metric that mattered. Give the ISR a tiny piece of any deal as a bonus to be reward him for bringing in bigger, more qualified leads, but don't punish him if the sales folks can't sell.

Incidentally, this virtue also covers the case of payees getting rolled credit for transactions for which they didn't influence the sale. Getting paid for business the payee didn't have a role in bringing home is wasted incentive comp money – much as the payee might like it. My rule of thumb is, *if the payee didn't know a sale happened, then the payee shouldn't be compensated for it.*

COMP PLAN METRIC REWARDS MUST BE MOTIVATING

There are really two pieces to this. One is to understand the motivation – especially the financial motivation – of your payees. I've seen comp plans for high-priced sales reps, people who expect to bring home 5-figure commission checks every month that had "Update the CRM System Weekly" kinds of metrics that were worth, oh, easily several hundred dollars per quarter. Those reps wouldn't get out of bed for several hundred dollars, let alone change their behaviors to put their contacts into the CRM system when they're just as happy keeping them on their phones. On the other hand, a retail sales associate will absolutely notice a several hundred dollar reward, and might even ask if you want help hiding the body, at least if my experience in retail is anything to go by. Same money, very different results in terms of behavior change.

Which ties into the second piece we discussed – too many metrics dilute the value of all of the metrics on the plan.

THE BOOK ON INCENTIVE COMPENSATION MANAGEMENT

If the payee has a given amount of pay at risk that is managed by the comp plan, wasting some of the motivation of that pay at risk with what amounts to noise-level metrics means that the really important thing – revenue, new customers, or margin – is worth relatively less. The common benchmark being thrown around in the ICM industry is that anything less than 15% of total pay – fixed and variable – probably won't be much of a motivator. If the update-the-CRM-system metric is peanuts – far less than 15% of total pay – it's just noise. Don't hide the value you expect from the payee in a plan filled with either too many metrics, or metrics that will not drive actions.

Incidentally, sometimes **non-monetary** rewards work better than money. Sales guys can be incredibly competitive with each other. Tell them that the rep who brings in the biggest deal of the quarter gets to keep the pawn shop bowling trophy in her cube for the next quarter and they will sometimes fight each other tooth and nail to win. And a call center agent who gets to park in the "Agent of the Month" reserved space next to the entrance, or who gets her name on the plaque by the break room? That can be worth far more than the $100 bonus that might be on the plan.

COMP PLANS MUST NOT CONFLICT

This is one of the more challenging ones. You absolutely do not want metrics to conflict on a single payee's plan. An example of this would be revenue versus margin, or profitability. If revenue matters, then you lower your price on deals to bring in more of it. But that lowers your margin. If profitability matters, you might turn down deals that won't bring in a high enough margin. So having both metrics on a single plan might well make it impossible for the payee to perform well and optimize her commission check. Most people know not to put both on a single plan.

But what about plans for payees who interact with each other? If my metric is margin, but my manager's metric is revenue, my manager might well undercut a deal I'm trying to bring in to be sure he or she hits the revenue target. Our plans are in conflict.

I saw a similar situation once when working for the consulting arm of a software company. The consulting managers were being compensated on margin – making sure that all the Professional Services deals were at a high enough rate to make the business unit profitable. But the software sales people often needed our help to sell their products, and they were compensated on revenue. So they would come to us to ask for help with proofs of concepts for their customers or what have you, and our managers would refuse because it was counter to their plans. Eventually a VP would come along, slap our guys, and make us help the software sales people.

There were no bad guys there. Our comp plans measured and rewarded what we were told was the most important thing – margin. But that was in conflict with the product side of the house, whose sales folks were also optimizing the most important thing – revenue. Sometimes conflict is inevitable, but you should have ideas in mind for quota relief if the plans interfere with the business.

COMP PLANS MUST NOT BE USED IN PLACE OF MANAGEMENT SUPERVISION

The first place we see this in the ICM space is in comp plans that include administrivial metrics. I've made my views pretty clear on how effective I think that is. But increasingly, we are also seeing **pay-for-performance** – **P4P** – plans in the domain of Performance Management.

Performance Management is a fast growing and fascinating field. People are munging huge amounts of data to see how well their employees or agents are performing, and applying pinpoint coaching and support exactly where needed. Call center management is the bread and butter of this field, but really, any behavior that can be measured is a candidate. It's a small step to go from measuring to rewarding. Then it's a small step to expecting the rewards (or punishment) for the metrics to do your supervision. I am not a fan of this.

Firstly, the amount of pay at risk in plans like these P4P plans is usually pretty low, so the motivation factor isn't high. And sometimes people being paid for performance see the plan as a punishment for failing to achieve, rather than as a reward for achieving a high score. If all they get for hitting their targets is the pay they were receiving before they went on plan, you are likely just fostering resentment. Upside is key to making the plan into one that makes a payee want to overachieve.

You know your culture, you know what the expectations of your potential payees are, so you must decide who should be on a P4P plan. But my message has long been that *not everyone belongs on a comp plan*. You have managers and supervisors; they need to do their jobs of training, motivating, and course correcting their subordinates. Applying remote-management-by-comp-plan is an abdication of their responsibilities.

COMP PLAN METRICS MUST BE MEASURABLE

If you have a metric on a comp plan, there must be a way to actually measure performance. Seems obvious, right? So how come we sometimes see "Improve Customer Satisfaction" on the plan, but we don't have a mechanism in place to actually poll the customers to see how they feel? Maybe a great metric, but not measurable.

I worked for a Telco – a phone service provider – who wanted to pay its B2B – business-to-business – sales reps for new customers. But they didn't have a definition of what a new customer was, and they didn't have a way to identify them systematically. What the Comp Team ended up doing was looking at the logs of the installers to see if they could identify new service address and customer ID combinations, which they would then assume was a new customer. They missed a bunch, overpaid on a bunch of others, and mostly just made the sales reps unhappy. Again, it was the perfect metric for that kind of rep, but again, it couldn't be measured. The only two choices here are to either build or modify a system to track new customers, or to take the metric off the plan.

COMP PLAN GOALS, TARGETS OR QUOTAS MUST BE ACHIEVABLE

If you offer me $1M to sink 10 half-court free throws in 10 shots, I would certainly be motivated to try. But after I missed the first shot (if you've ever seen me on a basketball court, you know it's not a pretty sight), my motivation to try hard on shots two-through-ten would be pretty minimal. If I can't make my quota, I will only put enough effort into my job to avoid embarrassment or to satisfy my sense of professionalism. But my comp plan would end up limiting the work I do, rather than driving me forward.

I listened to some sales people commiserating with each other recently over the new comp plans they had just received. The plans called for them to sell in a quarter what they were used to selling in a year. There was not an ounce of motivation on display anywhere because they knew they were only working for salary at that point, not for commissions and bonuses.

Incidentally, "Stretch Goals" are fine. By all means, give the payees something to reach for. But it has to be a stretch from a reasonable baseline.

COMP PLANS MUST NEVER DEMOTIVATE PAYEES FROM SELLING

There are a variety of ways plans make payees stop selling. The most obvious one is the payment cap, which is almost incomprehensible to me as a plan strategy. Wind back the accelerated commission rate for selling over 150% or 200% of quota if you want, but if the rep is adding value and bringing in business, never tell them that they have earned all the commissions they will get this year.

Another sneakier way to demotivate, especially when the reps have some control over when business hits, is also related to the achievable goals idea. If it's October and a sales rep realizes he's not going to make quota this year, it's not uncommon for the rep to start slowing down the sales process for the deals in the pipeline. Why bring in these deals this year if the bonus won't get earned either way? Far better (in the rep's mind) to seed next year's business with these deals. Let's start the New Year off right with some revenue that should have been brought in this year. His incentive plan is incenting him to slack off and stop selling.

COMP PLANS MUST NEVER MOTIVATE PAYEES TO KILL BUSINESS

When does a plan go from just demotivation to actual sabotage? It doesn't happen often, but it's always a hoot when we see the situation. A year or two after I bought my house, I got a call from the friendly mortgage broker at my bank telling me that there was a better deal out there, no closing costs or points to me, how about stopping by and refinancing? My having paid commissions for mortgage brokers, it was obvious to me that the broker knew she would not be dinged for killing the old mortgage, and she would, in fact, collect a commission for generating the new one. This happens all the time when banks' systems can't tie the canceled mortgage with the new one. It saved me a buck or two so I was happy to do it, but the bank lost money on the mortgage and ended up paying a second commission for business they had already won a year or two before.

Another scenario I have seen is a bonus based on, say, percentage of booked business that is actually shipped or invoiced within a time frame. Mary got the customer to place the order, but for whatever reason, it won't be shipping before the end of the quarter. So Mary has her friend the customer cancel the order, then place it again at a more favorable time. Or maybe she tells them that the deal wasn't structured properly, so would they mind if she cancels and rebooks it – same price to them, same money, same PO, no problem. She'll lose the commission on the first order, get it back on the reorder, and then get the bonus for the next milestone.

The strangest case I ever saw was for a company that sold service contracts. It was very important to them that the contracts not be allowed to just expire at the end of their term – there had to be active closure of some sort. Ideally they wanted the reps to upsell – sell a more valuable contract to the customer. It was okay if they just got a renewal. But worst case, they wanted an active termination of the contract – an explicit "no" when it was time to renew. There was a bonus component to the plans that was based on the percentage of contracts that had a definite end – and upsell, renewal, or termination all counted equally.

The other interesting thing about this company was that they had a lot of turnover in their reps. So it became apparent to us as we built their plans that a rep who knew he was leaving could just call each of his customers to cancel their contracts. Even if 100% cancelled, the rep would earn the bonus. We pointed this out to the Sales Ops people we were working with, and collective gasps were deafening. That behavior had never occurred to the people who wrote the plans.[65]

COMP PLANS SHOULD PAY AS SOON AFTER THE SALE AS PRACTICAL

The analogy I've used on the past is that sales reps are like puppies. If you don't punish or reward them immediately, they won't associate the reward or punishment with the behavior that earned it. But sales reps don't like being compared to puppies, so just take that message away with you while I try to think of a less offensive analogy. If a rep makes a sale in February, and a check shows up in October, the rep might know intellectually that the sale is what earned the check, but it won't have as much impact as getting that check in March or April.

Incidentally, the ability to pay faster is one reason a lot of companies buy new ICM systems.

---

[65] This kind of thing is called **unintended consequences**. I find them to be endlessly fascinating. I'm kind of a collector of them.

COMP PLANS MUST ALWAYS BE WRITTEN TO RECOVER INCENTIVES IN THE EVENT THAT THE BUSINESS DOESN'T STICK

A comp plan must nearly always be about the value and performance a payee brings to the company. Bringing in a deal, then having the deal cancel, means that the value to the company is zero. You might have paid a commission for that deal when it came in, but that doesn't mean the rep has earned it. This seems pretty self-evident to me, so you can imagine my confusion when a customer tells me that *they don't want to recover commissions because the sales guys wouldn't like it*. Um… excuse me?

When we don't recover commissions when business goes bad, we end up with rewards that aren't supported by the revenue that was supposed to earn them. If we have non-linear calculations, there is the practical matter of figuring out how much to compensate the reps for new business when the existing attainment doesn't map to reality. And there is yet another place where the payees can get creative with the way they generate and report business to take advantage of the plans (see the GAMING THE COMP PLAN section). I cannot think of any reasons why it would make sense not to keep the commissions consistent with the revenue.

I have heard that there are some countries where it is illegal to recover, although I suspect that the plans could be written in such a way as to make it legal. Say, by specifying that commissions are *earned at the end of the plan year based on total committed revenue*, and that monthly payments are an *advance on earned commissions*, not commission payments themselves. But hey, I'm not a lawyer. I'm just a guy trying to figure out how to make the math work in the ICM system, and who is trying to pay the reps what they're worth, but no more than that.

COMP PLANS MUST ALWAYS BE CLEAR AND UNAMBIGUOUS

Remember those discussions we had back in the REQUIREMENTS WORKSHOP sections about completely nailing down what the comp plan requirements are? Every single one of your payees has the same problem. If the plan is complex, with interlocking terms and conditions and metrics that can be interpreted in various ways depending on which system you are looking at, and rewards that require an advanced degree in Fourth-Dimensional Irrational Number Theory to understand, then the plan cannot be followed and behavior will not be improved by putting a payee on it. If you have conditions built in where the order of transaction processing can affect the result, you will never get agreement that the plan is working.

In other words, lots of Weirdness cuts into the ROI of your incentive program. The payees should never have any questions about what is expected, what performance they should be optimizing, and how the math will work. If they do, you are wasting your incentive dollars.

Gaming the Comp Plan

Gaming the comp plan is the glorious tradition and the national sport of Saleslandia. No professional sales person would ever consider the possibility that the loophole that sneakily appears in the comp plan (when you look at it upside-down) (with a detailed knowledge of some gaps in the source data systems) (and a devious mindset) wasn't placed in the plan on purpose by the Sales Finance group for reasons of sales plan effectiveness and company success. So if the loophole is there, it would be wrong – nay, *criminal!* – not to take advantage of it. Because obviously the company wants us to, right? Only stands to reason.[66]

The fact that the intent of the plan is obvious is immaterial. If I can make a convincing case that the words were

---

[66] I've been admonished any number of times to stop making cynical remarks about sales people. I've even been given that directive as an MBO on my comp plans occasionally. I usually ask, "So you mean I am mistaken about them?" Well, no, but it isn't nice to say all those mean things and it hurts their feelings. Alrighty then.

open to misinterpretation, then I will do my best to misinterpret if the wrong interpretation goes my way. You can say, *"You knew what we meant!"* all you want, but a look of hurt innocence is my defense if I get caught. If I can make a sad, disillusioned little tear gather at the corner of my eye when I say, *"But the plan said!"*, so much the better.

A few months into a new plan year, the Comp Team will begin to see how the reps are subverting the spirit of the plan by following the cherry-picked letter of it. So new terms and conditions are created and applied to the next year's plan to try to close the loophole. But like the tax code, that opens up others. Eventually you end up with a comp plan that consists of a page and a half of metrics and rewards and 15 pages of T&Cs explaining what revenue is, what it isn't, what makes a payee eligible, and all the other legalese that makes comp plans such a pleasure to read by the fire on a cold winter's eve.

So here's **Ol' Unka DK's First Law of Avoiding Unintended Consequences**:

- *Write* the comp plans *"top-down"* – reflecting the company's goals and the desired behaviors. Then *read* the comp plans *"bottom-up"* – from the perspective of the payees, and with the payees' agendas in the front of your mind.

By this I mean, yes, make the comp plans reflect the company's strategy – that's the first comp plan virtue, and it's a key one. But then clear your mind of what you mean the plans to do and look at them the way someone interested in optimizing pay checks in return for the minimal amount of work would do. *Actively look for the gotchas*. Because believe me, the sales guys will spend most of Q1 looking for them too.

Ideally, you also know the limitations of the data and the systems that will be used to administer the plans. For instance, on a project at one Telco, we discovered that the source POS systems[67] could not tie a new contract opened at one store with the cancellation of that contract made at a different store. It's a safe bet the store personnel knew all about it. So if there was a sales contest, how often did store staff get their friends to buy a contract at their store on the last day of the month, then cancel it a couple of days later at a different store? Not saying they all did that, but you know some of them did. Keep that kind of system weakness in mind when reading the plan you just wrote (the sales associates surely will!), and maybe a few unintended consequences will rear their ugly heads and present themselves to you.

It's amazing how many companies don't seem to follow this law, but it's obvious that in many companies, no one has ever read the plans from the perspective of the readers. It's not only about unintended consequences, by the way. Sometimes the complete incomprehensibility of the plan pops out when you read it bottom up. It's just a good practice.

And hey – if you can find the oldest, wiliest sales guy and give him a grand for every loophole he points out for you, you'll catch the easy 80% right there. He's saving the sneakiest 20% for himself, of course.

---

[67] POS stands for Point-of-Sale. It is the retail systems used to track business. It is not a value judgment on the systems.

CHAPTER NINE – CONCLUSION & ROUSING CALL TO ACTION

Lessee, comp is hard, the words don't mean what the words mean, requirements matter, the math has to work. I think that's pretty much what I had to say about ICM. But I think maybe I've missed coming out and saying something important.

Everyone in the space has ICM system or operations horror stories to tell, Weirdness to wallow in, and a history of mind-boggling challenges we have faced. It's just part of the domain. The point I'd like to make, though, is that many of these issues come about because we – and I'm alluding to customers, vendors, and implementers in that "we" – inflict them on ourselves. We all fool ourselves about what's going to happen on the next project, and we end up running into every roadblock and pothole. But if we look at the situation without our rose-colored glasses on, we could head off a lot of the issues that make incentive comp such a corporate challenge. Then we could turn it into the smooth-running back-office function it was meant to be.

Smoothness and elegance will happen when the customer execs treat the function with the respect it deserves and the rigor it needs in order to work. Exceptions weaken the plans and make all systems more complex, so they should be granted only when they make the business work better, not just because it's easier than hurting the sales guys' feelings by following the rules in the plan they signed off on.

It will happen when vendors stop saying it'll be easy-cheap-'n'-fun to implement the system, just plug it in and you'll be paying out of it in minutes. ICM projects run longer than other comparable IT projects – they just do. You are not doing yourself or the customer a service when you estimate an 18-month project at 8 months. And customers – you are not doing yourself (or the more honest vendors) a service when you punish the ones who tell you the truth, and hire the ones who tell you all the sweet little… untruths… you want to hear instead.

And it will happen when implementers are more up front about what they can and cannot do with the system. They need to be more consultative with suggestions to make things work better when unsustainable requirements come up. And the customers have to at least be open to listening to those suggestions. Implementation must be a partnership.

I get a lot of flak in the industry because I do spend a lot of time (too much time) on the "ICM is hard" message. I do it because I haven't seen enough acknowledgement of that point. Only by understanding that there are problems to be faced can we then look to find the solutions for them that let us get down to dealing with the business problems. In other words, admitting there's a problem is the first step towards a cure.

In the meantime, if you have any sense of adventure, ICM is the most endlessly intriguing of all back-office systems and functions. In the words of a consultant I know who escaped the domain, and then came back intentionally, once you have dealt with ICM challenges, everything else is boring. When you think you have seen it all, every day ICM shows you something new.

And if you're a connoisseur of unintended consequences like me, it's often pretty entertaining.

Hey, look at that! We'll be landing in Australia in a few minutes! It was great chatting with you! Let's keep in touch, whaddya say?

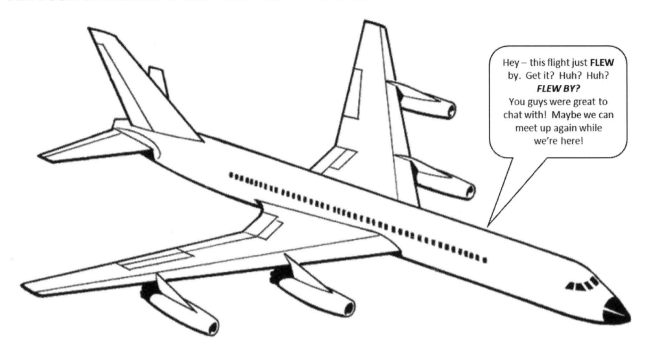

Figure 46 - All Good Things Must Come to an End

APPENDIX ONE – GLOSSARY

As stated ad nauseum throughout this book, human language is often insufficient to the task of describing the ICM domain. That has not prevented us from creating verbiage and TLAs[68] to add to the confusion. As I've used terms for which there might be confusion or ambiguity, I've tried to define them in this chapter. Because no one in the ICM world can agree on anything ("commission" vs. "bonus", anyone?), I'm sure that there will be grumbling over some of my definitions. But they'll at least do for a start, and should help clarify points I've made in the book.

Term	Definition
Accelerated Commission Rate (ACR)	The commission rate for revenue over quota for comp plan components based on attainment. Often expressed as a factor of Base Rate. Also called "Accelerators". Contrast with "Base Rate".
Accumulate Stage	The part of the logical incentive compensation calculation process in which Transactions are allocated to payees in the form of Credits. Compare to "Aggregate Stage", "Reward Stage", and "Pay Stage".
Agents	For purposes of this book, staff who are compensated by, but are not employees of, the customer company.
Aggregate Stage	The part of the logical incentive compensation calculation process in which Credits are "bucketized" into Metrics. Compare to the "Accumulate Stage", the "Reward Stage", and the "Pay Stage".
Agile Methodology	A project methodology in which short development cycles - sometimes called "sprints" are conducted with the intent of creating working software in every sprint. Contrast with "Waterfall Methodology".
Analytics	A presentation of data with a focus on numerical trends or relationships from the system. Compare to "Report" and "Query".
Application-Agnostic (or System Agnostic)	In techie language, written without reference or regard to the functionality of a particular system or software.
Attainment	Actual performance compared to target performance. Often expressed as a percentage. If I have a target (or quota) (or goal) to sell 20 widgets, and I have sold 15, I would be at 75% attainment.
Attribute	Part of the definition of an Object, often represented by a column in a database. ID, name, IQ, or shoe size might be attributes for a Payee Object.

---

[68] TLA – "Three Letter Acronym". Humans have a propensity to create three-word descriptors for domains and concepts, and then to just refer to them by their initials. "ICM" is a TLA. "TLA" is the TLA to rule them all.

Term	Definition
Base Commission Rate, or Base Rate	The commission rate for revenue under quota for comp plan components based on attainment. The standard formula for Base Rate is ((Target Variable Comp * Component Weight) / Quota)). Also called "ICR" (Incentive Commission Rate). Contrast with "Accelerated Rate".
Best Practice	Whatever works best to solve this particular problem. Might be the opposite of the Best Practice to solve tomorrow's problem.
Black Box Testing	Testing based on validation of final results without taking into account the internal logic of the system to determine root causes of any defects found.
Bluebird	A large sales deal that can out of nowhere and that was not a result of skillful selling.
Bonus	Incentive that is rewarded based on achieving performance conditions.
Boutique	An SI that specializes in one particular kind of project.
Bucketize	A linguistic abomination referring to the tallying of Credits into Metrics and generating periodic values of the Metrics.
Build Phase	The part of the project during which the design is implemented in software.
Business	Shorthand for the side of the house dealing with policies, procedures, Payees, Comp Plans and the like. Contrast with "IT".
Business-as-Usual (BAU)	The ongoing operations of the system or process in production.
But Your Sales Guy Said!	The source of many conflicts on ICM projects.
Child	A record lower in a particular hierarchy than the parent record being referenced. Compare to "parent"
Collaborative Build	A project performed by both the implementation team and the customer team working side-by-side during the Build Phase.
Commission	Incentive that increases incrementally with additional performance.
Comp Team	The collection of operations staff - business and IT - who administer variable compensation and who run the ICM system. See: "Tammy".
Compensation (Comp)	Monetary or non-monetary rewards for staff or agents. Compensation can include salary, commissions, bonuses, and recognition awards for high performance.

Term	Definition
Compensation Center of Competency (CCC)	The representatives of different parts of the organization who provide guidance and planning for ICM operations. Compare to "Steering Committee".
Compliance	Following the company's policies, the law, or the rules.
Component	The end to end logic and formulas to calculate a particular incentive on a Comp Plan. A Comp Plan might be made up of many Components.
Contingency	The fudge factor built into an estimate or contract.
Credit	The joining of a Payee and a Transaction. Payees might receive Credit for many Transactions, and a Transaction might be credited to multiple Payees. Compare to "Transaction".
CSV	Comma Separated Values. A data format that can be read by spreadsheets or loaded into database tables. Not pretty to look at.
Customer	For purposes of this book, the business entity acquiring, implementing and using an ICM system..
Date Effectivity	The "stateful" storage of data in the system. Date effectivity lets me ask, "What did this object look like at this point in time?" Contrast to "Snap Shot".
Day Job	The thing that keeps the customer project team members from committing 100% of their time and resources to the implementation project.
Debook	A sales order that is cancelled for whatever reason, though generally by the customer.
Delivery	The project team that will implement the new ICM system, as opposed to operating it.
Delta	The difference between the previous state of a calculation and the current one. If you were paid $250 in commissions for January, then the period was reprocessed and you should have earned $270 instead, the Delta would be $20.
Demonstration, or Demo	The display of the product to the customer. Nerve-wracking.
Demotivation	An unintended consequence of a bad Comp Plan design. When your ICM process convinces Payees that not performing is preferable to performing. Payment Caps are the most obvious one, but there are many ways to demotivate.

Term	Definition
Design Phase	The part of the project concerned with taking requirements and translating them into a system architecture that will support them.
Direct Credit	The sales credit generated for the rep or reps who most directly made a sale or were otherwise interested in an event.
Draw	A lump-sum payment to protect the sales rep during periods when earnings are expected to be low, such as the first few months in a position or territory. May be Recoverable or Non-Recoverable. Compare to "Guarantee".
Enterprise	The company.
Enterprise Architect	The person responsible for ensuring that the technical infrastructure for a company is sound and rational, and that all relevant systems play and share well together.
Event	An atomic occurrence that is relevant to the business and function of paying incentive compensation. See "transaction".
Exception	The bane of complex systems.
Executive Sponsor	The person on the customer side who "owns" the project, usually due to owning the budget that's paying for the project.
Finance	The generic name for the staff of the company responsible for crunching and analyzing the numbers.
Fixed Price	A project contract that sets a price for the entire project, payable on achieving milestone, regardless of the level of effort needed to achieve them. Contrast with "Time & Materials (T&M)".
Gaming the Comp Plan	Looking for the unintended consequences that will result in higher payments for less or no work.
Gate	A comp plan component that serves as a condition for higher rates for a second component. A Payee might not be allowed to receive overattainment rates for Widget Revenue unless the Payee is also over quota on Rugalator Revenue. The Rugalator Revenue attainment is the Gate for the higher rate for Widget Revenue.
Goal	A predefined level of acceptable or desirable performance. Often used in compensation calculations. See also "quota" and "target".
Gold Copy	A milestone system configuration known to be good. The foundation for the next set of development, which should theoretically generate the next Gold Copy.

Term	Definition
Guarantee	A make-up payment to bring a sales rep to a minimum level of earnings during periods when earnings are expected to be low, such as the first few months in a position or territory. May be Recoverable or Non-Recoverable. Compare to "Draw".
Handoff Phase, or Go-Live	The end of the implementation project. The time at which the customer begins to run the system in daily operations.
Hosting	When the vendor provides the infrastructure to run the software. Compare to "Software-as-a-Service (Saas)", contrast with "On-Premise".
Incentive	The reward dangled in front of the Payees to convince them that they should align their best efforts to company goals.
Incentive Compensation Management (ICM)	The processes and technology involved in calculating and paying variable compensation. Compare to "Sales Performance Management (SPM)"
Indirect Credit	Sales credits for payees other than the direct credit receiver. Compare to direct credit.
IT	Shorthand for the side of the house dealing with systems, data and the like that support business processes in a company. Contrast with "Business". It stands for "Information Technology".
Key (Logical or Physical)	A database term to describe the way a record in a table (or an object in "real life" is identified. Sometimes it's just an artificial record sequence number, but it can be a combination of fields that, together, form a unique ID for the object. HINT: for people, "name" is not generally a good "unique-ifier".
Logical Design	The "story" of how the system will be built. More application-specific than the requirements document, but showing pseudo-code rather than specific configurations and code. Compare to "Physical Design".
Managed Services	An ongoing consulting engagement in which the consulting provider operates the system in partnership with the customer.
Many-to-Many	A kind of relationship between objects in which zero, one, or several Objects can be formally linked to zero, one, or several other Objects. Many Payees might receive Credit for a single Transaction, and many Transactions might be credited to a single Payee. So Transactions and Payees have a many-to-many relationship. Compare to "One-to-Many" and "Many-to-One".

Term	Definition
Many-to-One	A kind of relationship between objects in which zero, one, or several Objects can be formally linked to only a single other object. Many Components might be included on one Comp Plan. Compare to "One-to-Many" and "Many-to-Many".
Metric	A class of performance for which a payee might be incented. It often represents a component on a comp plan.
Non-Cash Reward	Goods, services, or recognition rewarded for high performance.
Non-Linear	Any calculations that have rates that vary depending on performance. See "Base Commission Rate" and "Accelerated Commission Rate".
Non-Recoverable	For Draws and Guarantees, the policy of letting payees keep the advance, as opposed to having it repaid out of future earnings. Contrast with "Recoverable".
Object	A class of data, like products, transactions, or payees. Also, an instance of a class of data, often represented by a row of data in a table. "Payee" might be an object in the ICM system. "Mary Jones" might be a payee, and the "Mary Jones" record in the database is also an object in the system. Compare to "Attribute".
One-to-Many	A kind of relationship between objects in which a single Object can be formally linked to zero, one, or several other objects. One manager might have many subordinates. Compare to "Many-to-Many" and "Many-to-One".
On-Premise	Software bought, managed, and hosted by the customer in its own IT ecosystem. Contrast with "Software-as-a-Service (SaaS)" or "Hosting".
Operations Guide (or Ops Guide)	The user manual describing the specific operations a company will perform in the system. The cookbook for performing ICM operations left behind by the implementation team.
Organizational Change Management (OCM)	A project discipline concerned with defining a better "to-be" state - the future state after the project is completed, and helping prepare the customer's staff for the changes to their operational processes.
Overlay	A mechanism to provide indirect sales credits to payees in an enterprise. It typically uses hierarchies to determine the parent in a given relationship of the direct payee "child" record. Sometimes called "rollover" or "roll down". Compare to "rollup".
Parent	A record higher up in a particular hierarchy than the child record being referenced. Compare to "child".

Term	Definition
Pay Mix	The ratio between fixed (salary) and variable pay for achievement of exactly 100% of target, quota, or goal. Often expressed as a number pair that usually totals 100 - 90:10, 75:25, 50:50, etc.
Pay Stage	The part of the logical incentive compensation calculation process in which payments to payees are generated and managed. Compare to "Accumulate Stage", "Aggregate Stage", and "Reward Stage".
Payment Cap	The maximum amount a Payee will be paid during a period. See: "Demotivation".
Performance	Actual achievement against desirable metrics.
Physical Design	The detailed description of how the system will be coded or configured. Compare to "Logical Design".
PMO	Program Management Office. Or Project. Or Organization. The folks in the company who support large-scale projects.
Posted Payment	The finalized payment amounts that will be or have been communicated to Payroll or Accounts Payable. These payments are "written in stone", and from this point onward, new payments for the fiscal period will be communicated as deltas to the posted payments. Compare to "Trial Payment".
Preprocessing	Working with data to beat it into shape prior to the load into the ICM system for compensation processing. Any medium-to-large ICM system architecture will almost certainly need some.
President's Club	The carrot. And the stick. The trip to a luxurious resort awarded to the most successful sales people and selected others.
Project Manager (PM)	The administrative head of a project team. Often there is a PM on both the customer and the vendor side.
Project Readiness Consulting	A short engagement during with the implementers will assess the customer's level of preparedness for the upcoming project.
Query	A less formal presentation of data from the system via the user interface or by way of the database.
Quota	A predefined level of acceptable or desirable performance. Often used in compensation calculations. See also "goal" and "target".
Rate Table	The layout of commission rates, often as a function of Attainment against Quota.

Term	Definition
Recoverable	For Draws and Guarantees, the policy of having the advance repaid out of the payees' future earnings, as opposed to letting them keep it. Contrast with "Recoverable".
Redlines	Contract terms and conditions that are completely unacceptable, completely. Change this or this deal is dead.
Report	A formal, scheduled and formatted presentation of data from the system. Compare to "Analytics" and "Query".
Request for Information (RFI) or Request for Proposal (RFP)	Purchasing tools used by customers when selecting vendors. RFIs and RFPs are questionnaires about the product, the implementation, and the vendor company.
Requirements Phase	The part of the project concerned with gathering and documenting the full set of system functionality needed to support business operations. It may not be defined or documented in terms of system functionality.
Requirements Specification Document (RSD)	For purposes of this document, the complete set of system requirements. There are million different names for this.
Reward Stage	The part of the logical incentive compensation calculation process in which incentives are generated for the performance achieved against the metrics in the "Aggregate Stage". Compare to "Accumulate Stage", "Aggregate Stage", and the "Pay Stage".
Rollup	A method of providing indirect credit to payees. Generally, a manager will receive rollup credit from her subordinates. Compare to "overlay".
Rugalator	A product sold by ConGlomCo. Like a "Widget", only different.
S1P1	A system defect that brings the system to its knees and which must be fixed NOW! In other words, every system defect ever discovered.
Sales Finanace	The staff responsible for recognition of revenue and expenses based on the sales process. Often part of Sales Ops, often separate from Corporate Finance.
Sales Operations (Sales Ops)	The staff who support the Sales function at a company.
Sales Order Management	The generic name for the applications or systems with which a company enters and fulfills business with its customers.
Sales Performance Management (SPM)	The processes and technology involved in optimizing the corporate sales process. Compare to "Incentive Compensation Management (ICM)"

Term	Definition
Sandbagging	A time honored sales person trick. Holding orders until commission conditions are more favorable to the payee, usually as a result of poorly written or demotivating comp plans. See "Unintended Consequences".
Sarbanes-Oxley	A law created to strike fear into the hearts of financial folks everywhere. SarbOx, or SOx, requires that you have documented and auditable processes. The processes can be lousy, but as long as they are documented and you follow them, you are probably compliant. Before people understood that, fear of SOx sold a lot of ICM systems.
Shadow Accounting	When Payees don't trust the ICM system, they do their own ICM calculations to validate (or better, improve) the results from it. Shadow Accounting wastes a lot of people's time.
Silo	Tight segregation of groups in the enterprise, sometimes resulting in people working at cross purposes.
Single Point of Contact (SPOC)	A *nice* idea. Really. But not always a *good* idea.
Snapshot	The storage of a single view of an object: what that object looks like today. When data is stored in Snapshots, I cannot determine what the object looked like at any time in the past -even 5 minutes ago. Contract to "Date Effectivity".
Software-as-a-Service (SaaS)	A provider of software for which a customer might buy by subscription, rather than by way of "perpetual license" for On-Premise implementation. A cloud-based solution. Contrast with "On-Premise".
SPIF	It stands for "Special Product Incentive Fund". Or something else. At any rate, a SPIF is a short-term, tactical response to market conditions. It generally represents a short-term goal, plus the associated rewards.
Split, or Credit Split	Where more than one payee shares in the direct credit for a transaction. This reflects shared contribution to a sale, rather than rollup or overlay. Splits often, but do not always, total 100% of the transaction value.
State Machine	A tool that can be used for requirements gathering, design, and test case generation. A mindset.
Steering Committee	The representatives of different parts of the organization who come together to provide guidance for the project. SteerCos can be more or less active. More is better. Compare to "Compensation Center of Competency".

Term	Definition
Subject Matter Expert (SME)	The person who knows. Could be business or IT. The person the project staff goes to for information and requirements. But try to not think of a Dr. Seuss book when you say it.
Systems Engineer	The more technically-minded members of the vendor sales team. SEs typically run the demos and answer the hard questions.
Systems Integrator (SI)	Consulting companies that specialize in implementing systems. Typically SIs do not sell their own ICM product, but might build a custom system for a customer if desired.
Tammy	The legendary and possibly apocryphal Comp Team Lead.
Target	A predefined level of acceptable or desirable performance. Often used in compensation calculations. See also "goal" and "quota".
Temporality	See "Date Effectivity"
Territory	The multidimensional representation of the business domain or space in which a sales rep sells, and for which the sales rep will receive sales Credit for Transactions. A Territory might consist of a combination of products, customers, geography, sales channels, or any other business category.
Test Lead	The customer project team member who is responsible for developing the strategy, tactics and deliverables for the Test Phase. Ideally, the Test Lead is active from the Requirements Phase onward.
Test Phase	The part of the project during which the system design and build is validated to be sure it meets requirements.
Threshold	A minimum level of performance below which commissions will not be paid.
Time & Materials (T&M)	A project contract that calls for the customer to pay by the billable hour. Often limited with a "not-to-exceed" clause.
Total Target Earnings	One of many ways to express the fixed and variable incentive to be earned by a payee at exactly 100% of attainment against target performance.
Transaction	A record for a business event brought into the ICM system as the basis for incenting a Payee or many Payees. It often, but not invariably, represents a line from a sales order. Compare to "Credit".
Trial Payment	A preliminary report of payments amounts generated by the ICM system but not yet communicated to Payroll or Accounts Payable. Often the trigger for the payment approval workflow. Compare to "Posted Payment".

Term	Definition
Turn-Key	A project on which the implementation team builds the system without the active involvement of the customer team. Compare to "Collaborative Build".
Unintended Consequences	Different, and usually worse, outcomes than the planner had in mind. Often quite amusing when they don't impact you directly.
Unmaking the Omelet	The desire to unpack a highly non-linear calculation to determine the contribution of a small piece of it. A lot of work for minimal returned value.
Variable Compensation	The practice of rewarding staff or agents for performance against predetermined metrics.
Vendor	The company that sells ICM system software, or the company that implements it. One company might do both.
Vendor Evaluation	A consulting engagement in which a Systems Integrator will assist the customer in selecting a system vendor.
Veneer of Legality	Changing data or comp plan rules in order to make the system calculate the amount you already planned to pay. But hey, the system told us it was the right answer, so it must be right.
Waterfall Methodology	A well-defined sequence of project phases that (theoretically) are conducted in series, with the next phase not commencing until the previous one is complete. In fact, there is usually a little overlap. The ICM waterfall usually encompasses (at least) Requirements - Design - Build - Test - Handoff. Contrast to "Agile Methodology".
Weirdness	The thing your company does that makes Incentive Compensation Management software turn sideways. A strange confluence of data, processes, and plans that requires creativity or brute force to model in the application.
White Box Testing	Testing with knowledge of the internals of the system in order to determine root cause of any defects. Contrast with "Black Box Testing".
Widget	A product sold by ConGlomCo. Like a "Rugalator", only different.

APPENDIX TWO – THE COMPENSATION CENTER OF COMPETENCY

An idea that has been rearing its head in recent years is to create a cross-functional team of interested parties to act as the steering committee for all matters compensation for a company. This team has been called various things in the companies I've worked with, but Compensation Center of Competency (or Excellence, but Competency means you can call it the **CCC**, or Triple-C, or C-Cubed, or lots of other cute names) is one that seems to be sticking.

Simply, it is made up of interested, committed, and knowledgeable people from all the constituents of the ICM world. It might include members from:

- Sale Finance
- Sales Management
- IT Support
- HR
- Corporate Finance
- And absolutely, Tammy from the Comp Team

The idea is for the CCC to meet on a well-defined periodic basis to discuss how the plans are working now, proposed changes for the coming year, any course corrections that might be appropriate, and systematic issues that could affect the company's ability to respond to changes in market conditions that might come up.

The critical factor here is to get people who need comp operations to work, on the one hand, and who have the ability to help improve it when it doesn't, on the other. When Sales Finance proposes a new comp plan, for example, people who can point out that the current data feeds don't support measuring the performance needed for the metric can catch the problem early. It might mean changing the plan, or it might mean changing data feeds, but either way, when the plan plops onto her desk in January, Tammy won't be blind-sided by it.

At a minimum, the CCC should meet on a schedule roughly like this for a company that has year-long comp plans:

Figure 47 - Compensation Center of Competency Schedule

Of course, meeting more often is better, but let your company's culture drive. The important thing is, incentive compensation is too important to be planned in silos and administered by a group that doesn't control the data and systems needed to make it successful.

APPENDIX THREE: CONTRACT HIERARCHIES IN INSURANCE & FINANCIAL SERVICES

One of the bigger challenges in implementing ICM systems in the Insurance and Financial Services verticals is the problem of multiple instances of independent producers (payees), and the multiple hierarchies they live in. It stems from two fundamental aspects of the business model:

- The fact that independent agents move around over time, and;
- The fact that policies for some products can be active for decades, and must be tracked and compensated based on who the producer was at the time of sale, not who she or he is now.

Let's look at how the first aspect of insurance might play out over the years. It's 1990, Meg Smith is fresh out of school and she is at loose ends. Her uncle, Hiram Jones, decides to give her a chance at his insurance agency. Hiram has a contract arrangement with Trusted Insurance (among others – remember, he's independent). It's Contract A, and his agency is rated as a Level 7 on the contract. He hires Meg as a Level 1 agent, and because the Jones Agency is on Contract A, so is Meg (See **COMMISSIONS IN THE INSURANCE & FINANCIAL SERVICES INDUSTRIES** section for a refresher on how commissions are calculated):

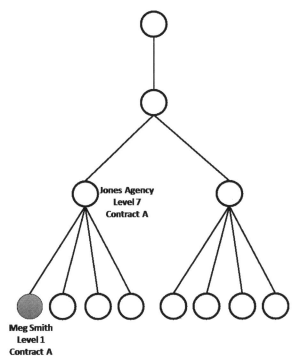

Figure 48 - Meg Goes to Work

One thing that's interesting about this is that, for a variety of regulatory reasons, Meg can't be paid her commissions directly – her check from Trusted Insurance must be sent to the Jones Agency for disbursement. Anyhow, it turns out that Meg is an insurance-sellin' fool – she's really good at it. That was a surprise to both of them. She's churning out policies left and right, and begins to wonder if she might not be worth more than her dear old uncle is paying her. Family is family, but a person has to make a living. So in 1993 she goes across town to the George Agency, which is on Contract B with Trusted Insurance (among other carriers), and she's a Level 3:

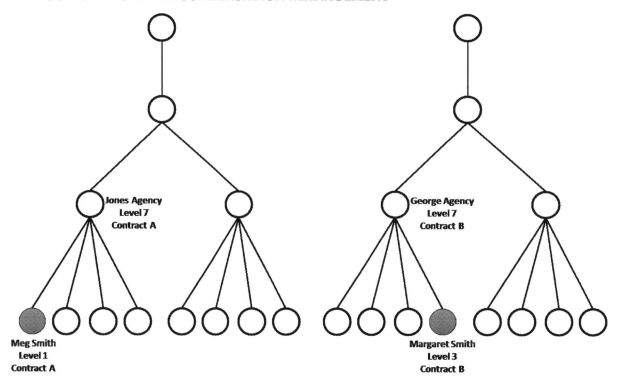

Figure 49 - Margaret Advances in the World

Oh, and don't call her Meg anymore – Margaret just sounds so much more professional. But let's not forget that Meg sold a lot of policies, and many of them are still active, so the commissions for residual premiums on them still go to her. Margaret is an insurance juggernaut, and Uncle Hiram isn't getting any younger. Margaret buys the old family agency in 1999:

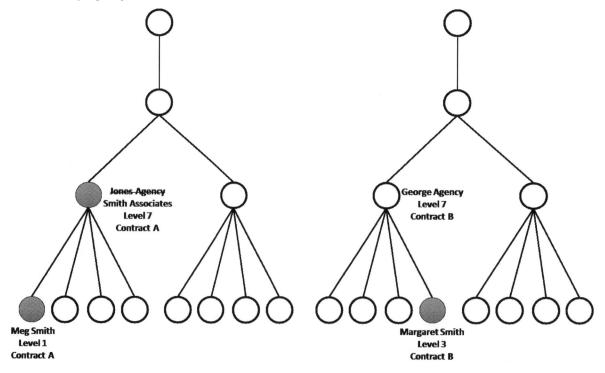

Figure 50 - Margaret is Unstoppable

Margaret, in buying the Jones Agency, also buys their active policies, including the policies she wrote as Meg, and she is taking over a contract relationship that already exists, so the terms to her as owner of the agency are the same terms Uncle Hiram had – Level 7 on Contract A. Essentially, Margaret has become Hiram. And Margaret is paying Meg – herself – commissions. She's also still collecting commissions for the active policies she sold at the George Agency as a Contract B, Level 3 agent.

In 2008, Margaret takes over the small Broker-Dealer operation that serviced the George Agency:

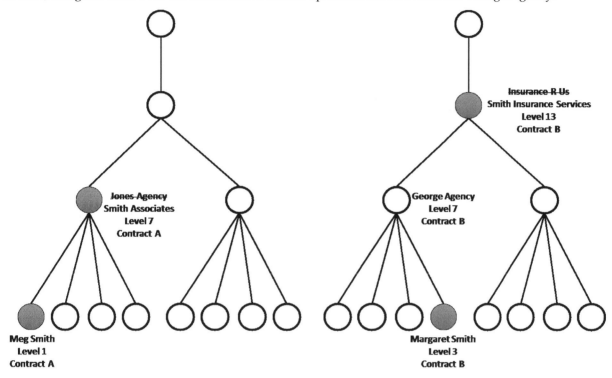

Figure 51 - Can Money Buy Margaret Happiness?

Margaret Smith is attached to Contract B at Level 13, and still gets commissions for the policies she wrote at the George Agency as a Level 3 all those years ago.

This is something of an oversimplification. The odds are, someone clawing her way up the insurance ladder would go further afield and be under more than just two contracts over time. A producer could exist in many more instances in contractual relationships with Trusted Insurance – plus all the other carriers she sells for.

The challenge for ICM systems – and the insurance company legacy applications that support them – is that every version of Meg, Margaret, the boss at Smith Associates, the CEO at Smith Insurance Services – each must be tracked and paid according to their different contract terms, whether the contract rates themselves (Contract A versus Contract B), or the producer levels at which they are calculated.

And commissions for policies, which can be active for decades, must be credited and calculated according to the state of the world at the time of issuance, not as the world looks today. So Meg's very first policy might still be collecting premiums and paying commissions – very small ones, but still, commissions – to the Meg version of Margaret until the 2030s. And Margaret has, essentially, "bought" the rights to Hiram's, the George Agency's, and the Insurance R Us Broker-Dealer's for all of their active policies.

So here's a hint: there will be pre- and post-processing for this ICM implementation. Plan for it.

APPENDIX FOUR: OL' UNKA DK'S LAWS & VIRTUES

The Laws

Ol' Unka DK's Only Law of Incentive Calculation Errors:

- Errors in variable compensation are *always in the payee's favor.*
  If you *underpay* them, they *will* report it to you so you can fix them.
  If you *overpay* them, they *might* report it to you.

Ol' Unka DK's First Law of Example Calculation Documentation:

- You may *never, ever*, use the numbers 1%, 10%, 1, 10, 100, or 1,000 in your calculation examples. *Ever."*

Ol' Unka DK's First Law of ICM System Design:

- Sometimes *there is no good answer.*
  Sometimes *there is only the least bad answer.*

Ol' Unka DK's Second Law of ICM System Design:

- The work *has to happen somewhere.*
  Moving it doesn't make it go away.

Ol' Unka DK's Third Law of ICM System Design:

- *Render unto SQL the things that are SQL's, and render unto application logic the things that are logical*
  - *Keep logic out of the preprocessor (whenever possible)*
  - *Keep data lookups out of the comp calculation engine (wherever possible)*
  - *Keep calculation out of the reports (whenever possible)*

Ol' Unka DK's Fourth Law of ICM System Design:

- *If implementing it in the system will make the system more onerous to manage than handling it as a manual exception would, then handle it as a manual exception*

Ol' Unka DK's Only Law of Data Exclusion:

- The *only objects*, and the *only attributes*, that belong in the ICM system are those needed for *crediting, commissioning, reporting, or researching compensation.* The ONLY ones.

Ol' Unka DK's Ninth & Tenth Laws of Exception Processing:

- Manual exceptions must be planned for
- Systematic exceptions have a cost

Ol' Unka DK's First Law of Avoiding Unintended Consequences:

- *Write* the comp plans *"top-down"* – reflecting the company's goals and the desired behaviors.
- Then *read* the comp plans *"bottom-up"* – from the perspective of the payees, and with the payees' agendas in the front of your mind.

The Virtues

Ol' Unka DK's Sometimes Contradictory System Virtues:

- **Accuracy**
  We have got to get the right answer.
- **Performance**
  We usually have to get the right answer in a screaming hurry.
- **Thoroughness**
  We want to create lots of usable data for reporting and analytics, but it takes longer to process lots of results than it does to process just enough results to pay on.
- **Flexibility**
  The system must work for what we do today, but also for what we might do in the future.
- **Robustness**
  The system can't be fussy. It should be like a train – it just goes. Let's just wire it up to do what it's supposed to do. But that conflicts with the flexibility we also want.
- **Automation**
  The system should do the job, and the whole job. Don't make the admins do all the work.
- **Maintainability**
  If the system is too complicated, it becomes a bear to maintain, now and in the future. So make the system do the right things that neatly fit inside its core functionality, and leave the rest for the admins. But we are now conflicting with the full automation we were hoping for.

Ol' Unka DK's Comp Plan Virtues:

- Comp plan metrics must be *aligned with company goals*
- Comp plan metrics must be *focused*
- Comp plan metrics must be *within the control of the payee*
- Comp plans must be *motivating*
- Comp plans must *not conflict*
- Comp plans *must not be used in place of management supervision*
- Comp plans must be *measurable*
- Comp plan goals, targets or quotas must be *achievable*
- Comp plans *must never demotivate payees from selling*
- Comp plans must *NEVER motivate payees to kill business*
- Comp plans should *pay as soon after the sale as practical*
- Comp plans must always be written to *recover incentives in the event that the business debooks*
- Comp plans must always be *clear and unambiguous*

INDEX

Accounts Payable 20, 91, 92, 96, 177, 180

Accumulate Stage.................................16, 171, 177, 178

Aggregate Stage 17, 171, 177, 178

Agile..132, 133, 171, 181

analytics...... 36, 38, 42, 58, 84, 92, 93, 95, 109, 137, 152, 153, 190

annualization 150

application-agnostic...11, 81, 107

attainment .. 15, 18, 51, 52, 141, 144, 145, 166, 171, 172, 174, 180

best practices...................................15, 34, 105, 139, 161

bonus 19, 22, 27, 34, 38, 50, 51, 52, 82, 98, 99, 100, 101, 102, 103, 147, 152, 154, 162, 163, 165, 171, 172

Build Phase ...75, 107, 116, 117, 118, 119, 122, 131, 172

build versus buy..33

call center 13, 42, 55, 163

CFO 20, 32, 92, 106

collaborative build 75, 117, 118, 119, 172, 181

commission 15, 19, 22, 23, 24, 25, 33, 34, 37, 38, 43, 46, 50, 51, 52, 62, 82, 87, 94, 131, 137, 140, 141, 142, 144, 145, 146, 147, 153, 155, 158, 162, 163, 164, 165, 166, 171, 172, 179

commission rate 19, 46, 51, 52, 53, 87, 140, 144, 146, 155, 158, 164, 171, 172, 176

Comp Lead..34, 35

Comp Plan Designer...36, 37

Comp Team 20, 31, 32, 33, 48, 49, 50, 59, 62, 65, 75, 78, 84, 87, 91, 93, 94, 95, 105, 107, 111, 114, 117, 118, 125, 126, 130, 131, 152, 158, 164, 167, 172, 180, 183

Compensation Center of Competency 183

Compensation Department 34, 35

compensation plan..9, 11, 13, 14, 16, 17, 24, 25, 28, 31, 32, 33, 34, 36, 37, 38, 46, 48, 52, 56, 57, 70, 75, 83, 84, 86, 97, 107, 112, 114, 115, 118, 121, 131, 139, 147, 154, 155, 158, 161, 162, 163, 164, 165, 166, 167, 171, 172, 174, 176, 181, 183

components.......................................56, 57, 86, 173, 176

contingency...66, 72, 73

credit 17, 18, 44, 45, 46, 48, 50, 53, 54, 65, 70, 82, 88, 111, 124, 138, 139, 140, 141, 158, 174, 175, 178, 179

credit split 17

crediting ... 17, 46, 49, 56, 69, 81, 86, 111, 132, 138, 139, 140, 141, 151

Customer Success...65

Data Integration 55, 65, 109, 110, 115, 151

date-effectivity...39, 40, 41, 129

demo 69, 70, 71, 74, 173

Deployment Phase..98, 128

Design Phase 82, 107, 108, 109, 114, 116, 117, 118, 119, 131, 133, 174

disputes 26, 31, 34, 36, 55, 84, 96, 131, 132, 142

draw 22, 36, 46, 74, 76, 85, 148, 149

Enterprise Architect...38, 63

Exceptions 24, 156, 158, 169

Executive Sponsor....................................62, 65, 95, 174

expected results....................................99, 124, 125, 126

Financial Services........................25, 140, 149, 153, 154

fixed price 72, 73, 117

Fred Brooks...77

gaming...25, 166, 174

General Ledger.. 50, 63, 91, See

goal...18

Gold Copy..123, 128, 174

Go-Live Phase...130

guarantee..33, 145, 148, 149

hierarchy 44, 45, 47, 49, 54, 176

insurance..17, 31, 44, 51, 108

Insurance.......................................21, 140, 149, 150, 153

Leave of Absence 89

LOA ....See Leave of Absence

Logical Design...................114, 115, 131, 133, 175, 177

Lookup Tables 51

Managed Services 130, 175

metric..16, 17, 18, 86, 162, 176

modeling 43, 83, 94, 95, 104, 154, 155

OCM .... See Organizational Change Management

Organizational Change Management 65, 105, 106, 130, 131, 176

overlay...............................17, 44, 46, 138, 176, 178, 179

Pay Stage 20, 171, 177, 178 payee13, 14, 16, 17, 18, 19, 20, 24, 28, 34, 40, 41, 42, 43, 44, 50, 51, 52, 54, 55, 56, 57, 66, 82, 83, 86, 87, 88, 89, 90, 91, 93, 94, 96, 97, 98, 99, 111, 112, 126, 128, 129, 130, 131, 132, 139, 140, 144, 145, 147, 148, 151, 152, 154, 156, 157, 158, 161, 162, 163, 164, 165, 166, 167, 171, 172, 173, 174, 175, 176, 177, 179, 180, 189, 190

payee engagement 43, 51, 140

pay-for-performance 13, 163, 164

pay-for-Performance 13

payment cap 24, 151, 164

pay-mix 13

Performance Management 163, 175, 178

Physical Design 115, 119, 133, 175, 177

posted payments..20

preprocessing 71, 110, 111, 112, 113, 114, 124, 138, 141, 146, 147, 189

Program Management Office...............10, 63, 120, 177

Project Manager 63, 64, 73, 77, 79, 83, 98, 116, 121, 128, 177

Project Readiness 74, 75, 177

proof of concept 69, 70

quota14, 18, 19, 20, 23, 24, 27, 39, 40, 43, 46, 50, 51, 52, 96, 99, 129, 141, 142, 143, 144, 145, 147, 163, 164, 171, 172, 174, 177, 180

ranking 58, 112

Rate Table 51, 140, 141

Readiness Assessment...............*See* Project Readiness

recalculation 27, 28, 40

Regulatory Reporting...153

reporting 9, 15, 19, 20, 22, 23, 27, 28, 31, 32, 33, 36, 37, 38, 44, 45, 55, 57, 58, 59, 64, 65, 67, 68, 70, 75, 83, 84, 87, 88, 89, 90, 91, 92, 93, 94, 95, 97, 105, 108, 109, 112, 114, 115, 117, 119, 120, 121, 122, 123, 124, 125, 126, 127, 128, 130, 131, 132, 142,151, 152, 153, 166, 180, 189, 190

Reporting 109, 115

reporting hierarchy..............................39, 43, 44, 45, 46

reprocessing......................23, 26, 27, 28, 39, 40, 68, 145

Requirements Phase . 63, 73, 76, 81, 83, 89, 96, 98, 105, 107, 116, 117, 122, 124, 125, 128, 129, 133, 178, 180

Requirements Specification Document..81, 82, 83, 96, 104, 114, 116, 117, 119, 122, 124, 178

return on investment....26, 36, 38, 66, 67, 75, 132, 139, 153, 161, 166

Reward Stage..............................18, 20, 171, 177, 178

RFI..68, 69, 71, 72, 74, 178

RFP..68, 74, 178

rollup 17, 44, 45, 46, 86, 138, 176, 178, 179

Sales Order Management .. 21, 32, 46, 55, 90, 146, 158, 178

Sales Performance Management 13, 14, 15, 26, 27, 93, 94, 175, 178, *See* Sales Performance Management

Sarbanes-Oxley 32, 67, 96, 106, 179

shadow accounting.....................................27, 67, 132

Single Point of Contact.......................................78, 179

Slam Jar 185

SME..28, 70, 75, 76, 77, 78, 83, 86, 88, 98, 100, 101, 102, 104, 159, 180

Software-as-a-Service.... 34, 68, 122, 123, 130, 176, 179

SPIF..147, 179

spreadsheet 27, 31, 32, 34, 48, 49, 51, 52, 54, 55, 56, 67, 84, 99, 104, 114, 121

State Machine . 98, 99, 100, 101, 102, 104, 113, 125, 179

SteerCo ....*See* Steering Committee

Steering Committee......................65, 66, 116, 173, 179

Systems Integrator 10, 64, 69, 72, 74, 180, 181

Tammy 34, 35, 36, 37, 46, 52, 58, 62, 63, 78, 84, 95, 106, 111, 112, 120, 126, 130, 131, 132, 142, 172, 180, 183

target...18

target earnings 19, 43, 50, 94

Tech Support 65, 111, 157

Telco 46, 164, 167

territory 14, 17, 20, 27, 48, 49, 50, 55, 82, 111, 138, 139, 174, 175

Test Data 121, 125, 128

Test Lead...63, 180

Test Phase 83, 96, 107, 119, 120, 121, 122, 125, 127, 128, 131, 133, 143, 180

testing ... 12, 19, 25, 32, 36, 63, 72, 74, 82, 83, 96, 97, 98, 104, 116, 118, 119, 120, 121, 122, 123, 124, 125, 126, 127, 128, 129, 130, 143, 172, 179, 181

threshold 24, 53

Time and Materials...............................72, 73, 174, 180

transactions 16, 17, 23, 27, 31, 32, 35, 49, 53, 55, 68, 70, 90, 94, 96, 108, 112, 122, 124, 125, 127, 128, 137, 138, 139, 146, 147, 157, 158, 176

trial payments 20

Turn-Key...117, 181

unintended consequences 15, 24, 26, 107, 165, 167, 169, 174

upside...13, 166

variable compensation13, 15, 16, 31, 35, 46, 55, 56, 66, 67, 137, 161, 172, 175, 189

Variables 50, 115

vendor selection...74

Veneer of Legality.......................................157, 158, 181 waterfall methodology 61, 132, 181

Weirdness.......16, 28, 43, 58, 66, 98, 106, 107, 111, 113, 116, 125, 133, 141, 166, 169, 181

workflows 93, 95, 96, 124, 180

workshop ... 25, 38, 82, 83, 84, 86, 88, 89, 90, 91, 92, 93, 95, 96, 97, 98, 128

Made in the
USA
Middletown, DE